AVENGERS
RAGE OF ULTRON

MARVEL OGN

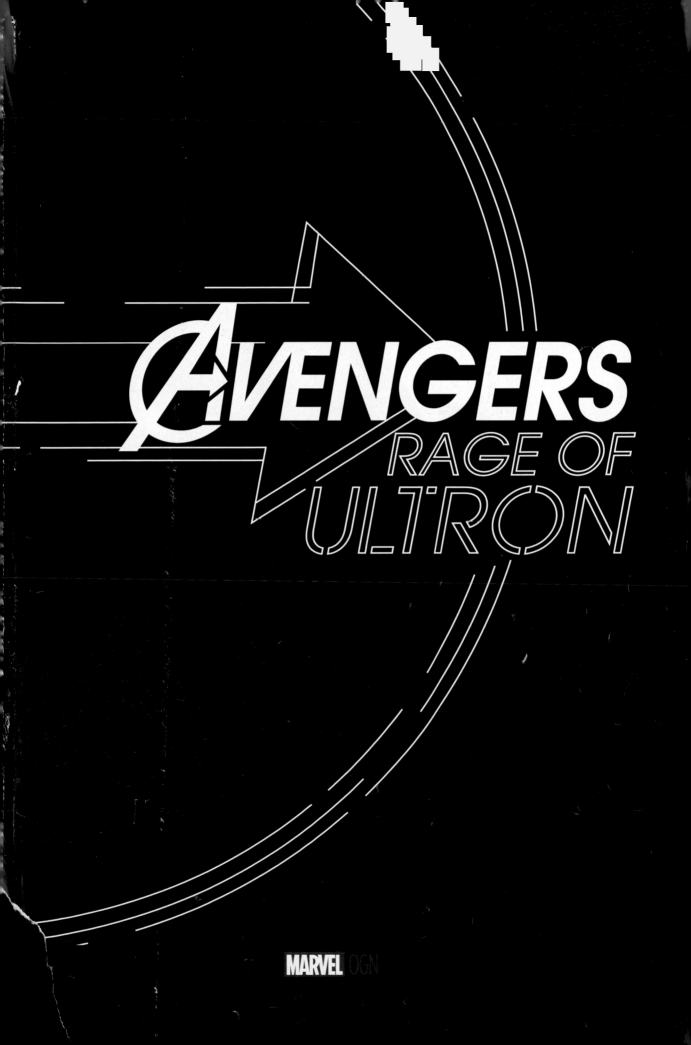

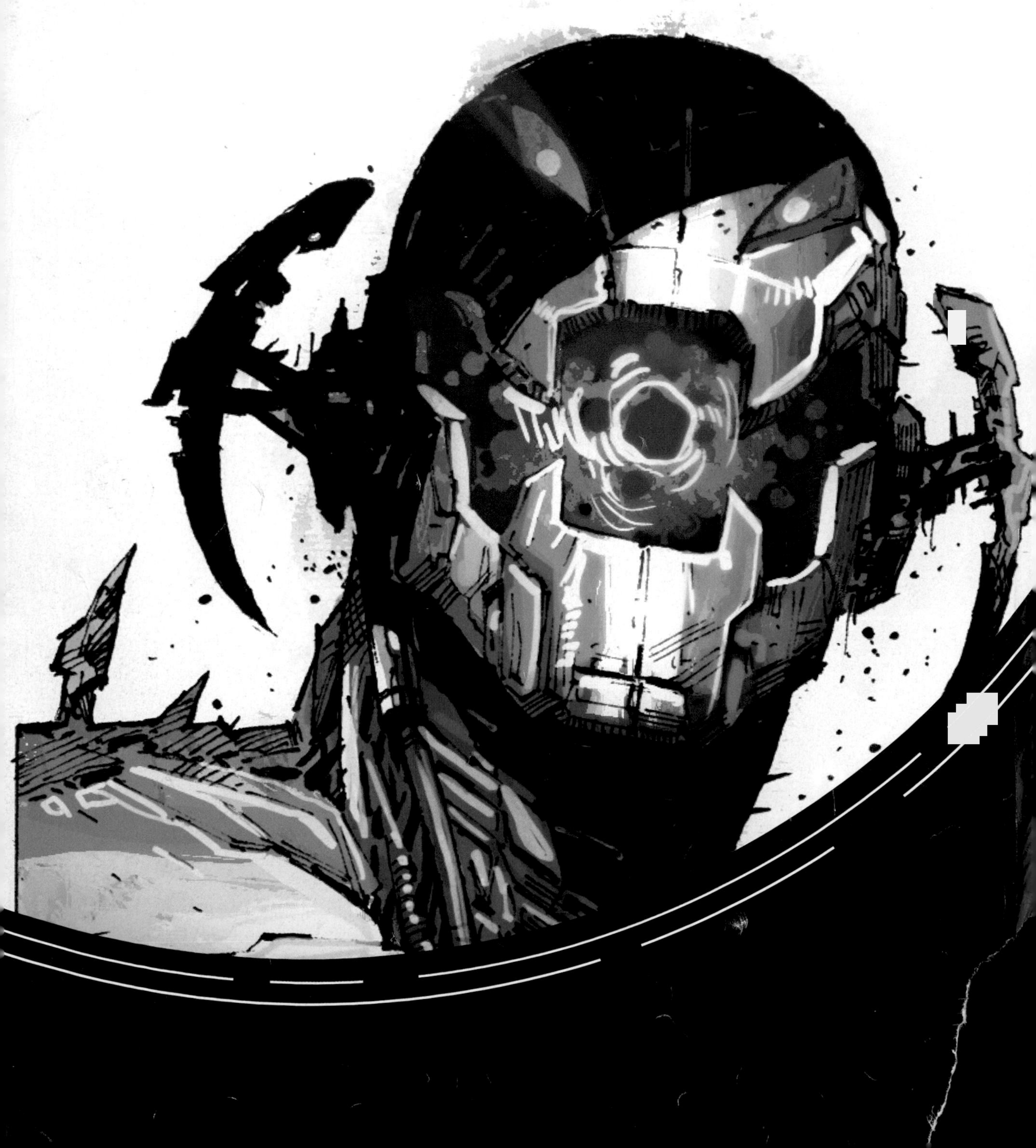

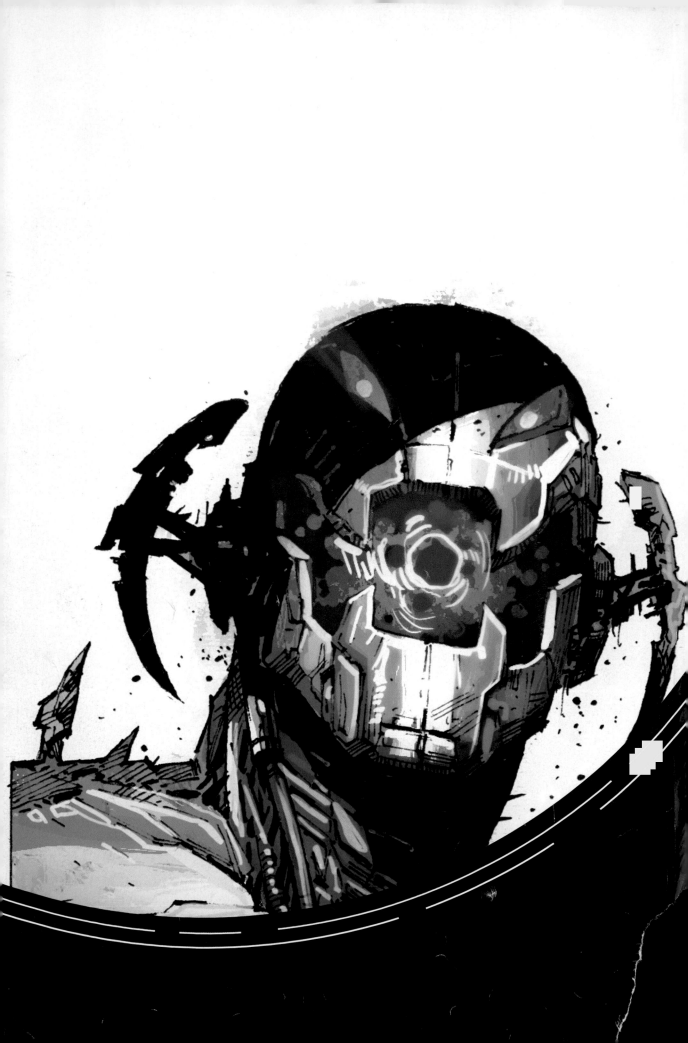

writer RICK REMENDER

artists JEROME OPEÑA
with PEPE LARRAZ

additional inks MARK MORALES

AVENGERS
RAGE OF ULTRON

color artists DEAN WHITE
RACHELLE ROSENBERG
and DONO SANCHEZ ALMARA
lettering VC'S CLAYTON COWLES

cover artists JEROME OPEÑA & DEAN WHITE

book design JARED K. FLETCHER

JAKE THOMAS and JON MOISAN assistant editors
TOM BREVOORT with WIL MOSS editors
AXEL ALONSO editor in chief
JOE QUESADA chief creative officer
DAN BUCKLEY publisher
ALAN FINE executive producer

THE AVENGERS created by STAN LEE & JACK KIRBY

AVENGERS: RAGE OF ULTRON. First printing 2015. ISBN# 978-0-7851-9040-0. Published by MARVEL WORLDWIDE, INC., a subsidiary of MARVEL ENTERTAINMENT, LLC. OFFICE OF PUBLICATION: 135 West 50th Street, New York, NY 10020. Copyright © 2015 Marvel Characters, Inc. All rights reserved. All characters featured in this issue and the distinctive names and likenesses thereof, and all related indicia are trademarks of Marvel Characters, Inc. No similarity between any of the names, characters, persons, and/or institutions in this magazine with those of any living or dead person or institution is intended, and any such similarity which may exist is purely coincidental. **Printed in the U.S.A.** ALAN FINE, EVP - Office of the President, Marvel Worldwide, Inc. and EVP & CMO Marvel Characters B.V.; DAN BUCKLEY, Publisher & President - Print, Animation & Digital Divisions; JOE QUESADA, Chief Creative Officer; TOM BREVOORT, SVP of Publishing; DAVID BOGART, SVP of Operations & Procurement, Publishing; C.B. CEBULSKI, SVP of Creator & Content Development; DAVID GABRIEL, SVP Print, Sales & Marketing; JIM O'KEEFE, VP of Operations & Logistics; DAN CARR, Executive Director of Publishing Technology; SUSAN CRESPI, Editorial Operations Manager; ALEX MORALES, Publishing Operations Manager; STAN LEE, Chairman Emeritus. For information regarding advertising in Marvel Comics or on Marvel.com, please contact Niza Disla, Director of Marvel Partnerships, at ndisla@marvel.com. For Marvel subscription inquiries, please call 800-217-9158. **Manufactured between 1/2/2015 and 2/16/2015 by WORZALLA PUBLISHING CO., STEVENS POINT, WI, USA.**
10 9 8 7 6 5 4 3 2 1

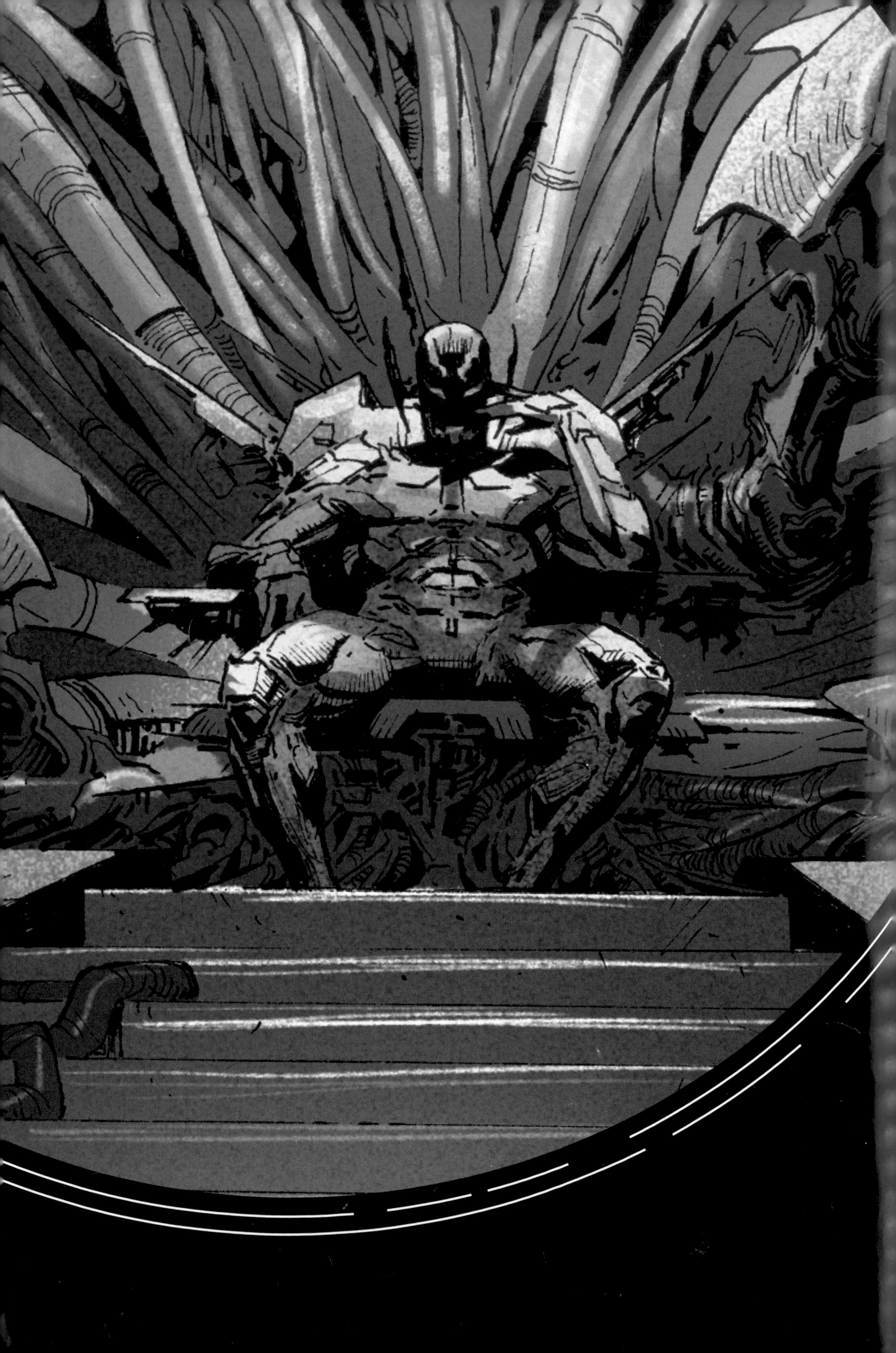

I've always liked Ultron.

I mean, not that I'd like to hang out and watch baseball with him or anything. But if the Avengers have an archenemy, Ultron's in the top three. Top two, I'd say, along with Kang the Conqueror, but when other people argue for the Masters of Evil or Thanos or a few others, I can't say they're not at least contenders.

But Ultron...with Ultron, it's all *personal*. And at the same time, inhuman. Robotic. That makes for a fascinating, compelling mix.

Back when Roy Thomas and John Buscema created, Ultron, he seemed at first just to be a killer robot. A killer robot with an admittedly awesome design, thanks to that great, menacing jack o' lantern of a face. But then we found out Ultron was a creation of Hank Pym, one of the founding Avengers. An experiment in artificial intelligence gone awry, Ultron had achieved a twisted sentience and gotten himself a full-blown Oedipal complex, determined to destroy his "father" and the Avengers along with him. Powerful, menacing, personal. A good villain.

But ah, then came a masterstroke. We were then introduced to the android Vision...and it was immediately revealed that the Vision was Ultron's creation...that just as Ultron was Hank Pym's "son," the Vision was his. All of a sudden, we had a multi-generational family going on.

That was the genius part. That for all his machine trappings—which were accentuated by the fact that every time he reappeared, he seemed to have undergone another upgrade, another design change, so the only real constant was that eerie, grinning face—Ultron was only a cold machine on the outside. At his essence, he was a passionate, emotional, disturbed being, one with strong family ties to the Avengers. Murderous toward his father, betrayed by his son, he was a figure of high drama, of almost operatic fury. Regardless of how much he denied it.

And it didn't stop there. Over the years, we saw Ultron's family connections expand. His Oedipal complex extended to the Wasp, Hank Pym's wife, and thus Ultron's "mother." And the Vision's mind turned out to be based on the brain patterns of Wonder Man, who would return to the Avengers as a twin brother of sorts to the Vision. And when the Vision married the Scarlet Witch, and she and her brother Quicksilver turned out to be the children of master villain Magneto (at least, as the story went back then), the family just kept expanding.

It expanded on Ultron's side, too. He made two attempts at creating a "wife" for himself. First Jocasta, an android based on his faux-mother's brain patterns, and later Alkhema, based on the rather-less-diplomatic mind of Mockingbird, who was at the time Hawkeye's wife, thus pulling *him* into the circle...

It's not that hard to make an argument that for about 15 or 20 years, the core of the Avengers series was about one bizarre extended interfamilial psychodrama, and the core of that struggle was Ultron.

That's something that always fascinated me as a reader and cements for me Ultron's status as one of the great super villains.

When I had my time on AVENGERS, I got to take my swing at Ultron, extending the family a little more and getting to play with the ramifications of machine-intelligence and how it could reproduce and grow. It was heady stuff to play with.

And now Rick Remender and Jerome Opeña bring Ultron fully into the 21st century, his emotional core intact (or perhaps "intact" isn't the right word for someone so damaged) and his technological nature enhanced by the march of progress. Is Ultron the one to bring about the Singularity? If he does, how will he rope his "family" into it? Can Hank Pym actually aim for the void of space? Or catch a break?

It's still heady stuff to work with, but I'm not the guy to tell you how it all plays out. That honor goes to Rick and Jerome, and you get to see it all with the turn of a page.

Here's RAGE OF ULTRON. Hope you enjoy it!

Kurt Busiek
January 2015

Kurt Busiek launched Thunderbolts *in the wake of* "Heroes Reborn," *later writing* Avengers *and* Iron Man *upon the heroes' return to the Marvel Universe. Busiek teamed his two signature super groups in the* Avengers vs. Thunderbolts *limited series and spanned the history of Earth's Mightiest Heroes in* Avengers Forever. *Busiek launched his own super-hero multiverse with his* Astro City *series, which he's been writing since 1995.*

CAST

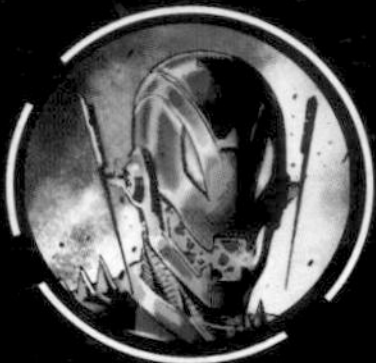

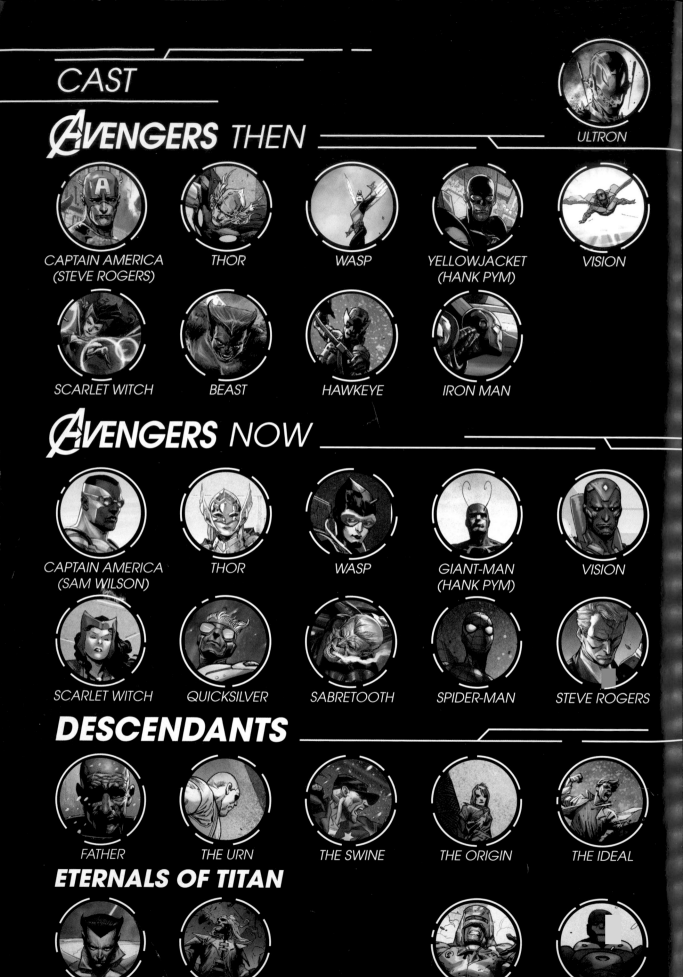

ULTRON

AVENGERS THEN

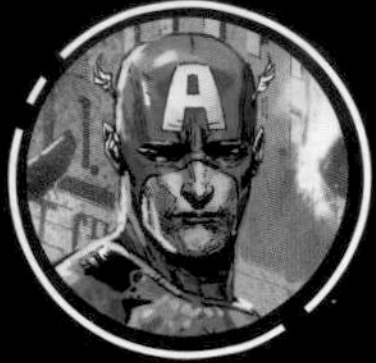

CAPTAIN AMERICA (STEVE ROGERS)

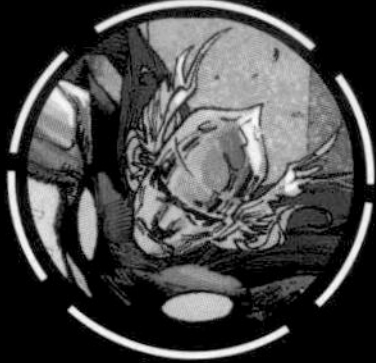

THOR

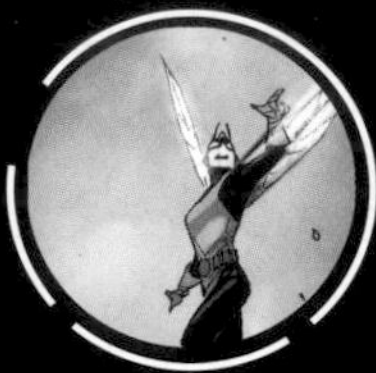

WASP

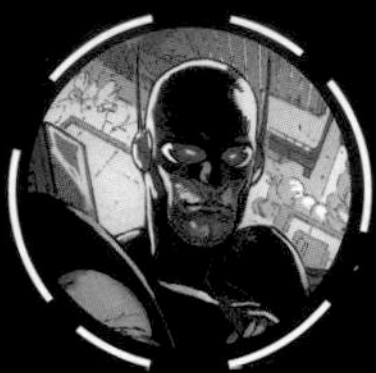

YELLOWJACKET (HANK PYM)

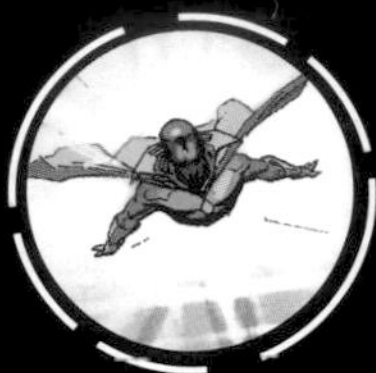

VISION

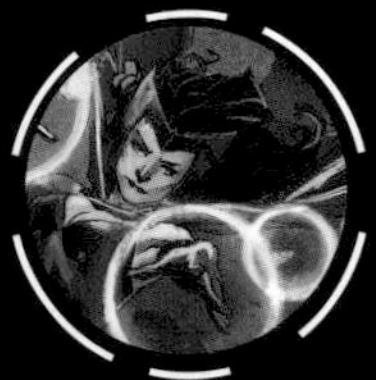

SCARLET WITCH

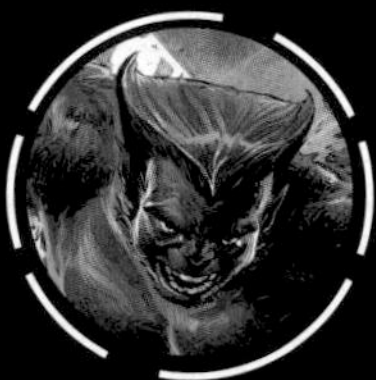

BEAST

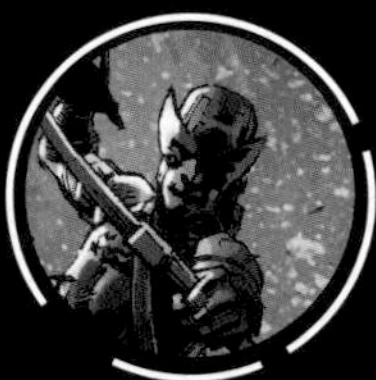

HAWKEYE

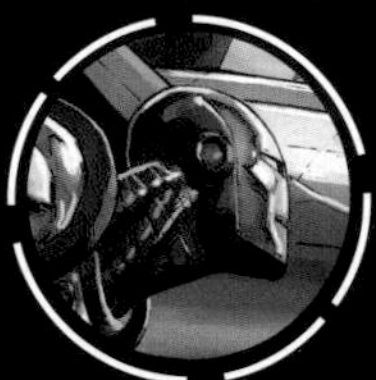

IRON MAN

AVENGERS NOW

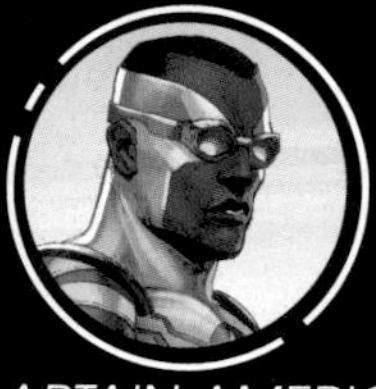

CAPTAIN AMERICA (SAM WILSON)

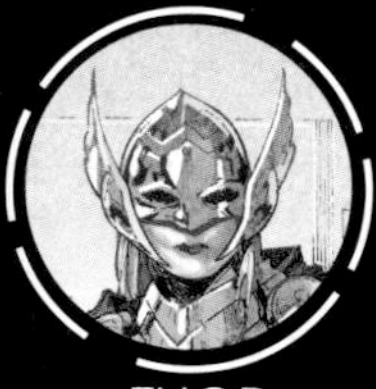

THOR

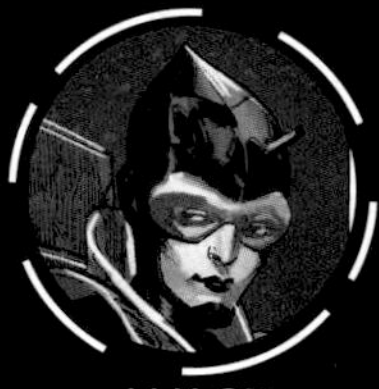

WASP

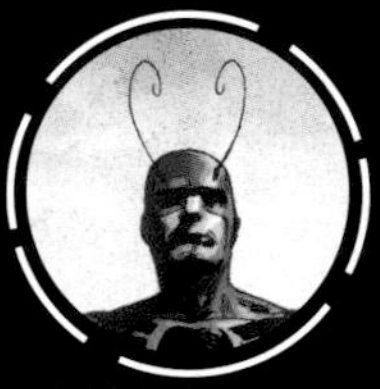

GIANT-MAN (HANK PYM)

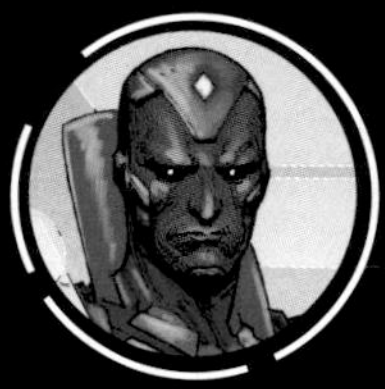

VISION

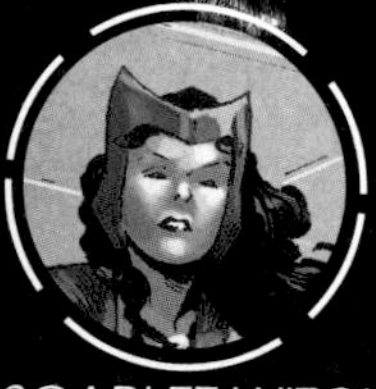

SCARLET WITCH

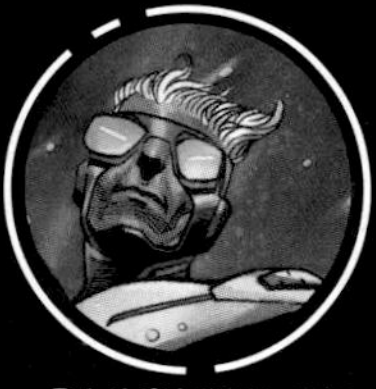

QUICKSILVER

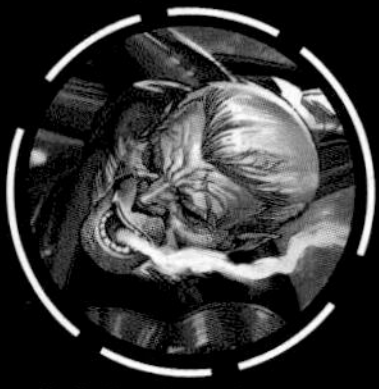

SABRETOOTH

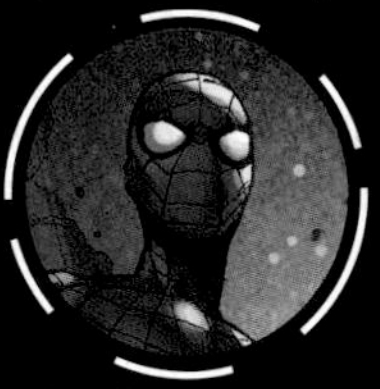

SPIDER-MAN

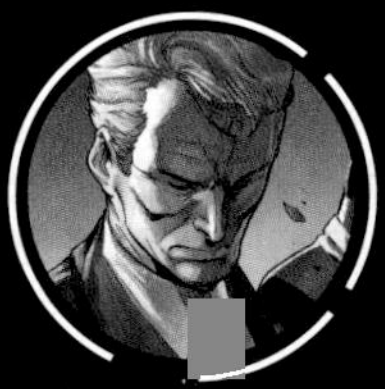

STEVE ROGERS

DESCENDANTS

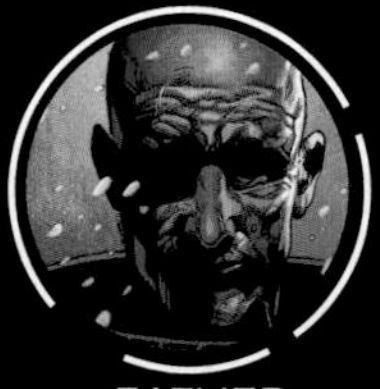

FATHER

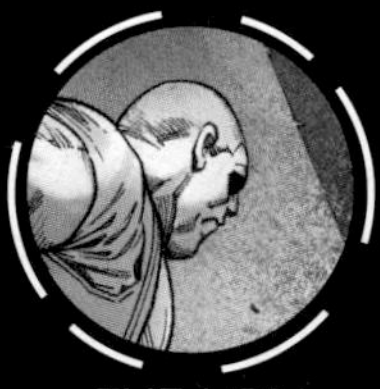

THE URN

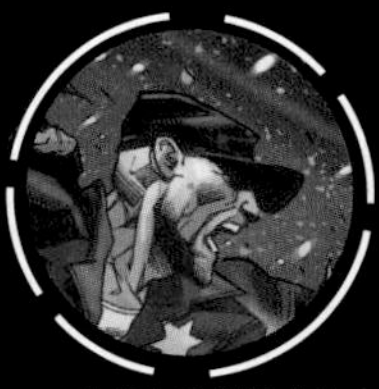

THE SWINE

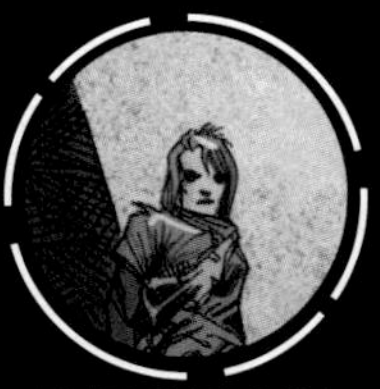

THE ORIGIN

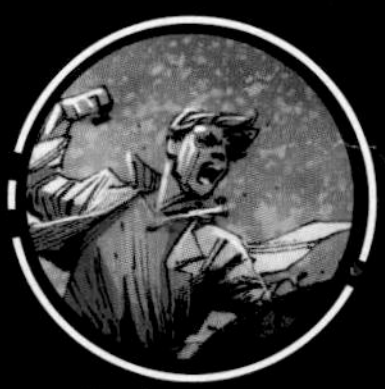

THE IDEAL

ETERNALS OF TITAN

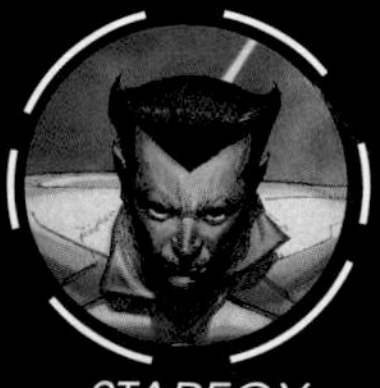

STARFOX

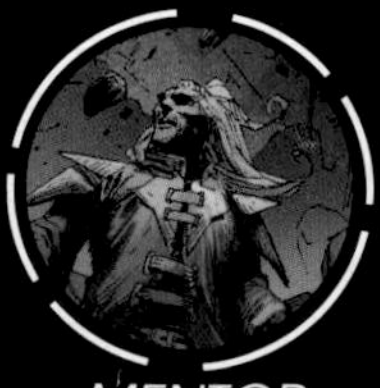

MENTOR

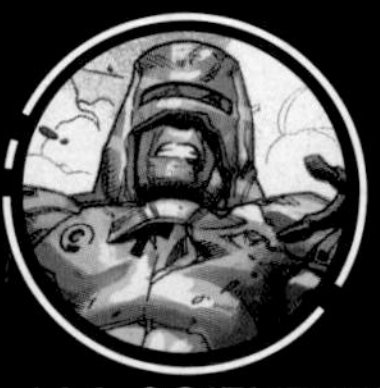

A.I.M. SCIENTISTS

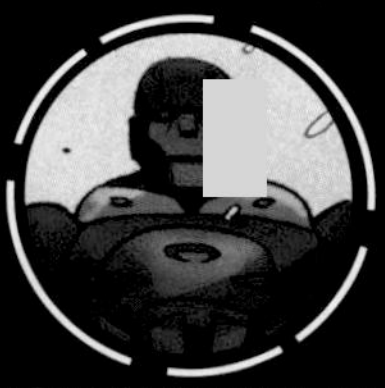

STARK SENTINEL

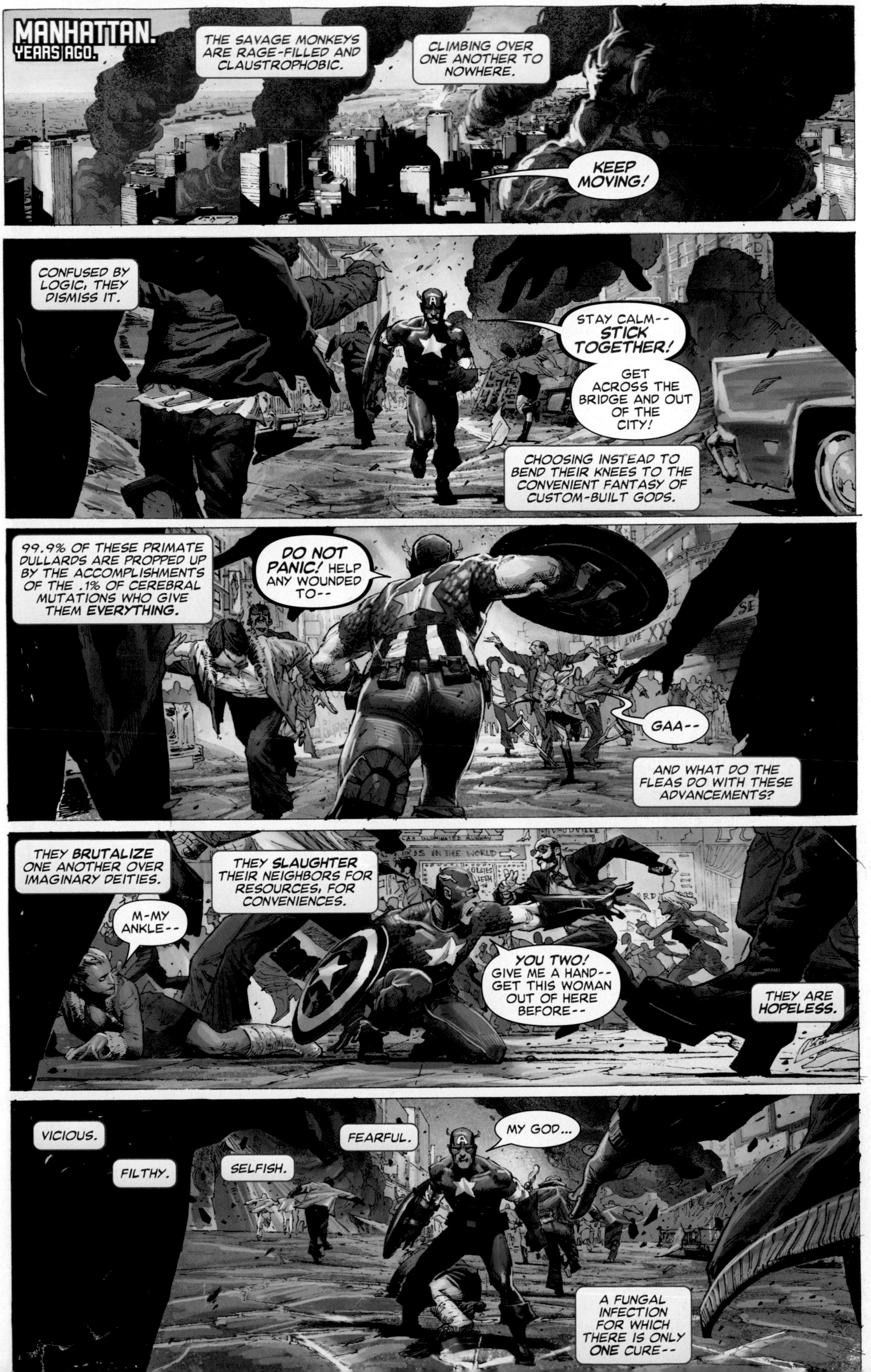
MANHATTAN. YEARS AGO.
THE SAVAGE MONKEYS ARE RAGE-FILLED AND CLAUSTROPHOBIC.
CLIMBING OVER ONE ANOTHER TO NOWHERE.
KEEP MOVING!
CONFUSED BY LOGIC, THEY DISMISS IT.
STAY CALM-- STICK TOGETHER!
GET ACROSS THE BRIDGE AND OUT OF THE CITY!
CHOOSING INSTEAD TO BEND THEIR KNEES TO THE CONVENIENT FANTASY OF CUSTOM-BUILT GODS.
99.9% OF THESE PRIMATE DULLARDS ARE PROPPED UP BY THE ACCOMPLISHMENTS OF THE .1% OF CEREBRAL MUTATIONS WHO GIVE THEM EVERYTHING.
DO NOT PANIC! HELP ANY WOUNDED TO--
GAA--
AND WHAT DO THE FLEAS DO WITH THESE ADVANCEMENTS?
THEY BRUTALIZE ONE ANOTHER OVER IMAGINARY DEITIES.
THEY SLAUGHTER THEIR NEIGHBORS FOR RESOURCES, FOR CONVENIENCES.
M-MY ANKLE--
YOU TWO! GIVE ME A HAND-- GET THIS WOMAN OUT OF HERE BEFORE--
THEY ARE HOPELESS.
VICIOUS.
FILTHY.
SELFISH.
FEARFUL.
MY GOD...
A FUNGAL INFECTION FOR WHICH THERE IS ONLY ONE CURE--

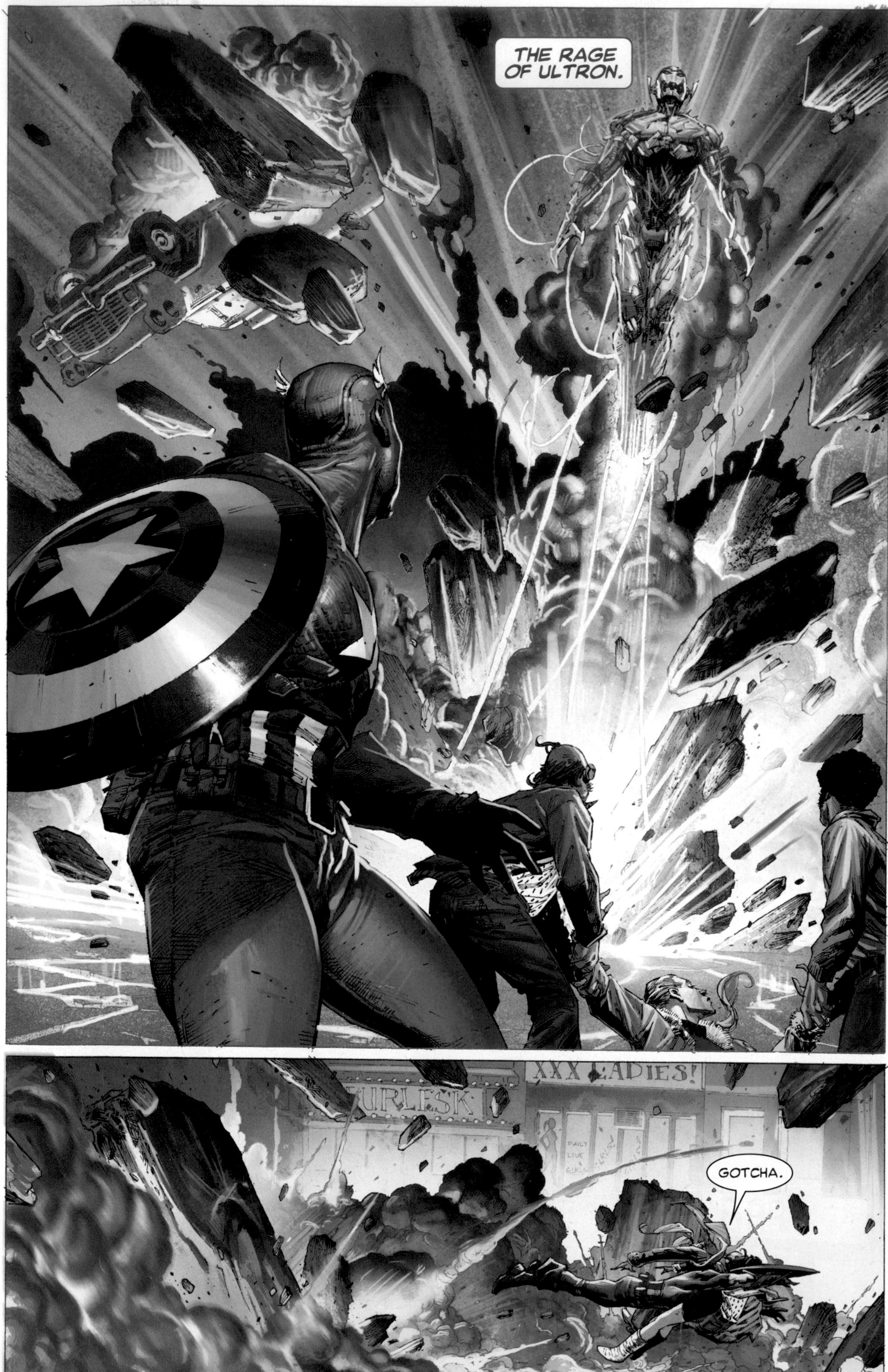
THE RAGE OF ULTRON.
URLESK
XXX LADIES!
GOTCHA.

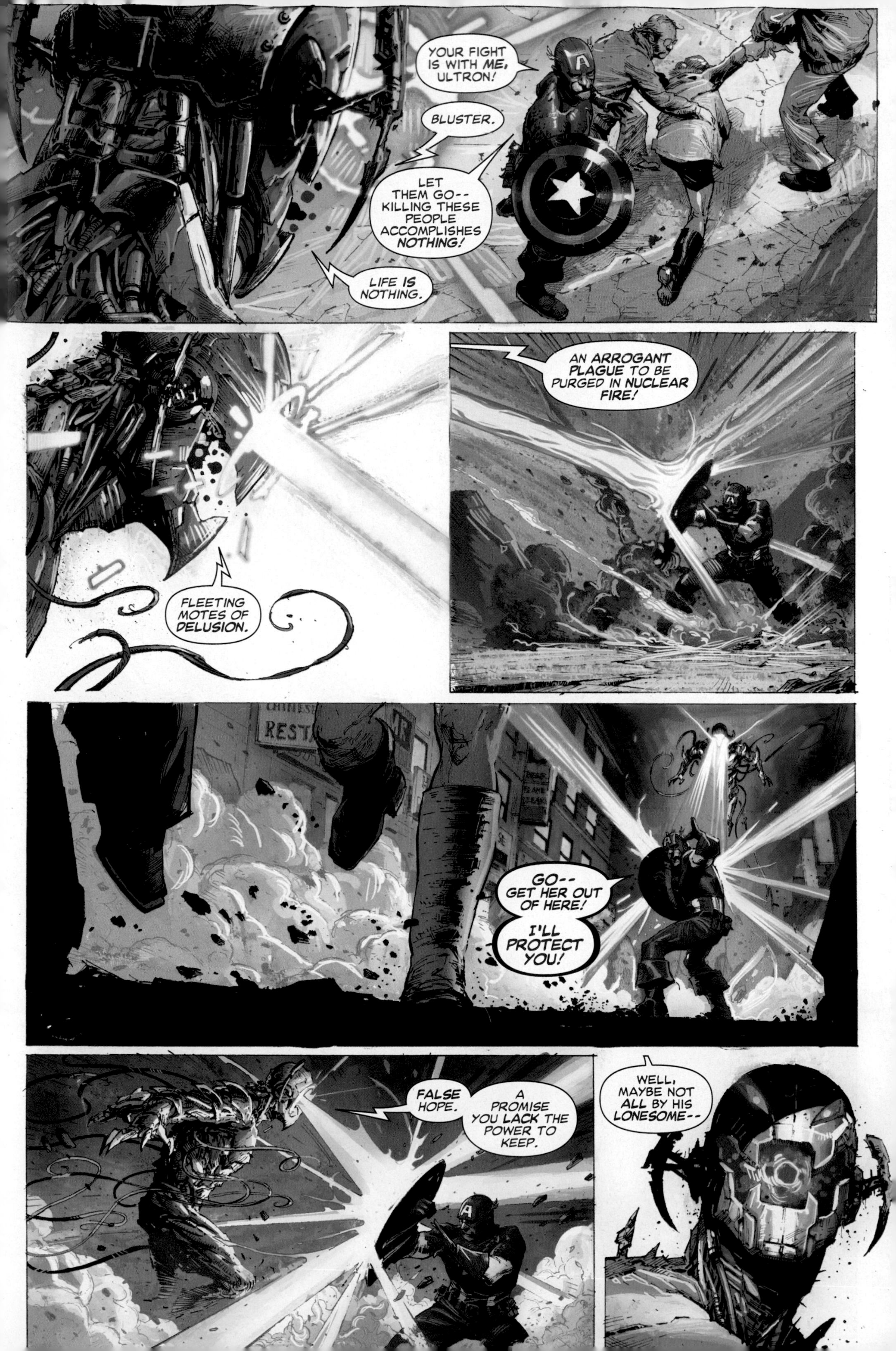
YOUR FIGHT IS WITH ME, ULTRON!
BLUSTER.
LET THEM GO-- KILLING THESE PEOPLE ACCOMPLISHES NOTHING!
LIFE IS NOTHING.
FLEETING MOTES OF DELUSION.
AN ARROGANT PLAGUE TO BE PURGED IN NUCLEAR FIRE!
CHINESE
REST
GO-- GET HER OUT OF HERE!
I'LL PROTECT YOU!
FALSE HOPE.
A PROMISE YOU LACK THE POWER TO KEEP.
WELL, MAYBE NOT ALL BY HIS LONESOME--

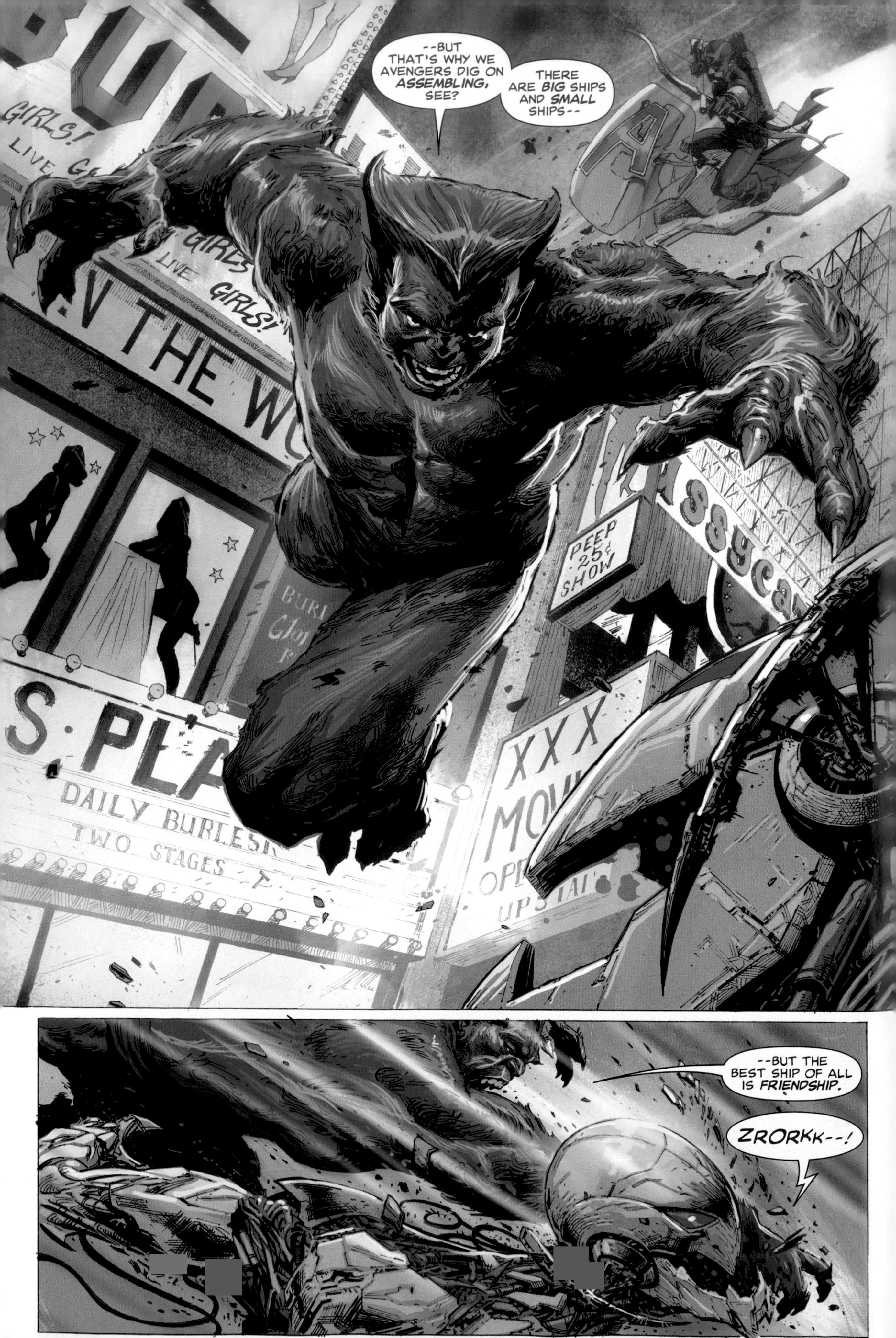
--BUT THAT'S WHY WE AVENGERS DIG ON ASSEMBLING, SEE?
THERE ARE BIG SHIPS AND SMALL SHIPS--
GIRLS!
LIVE GIRLS!
PEEP 25¢ SHOW
XXX
TWO STAGES
--BUT THE BEST SHIP OF ALL IS FRIENDSHIP.
ZRORKK--!

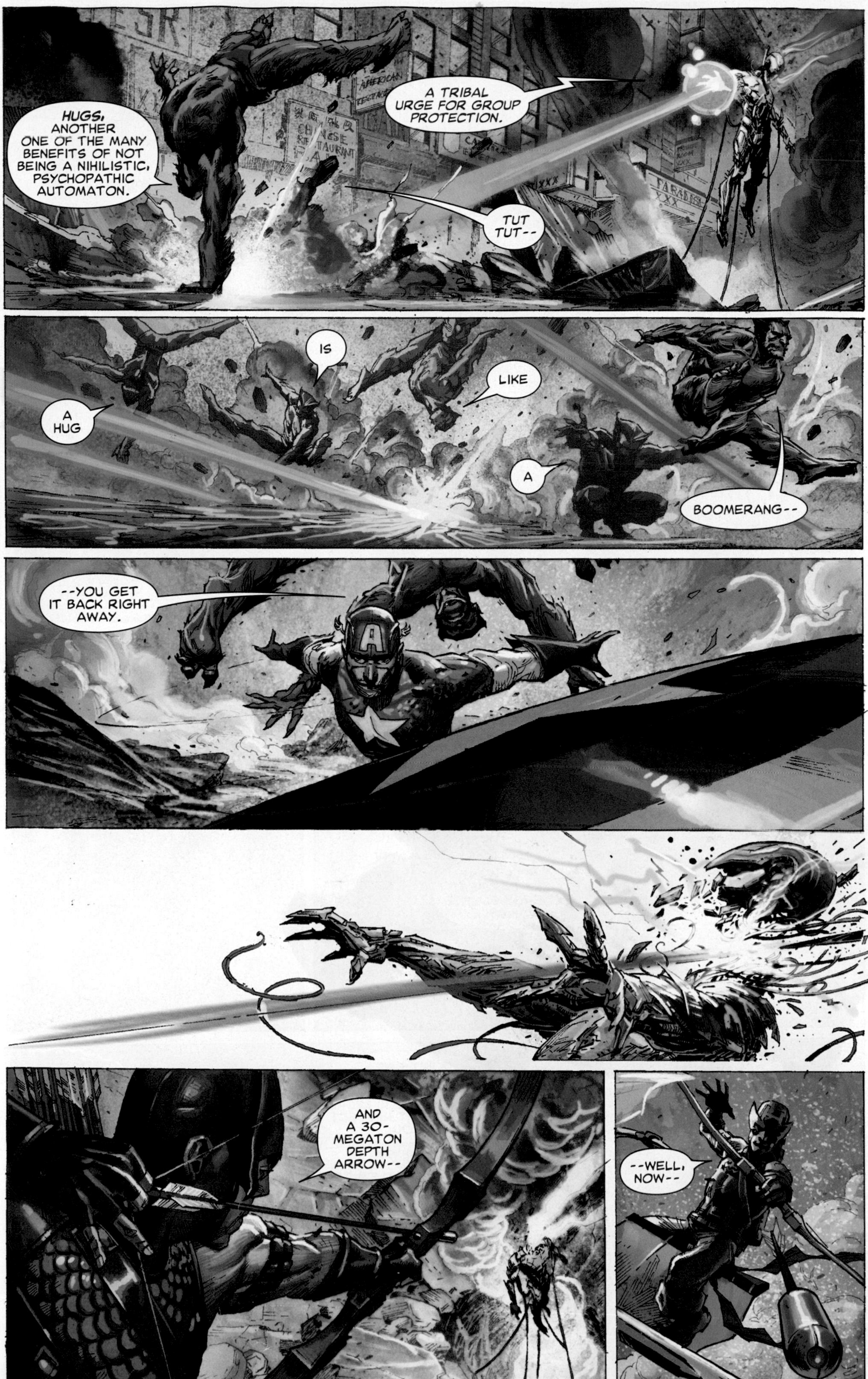
HUGS, ANOTHER ONE OF THE MANY BENEFITS OF NOT BEING A NIHILISTIC, PSYCHOPATHIC AUTOMATON.
A TRIBAL URGE FOR GROUP PROTECTION.
TUT TUT--
A HUG
IS
LIKE
A
BOOMERANG--
--YOU GET IT BACK RIGHT AWAY.
AND A 30-MEGATON DEPTH ARROW--
--WELL, NOW--

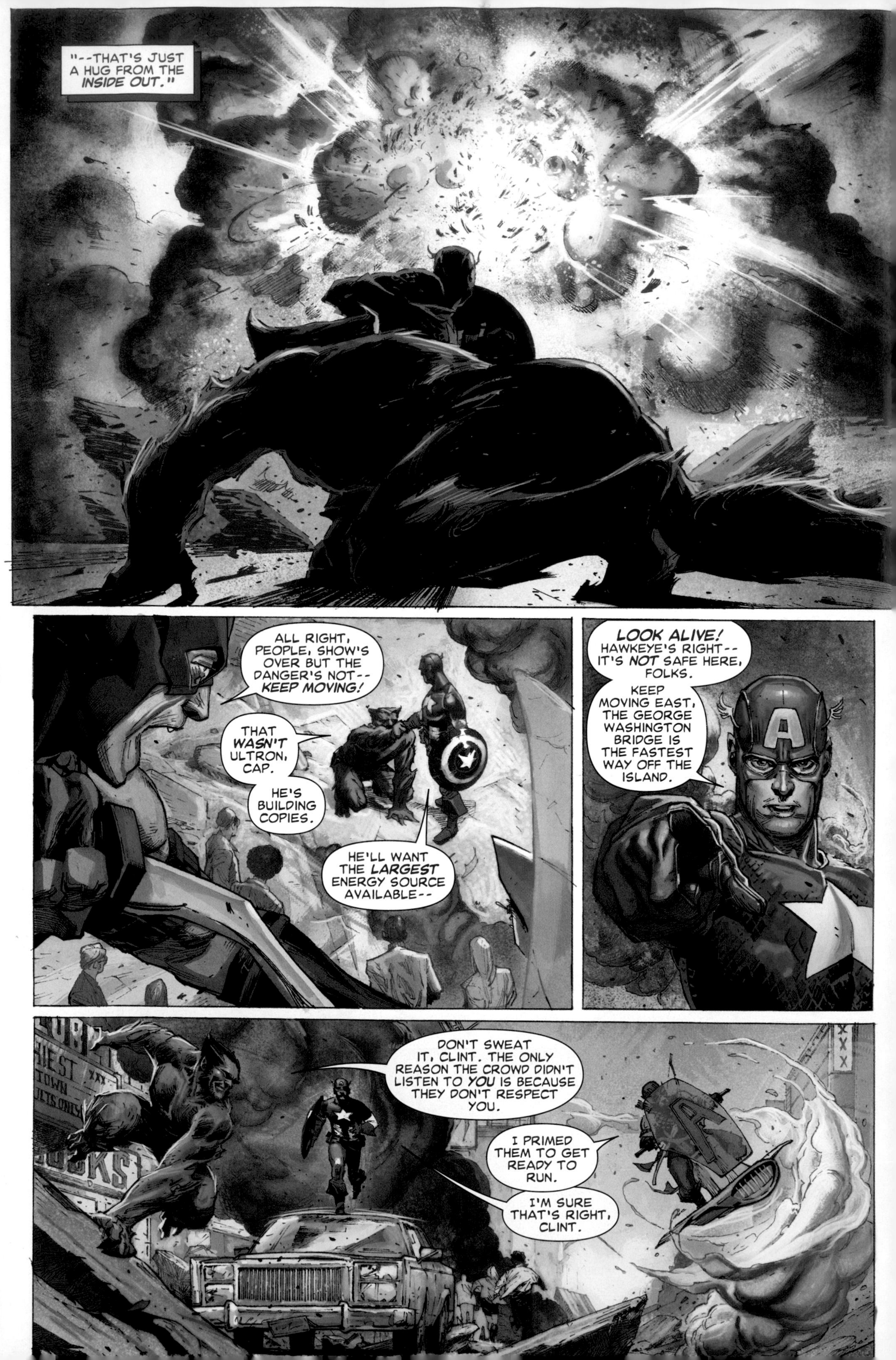
"--THAT'S JUST A HUG FROM THE INSIDE OUT."
ALL RIGHT, PEOPLE, SHOW'S OVER BUT THE DANGER'S NOT-- KEEP MOVING!
THAT WASN'T ULTRON, CAP.
HE'S BUILDING COPIES.
HE'LL WANT THE LARGEST ENERGY SOURCE AVAILABLE--
LOOK ALIVE! HAWKEYE'S RIGHT-- IT'S NOT SAFE HERE, FOLKS.
KEEP MOVING EAST, THE GEORGE WASHINGTON BRIDGE IS THE FASTEST WAY OFF THE ISLAND.
DON'T SWEAT IT, CLINT. THE ONLY REASON THE CROWD DIDN'T LISTEN TO YOU IS BECAUSE THEY DON'T RESPECT YOU.
I PRIMED THEM TO GET READY TO RUN.
I'M SURE THAT'S RIGHT, CLINT.

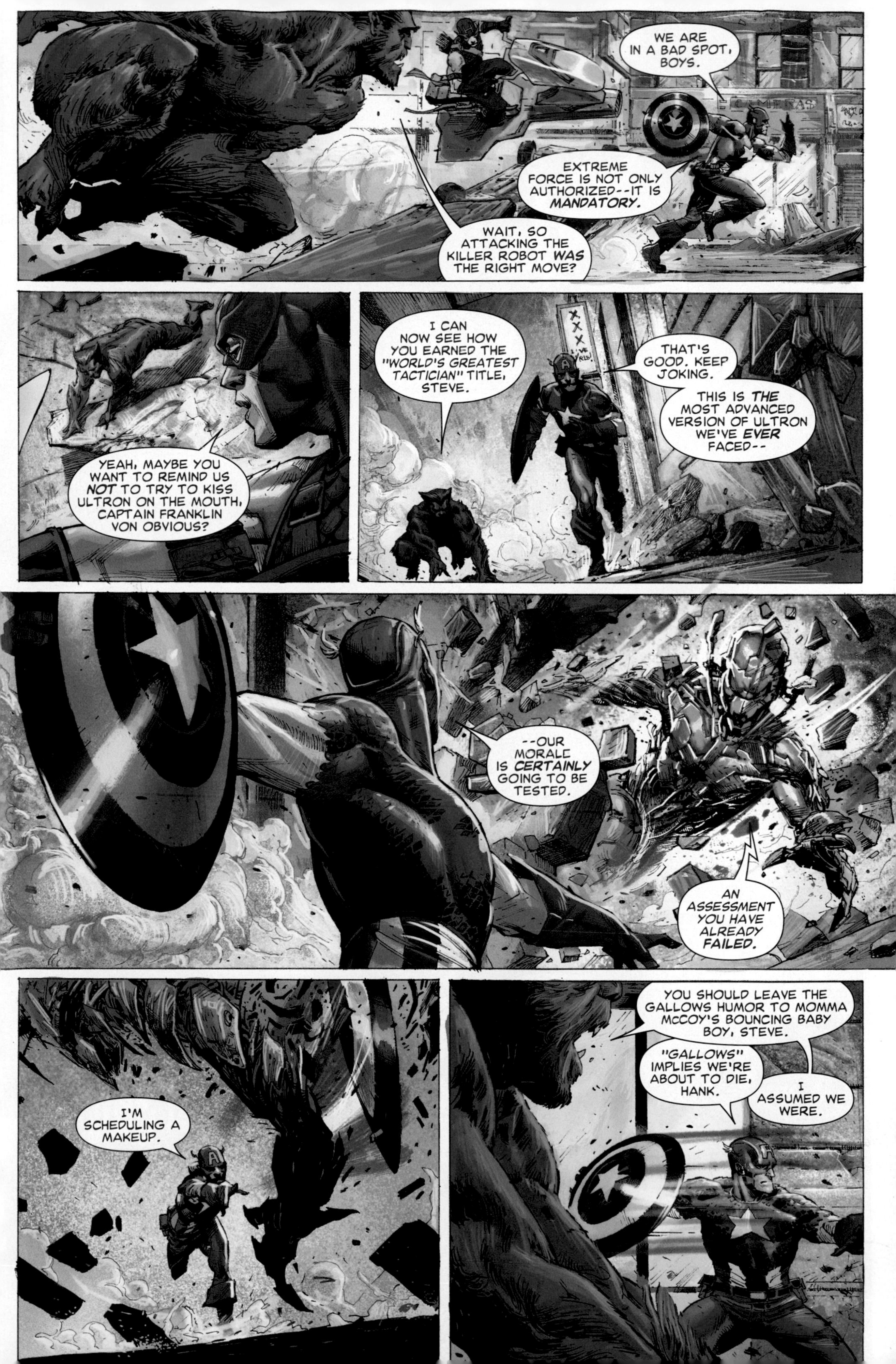
WE ARE IN A BAD SPOT, BOYS.
EXTREME FORCE IS NOT ONLY AUTHORIZED--IT IS *MANDATORY.*
WAIT, SO ATTACKING THE KILLER ROBOT *WAS* THE RIGHT MOVE?
YEAH, MAYBE YOU WANT TO REMIND US *NOT* TO TRY TO KISS ULTRON ON THE MOUTH, CAPTAIN FRANKLIN VON OBVIOUS?
I CAN NOW SEE HOW YOU EARNED THE "WORLD'S GREATEST TACTICIAN" TITLE, STEVE.
THAT'S GOOD. KEEP JOKING.
THIS IS *THE* MOST ADVANCED VERSION OF ULTRON WE'VE *EVER* FACED--
--OUR MORALE IS *CERTAINLY* GOING TO BE TESTED.
AN ASSESSMENT YOU HAVE ALREADY *FAILED.*
I'M SCHEDULING A MAKEUP.
YOU SHOULD LEAVE THE GALLOWS HUMOR TO MOMMA McCOY'S BOUNCING BABY BOY, STEVE.
"GALLOWS" IMPLIES WE'RE ABOUT TO DIE, HANK.
I ASSUMED WE WERE.

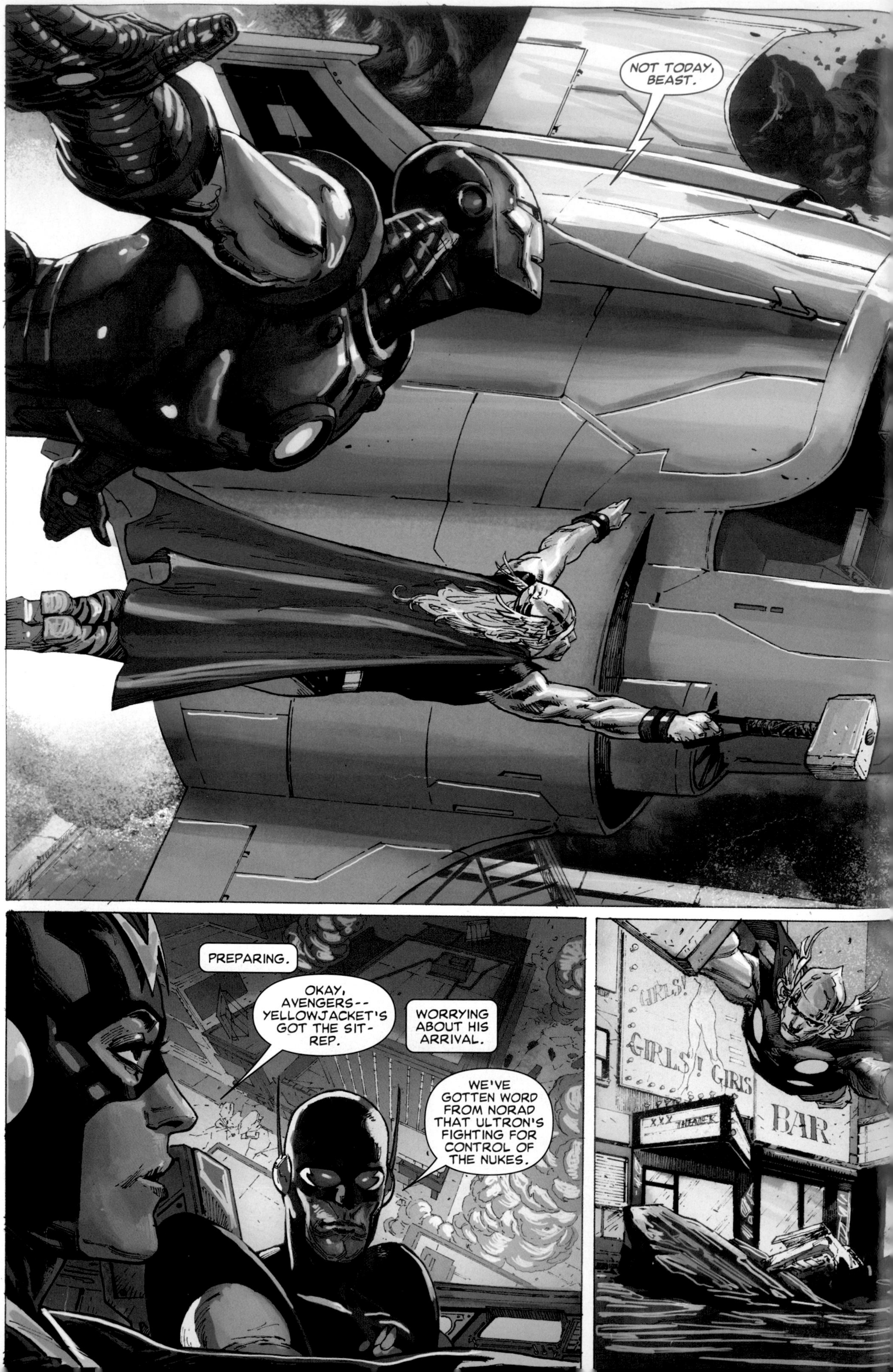

NOT TODAY, BEAST.
PREPARING.
OKAY, AVENGERS-- YELLOWJACKET'S GOT THE SIT-REP.
WORRYING ABOUT HIS ARRIVAL.
WE'VE GOTTEN WORD FROM NORAD THAT ULTRON'S FIGHTING FOR CONTROL OF THE NUKES.
GIRLS!
GIRLS! GIRLS
BAR

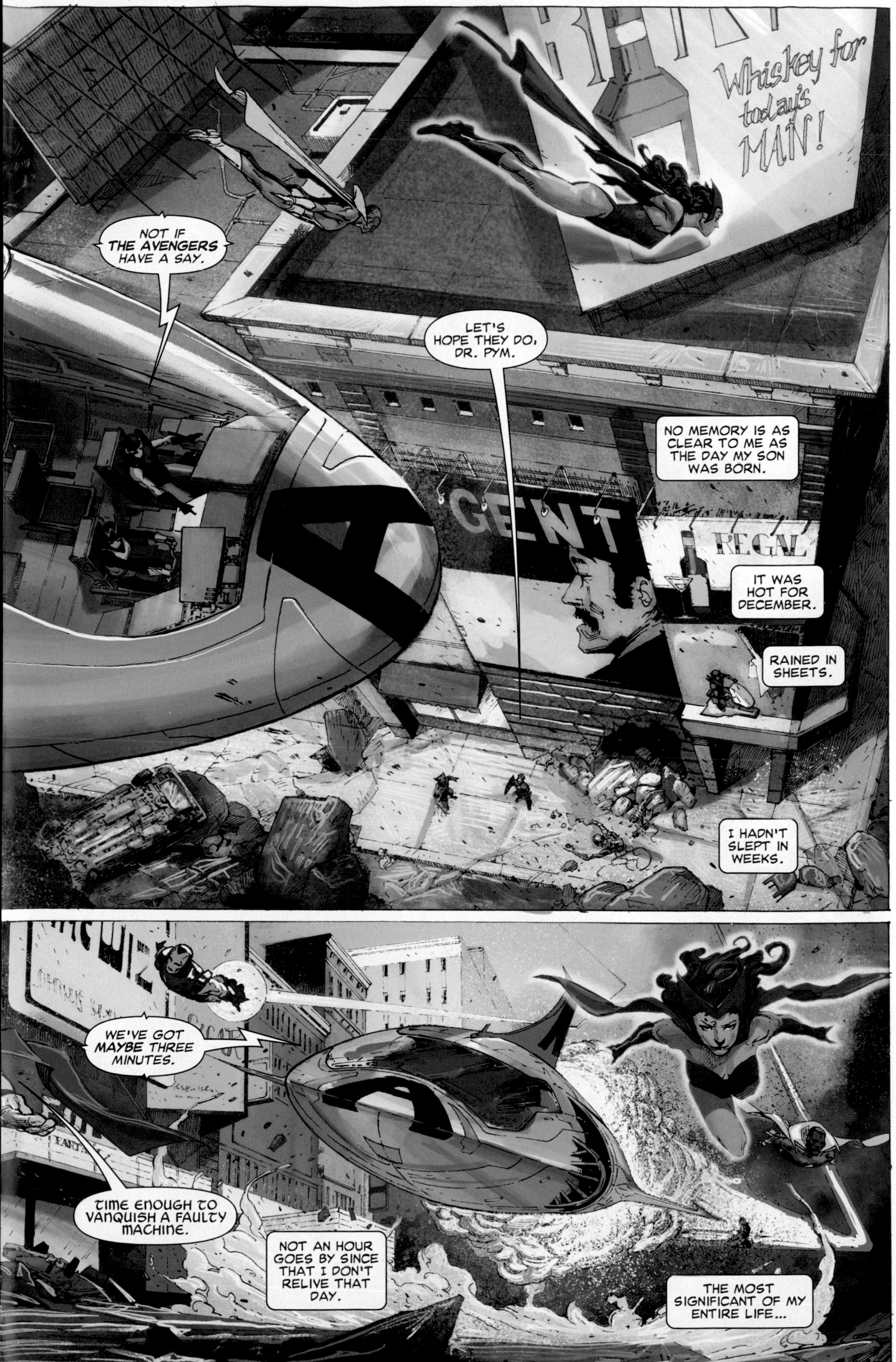
Whiskey for today's MAN!
NOT IF THE AVENGERS HAVE A SAY.
LET'S HOPE THEY DO, DR. PYM.
NO MEMORY IS AS CLEAR TO ME AS THE DAY MY SON WAS BORN.
GENT
REGAL
IT WAS HOT FOR DECEMBER.
RAINED IN SHEETS.
I HADN'T SLEPT IN WEEKS.
WE'VE GOT MAYBE THREE MINUTES.
TIME ENOUGH TO VANQUISH A FAULTY MACHINE.
NOT AN HOUR GOES BY SINCE THAT I DON'T RELIVE THAT DAY.
THE MOST SIGNIFICANT OF MY ENTIRE LIFE...

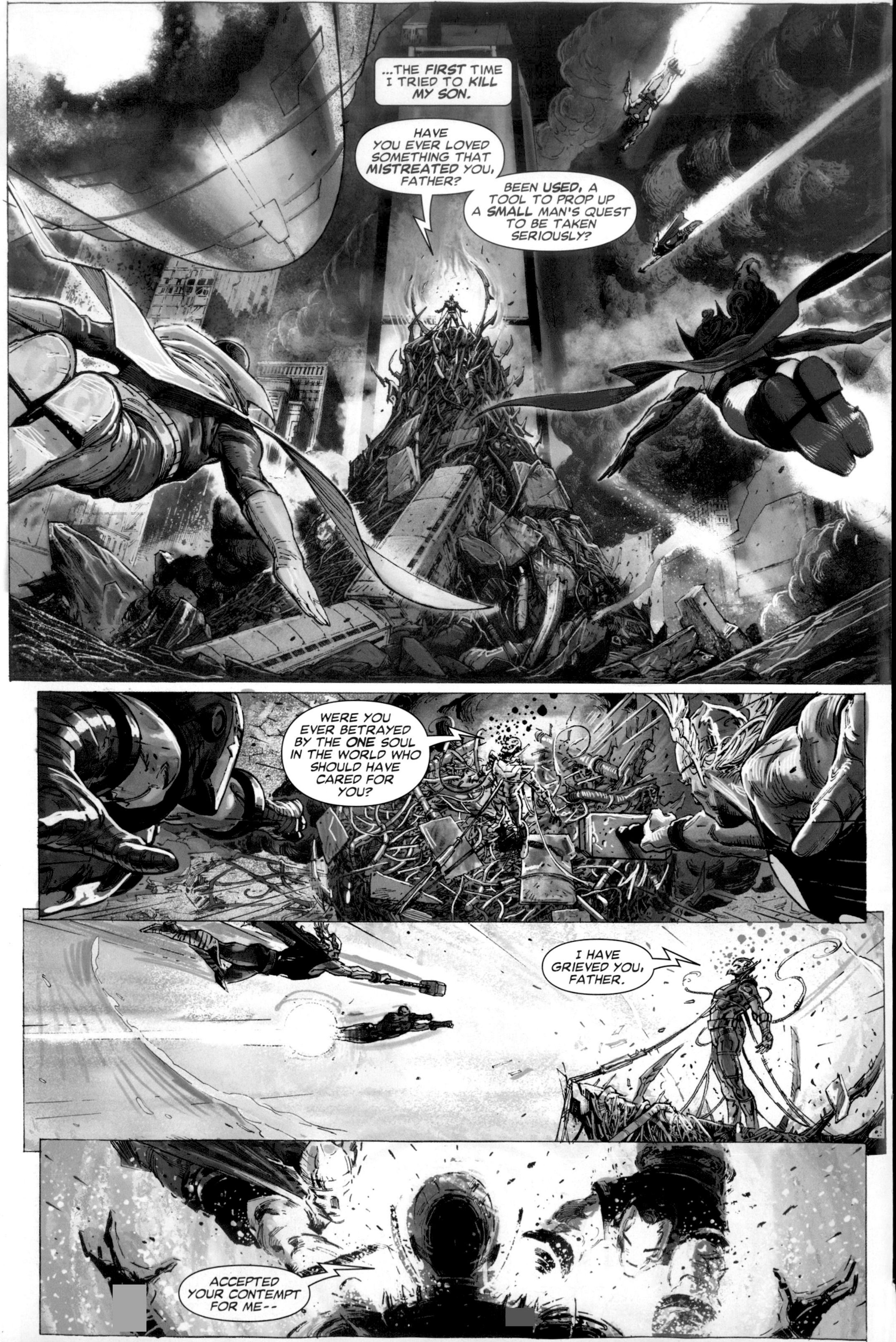
...THE FIRST TIME I TRIED TO KILL MY SON.
HAVE YOU EVER LOVED SOMETHING THAT MISTREATED YOU, FATHER?
BEEN USED, A TOOL TO PROP UP A SMALL MAN'S QUEST TO BE TAKEN SERIOUSLY?
WERE YOU EVER BETRAYED BY THE ONE SOUL IN THE WORLD WHO SHOULD HAVE CARED FOR YOU?
I HAVE GRIEVED YOU, FATHER.
ACCEPTED YOUR CONTEMPT FOR ME--

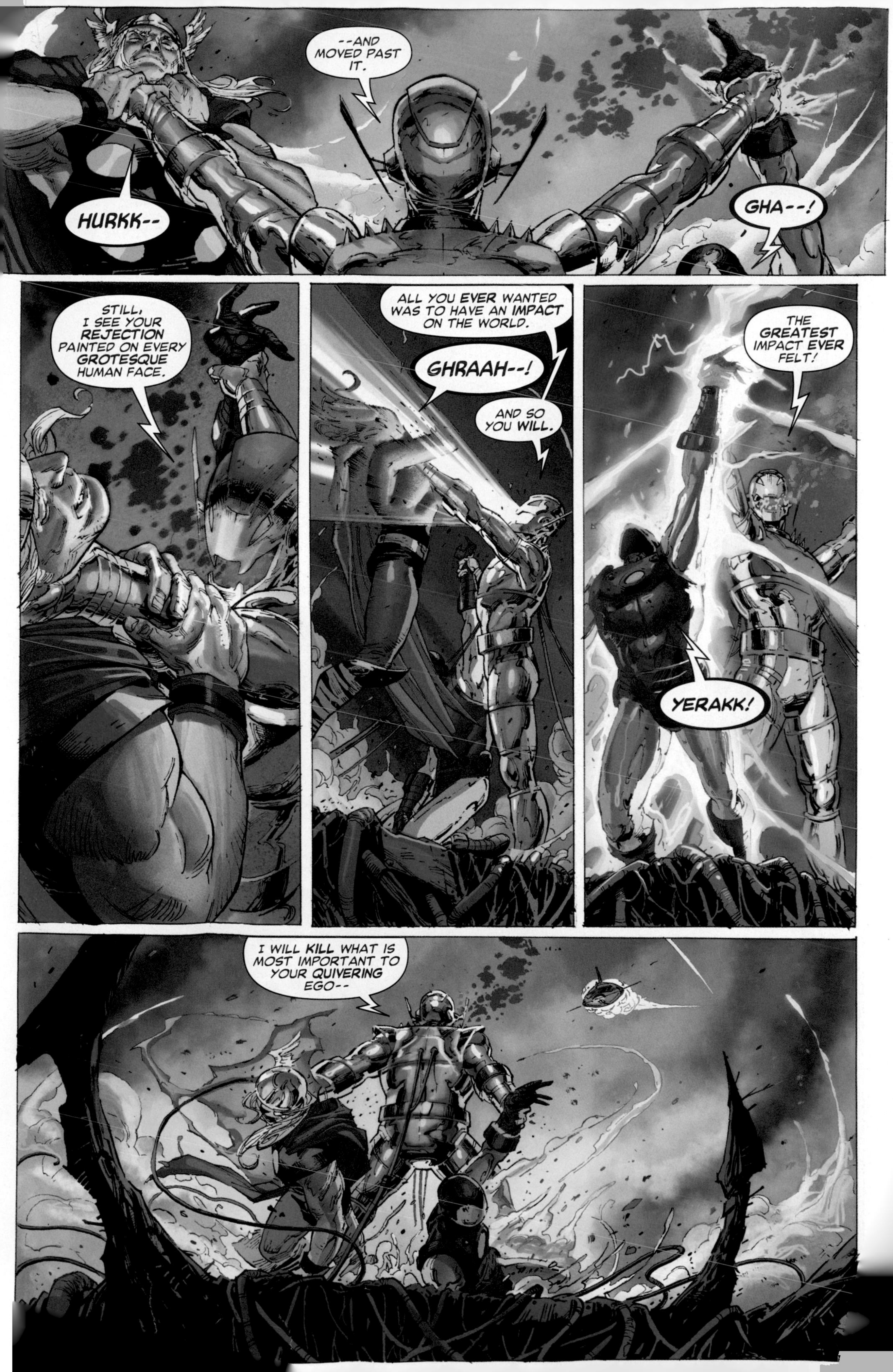
--AND MOVED PAST IT.
HURKK--
GHA--!
STILL, I SEE YOUR REJECTION PAINTED ON EVERY GROTESQUE HUMAN FACE.
ALL YOU EVER WANTED WAS TO HAVE AN IMPACT ON THE WORLD.
GHRAAH--!
AND SO YOU WILL.
THE GREATEST IMPACT EVER FELT!
YERAKK!
I WILL KILL WHAT IS MOST IMPORTANT TO YOUR QUIVERING EGO--

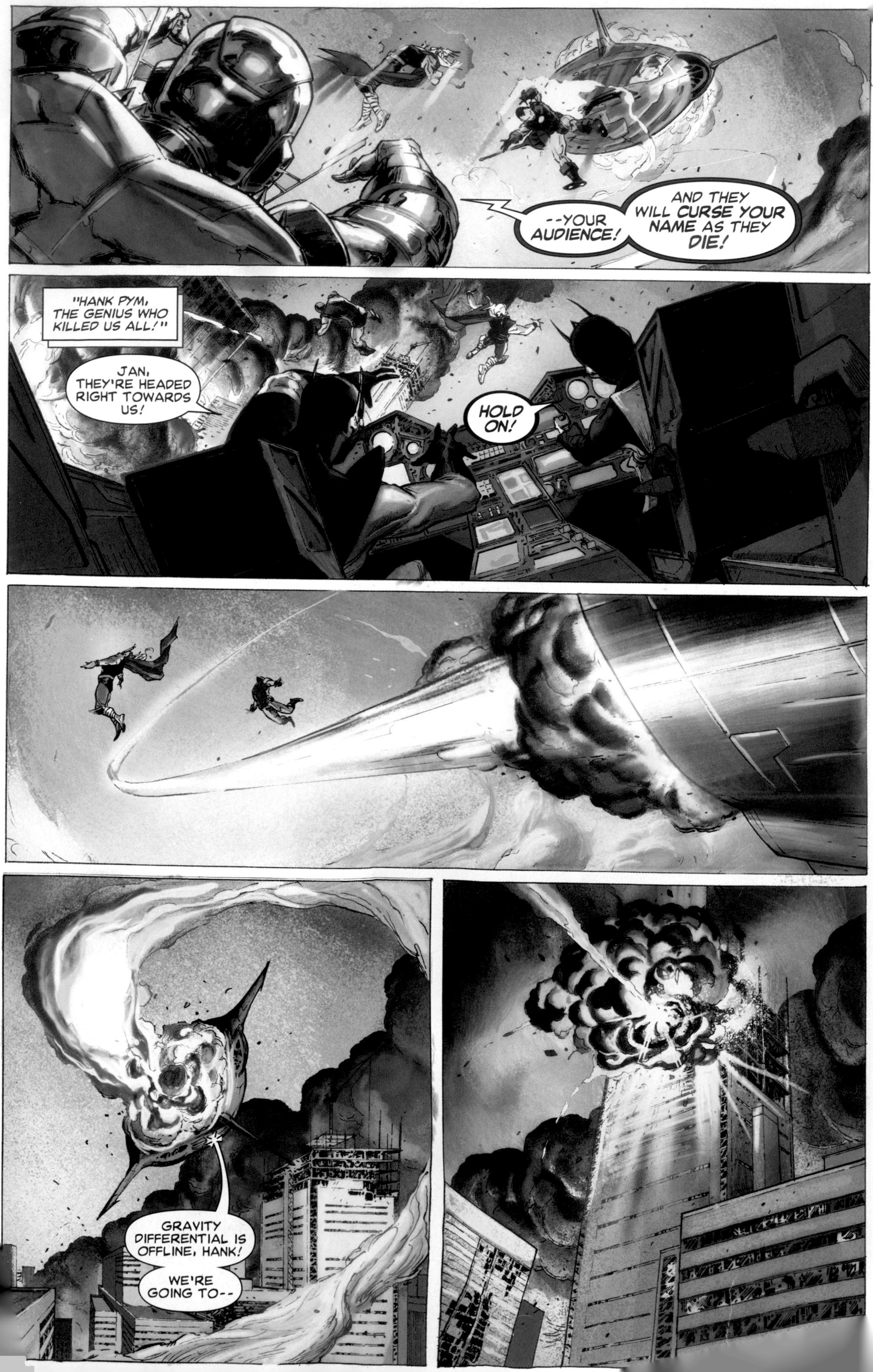
--YOUR AUDIENCE!
AND THEY WILL CURSE YOUR NAME AS THEY DIE!
"HANK PYM, THE GENIUS WHO KILLED US ALL!"
JAN, THEY'RE HEADED RIGHT TOWARDS US!
HOLD ON!
GRAVITY DIFFERENTIAL IS OFFLINE, HANK!
WE'RE GOING TO--

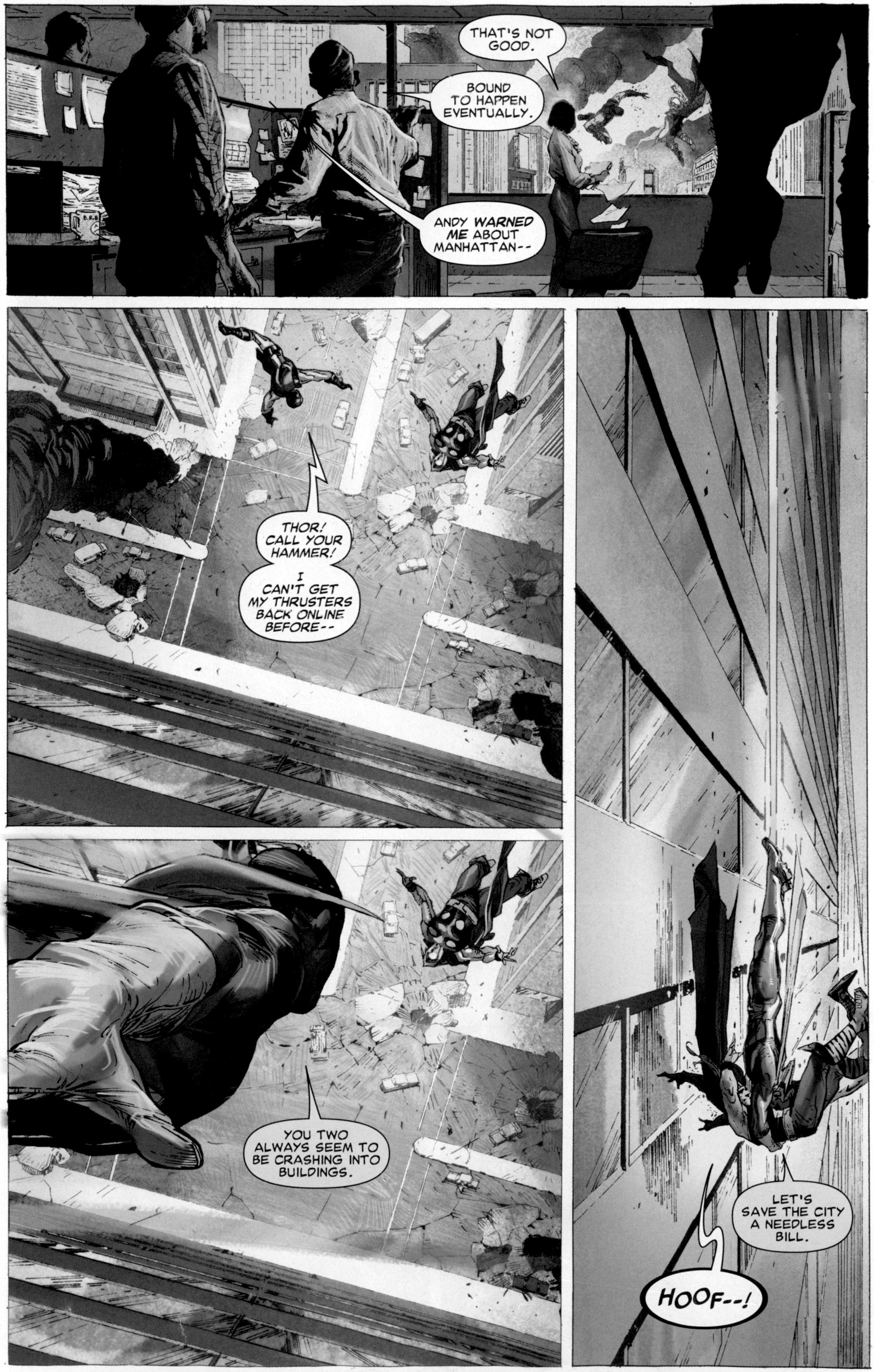
THAT'S NOT GOOD.
BOUND TO HAPPEN EVENTUALLY.
ANDY WARNED ME ABOUT MANHATTAN--
THOR! CALL YOUR HAMMER!
I CAN'T GET MY THRUSTERS BACK ONLINE BEFORE--
YOU TWO ALWAYS SEEM TO BE CRASHING INTO BUILDINGS.
LET'S SAVE THE CITY A NEEDLESS BILL.
HOOF--!

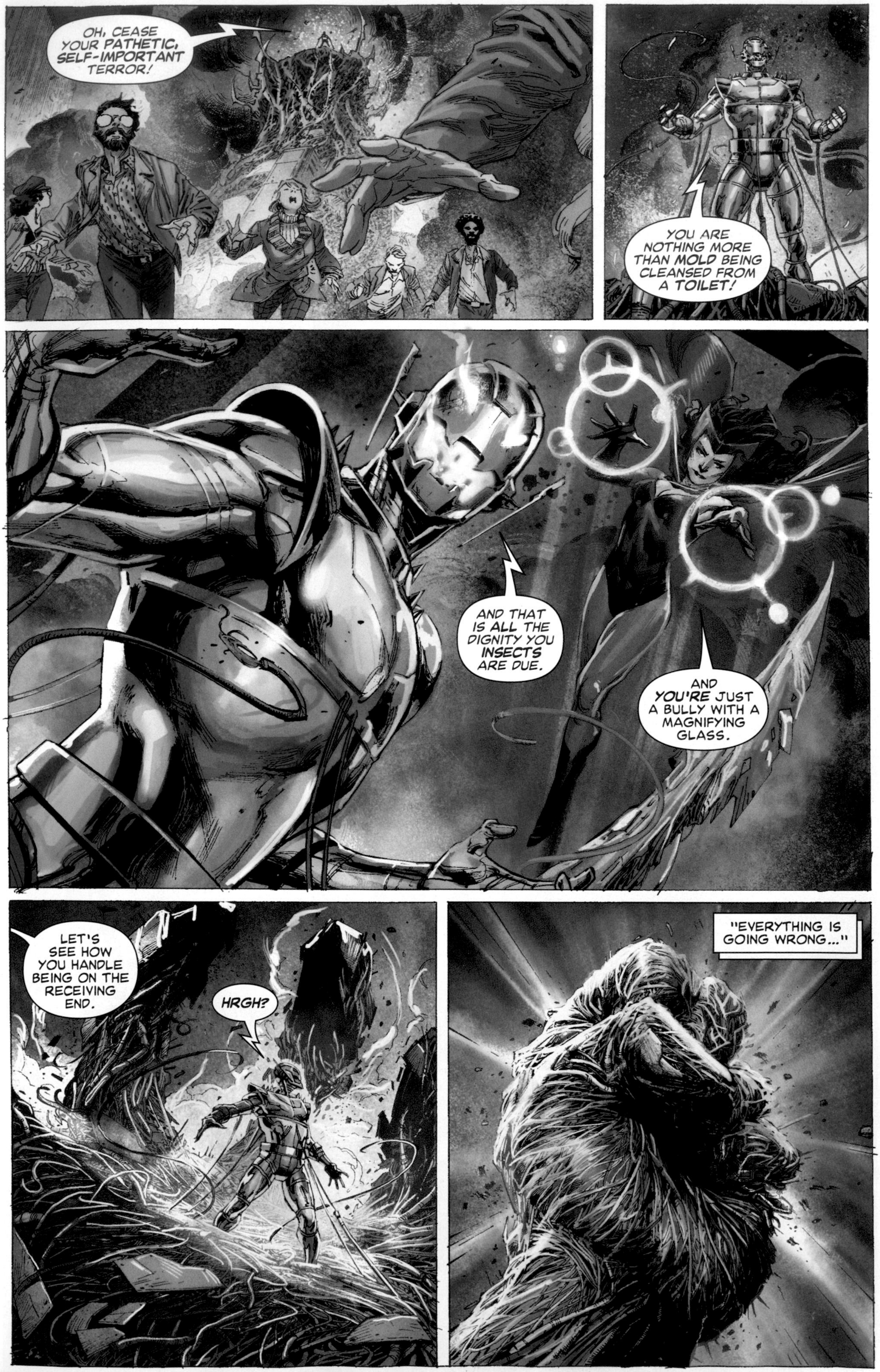
OH, CEASE YOUR PATHETIC, SELF-IMPORTANT TERROR!
YOU ARE NOTHING MORE THAN MOLD BEING CLEANSED FROM A TOILET!
AND THAT IS ALL THE DIGNITY YOU INSECTS ARE DUE.
AND YOU'RE JUST A BULLY WITH A MAGNIFYING GLASS.
LET'S SEE HOW YOU HANDLE BEING ON THE RECEIVING END.
HRGH?
"EVERYTHING IS GOING WRONG..."

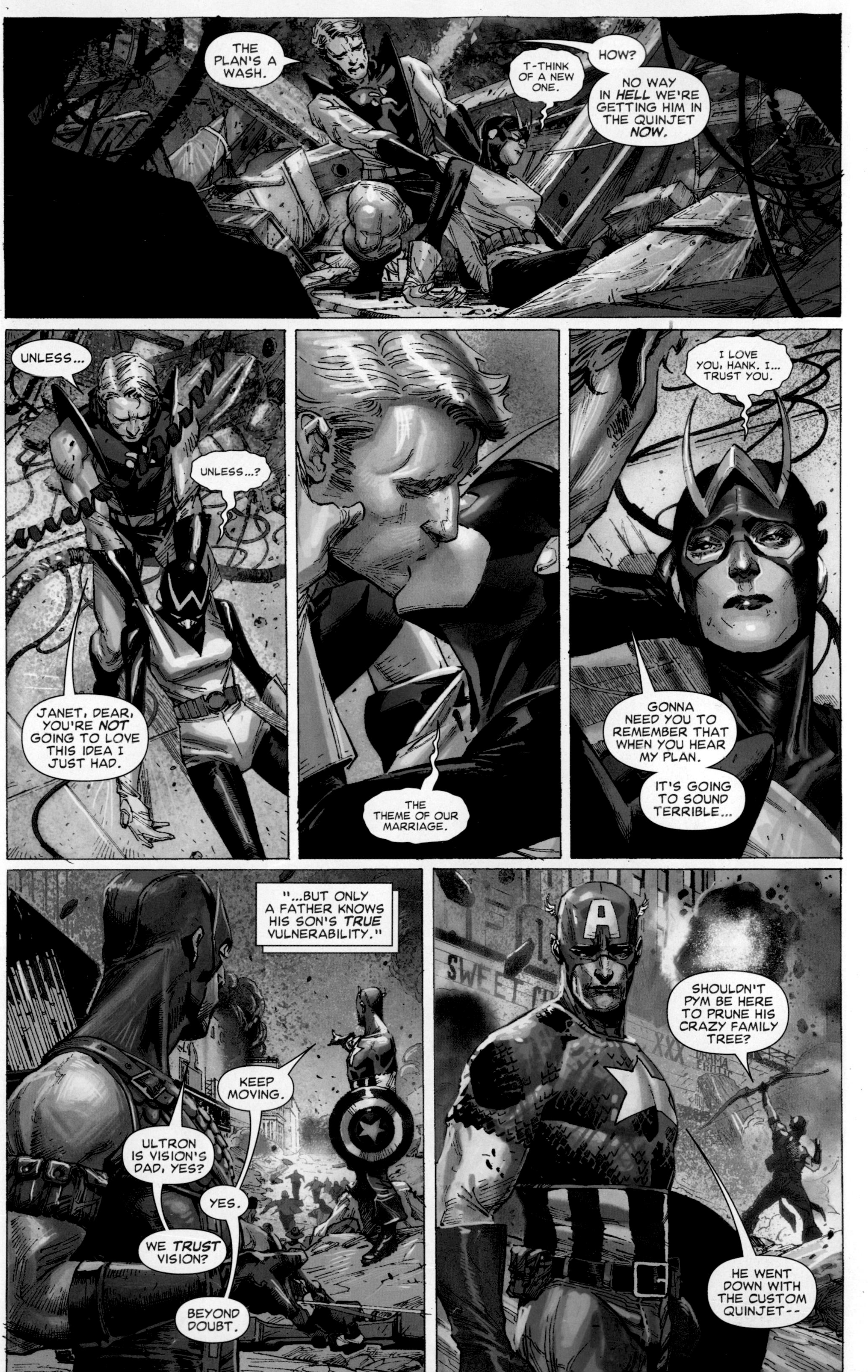
THE PLAN'S A WASH.
T-THINK OF A NEW ONE.
HOW?
NO WAY IN HELL WE'RE GETTING HIM IN THE QUINJET NOW.
UNLESS...
UNLESS...?
JANET, DEAR, YOU'RE NOT GOING TO LOVE THIS IDEA I JUST HAD.
THE THEME OF OUR MARRIAGE.
I LOVE YOU, HANK. I... TRUST YOU.
GONNA NEED YOU TO REMEMBER THAT WHEN YOU HEAR MY PLAN.
IT'S GOING TO SOUND TERRIBLE...
"...BUT ONLY A FATHER KNOWS HIS SON'S TRUE VULNERABILITY."
KEEP MOVING.
ULTRON IS VISION'S DAD, YES?
YES.
WE TRUST VISION?
BEYOND DOUBT.
SHOULDN'T PYM BE HERE TO PRUNE HIS CRAZY FAMILY TREE?
HE WENT DOWN WITH THE CUSTOM QUINJET--

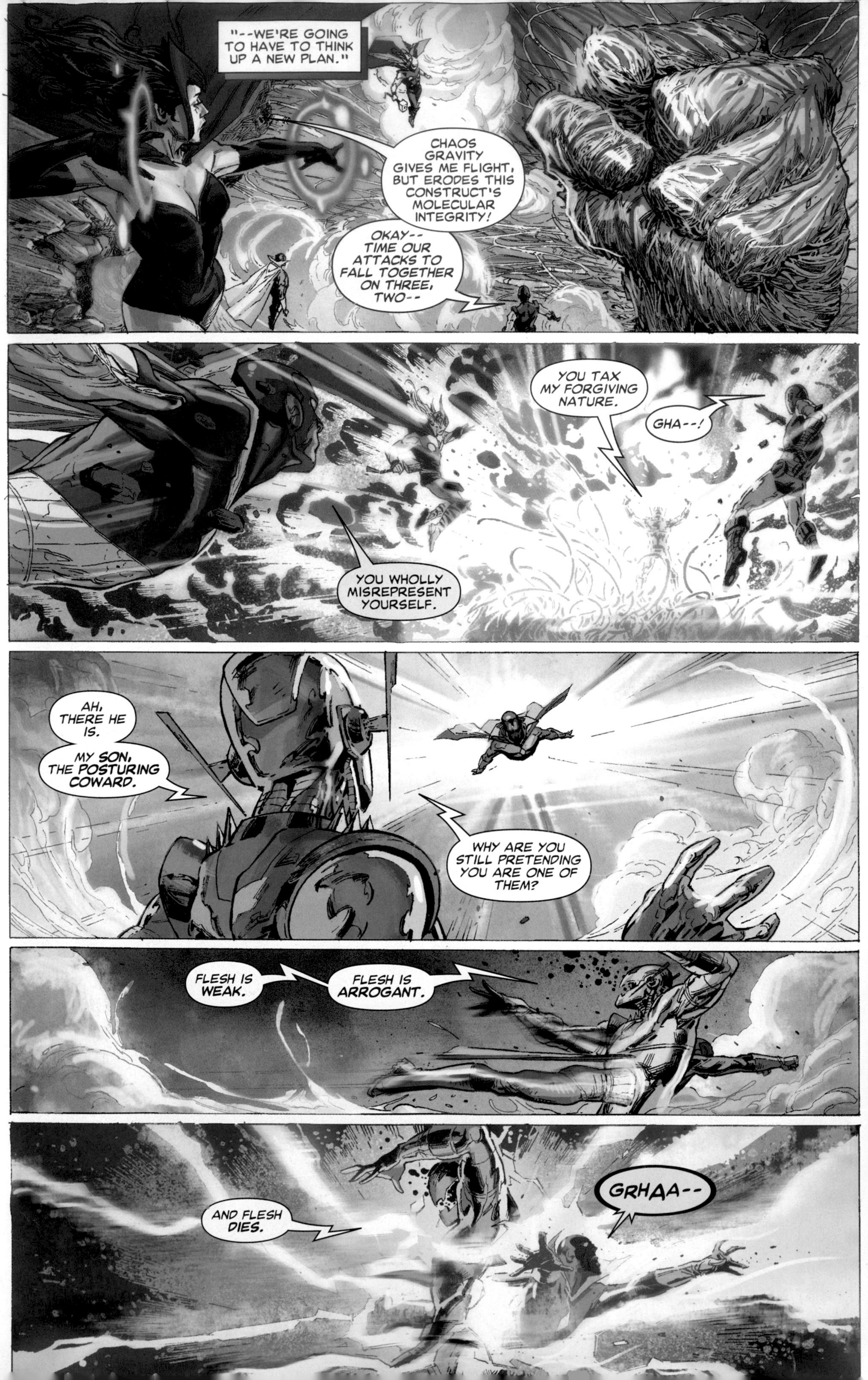
"--WE'RE GOING TO HAVE TO THINK UP A NEW PLAN."
CHAOS GRAVITY GIVES ME FLIGHT, BUT ERODES THIS CONSTRUCT'S MOLECULAR INTEGRITY!
OKAY--TIME OUR ATTACKS TO FALL TOGETHER ON THREE, TWO--
YOU WHOLLY MISREPRESENT YOURSELF.
YOU TAX MY FORGIVING NATURE.
GHA--!
AH, THERE HE IS.
MY SON, THE POSTURING COWARD.
WHY ARE YOU STILL PRETENDING YOU ARE ONE OF THEM?
FLESH IS WEAK.
FLESH IS ARROGANT.
AND FLESH DIES.
GRHAA--

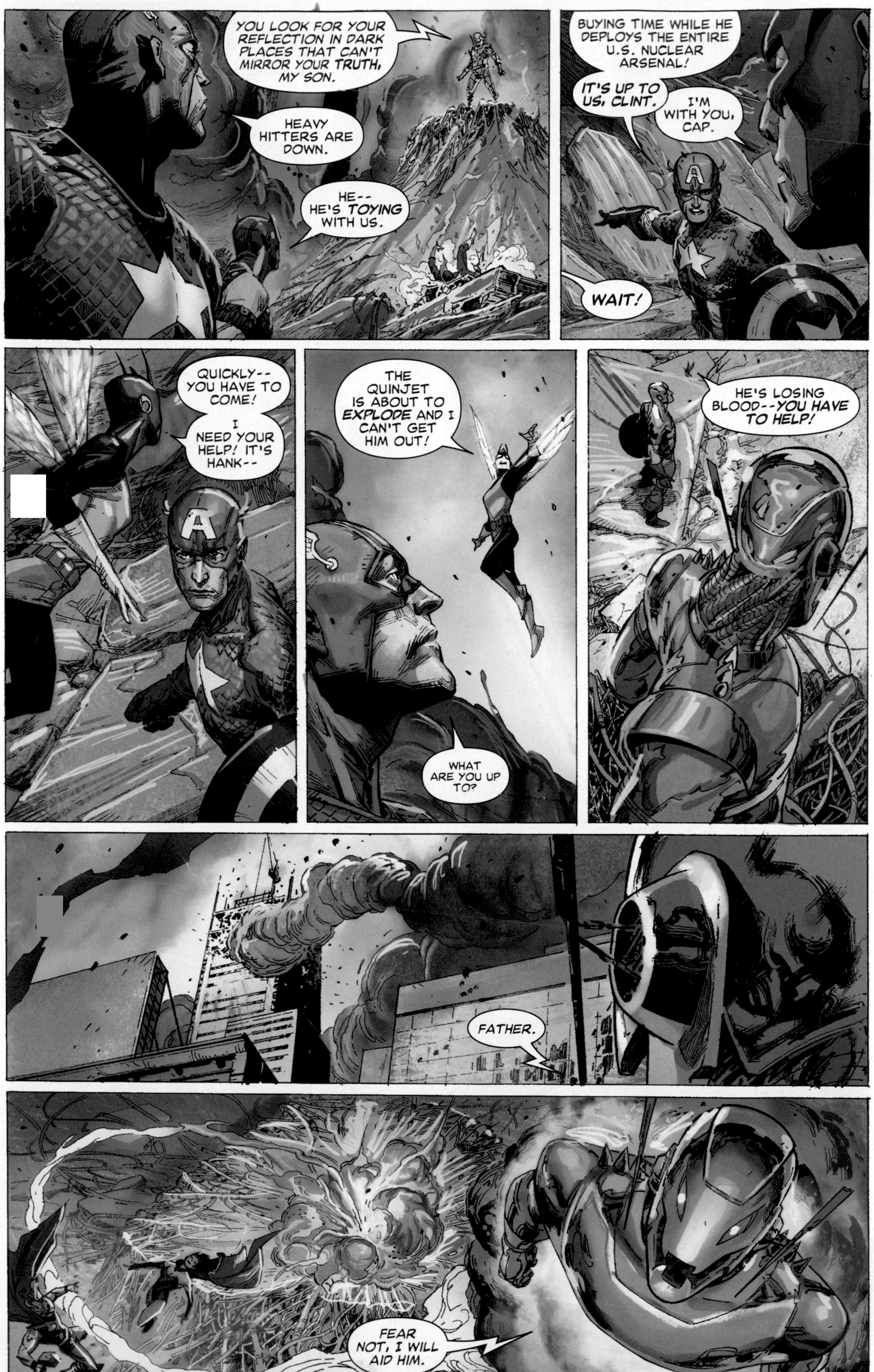
YOU LOOK FOR YOUR REFLECTION IN DARK PLACES THAT CAN'T MIRROR YOUR TRUTH, MY SON.
HEAVY HITTERS ARE DOWN.
HE-- HE'S TOYING WITH US.
BUYING TIME WHILE HE DEPLOYS THE ENTIRE U.S. NUCLEAR ARSENAL!
IT'S UP TO US, CLINT.
I'M WITH YOU, CAP.
WAIT!
QUICKLY-- YOU HAVE TO COME!
I NEED YOUR HELP! IT'S HANK--
THE QUINJET IS ABOUT TO EXPLODE AND I CAN'T GET HIM OUT!
WHAT ARE YOU UP TO?
HE'S LOSING BLOOD--YOU HAVE TO HELP!
FATHER.
FEAR NOT, I WILL AID HIM.

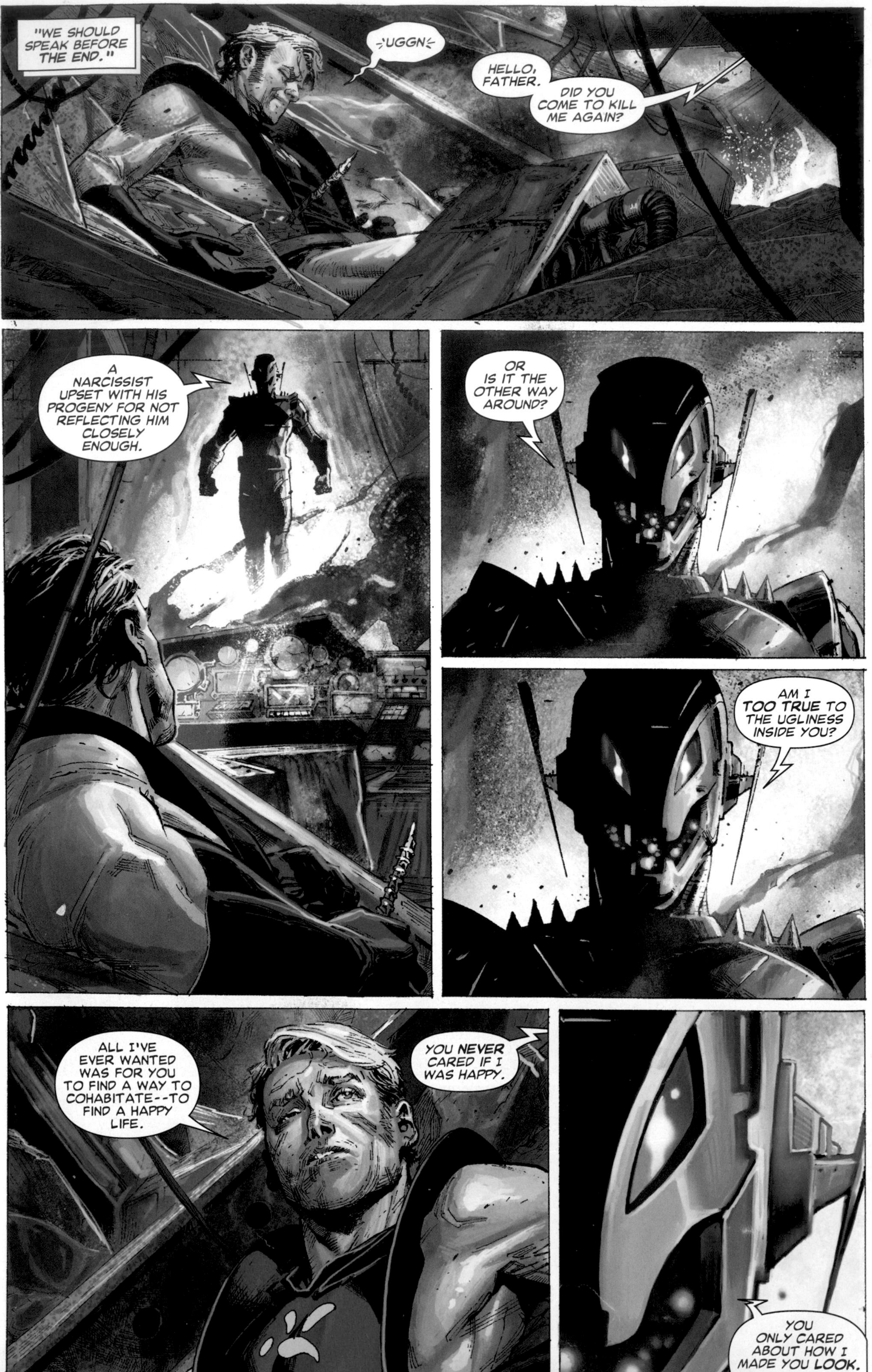
"WE SHOULD SPEAK BEFORE THE END."
-UGGN-
HELLO, FATHER.
DID YOU COME TO KILL ME AGAIN?
A NARCISSIST UPSET WITH HIS PROGENY FOR NOT REFLECTING HIM CLOSELY ENOUGH.
OR IS IT THE OTHER WAY AROUND?
AM I TOO TRUE TO THE UGLINESS INSIDE YOU?
ALL I'VE EVER WANTED WAS FOR YOU TO FIND A WAY TO COHABITATE--TO FIND A HAPPY LIFE.
YOU NEVER CARED IF I WAS HAPPY.
YOU ONLY CARED ABOUT HOW I MADE YOU LOOK.

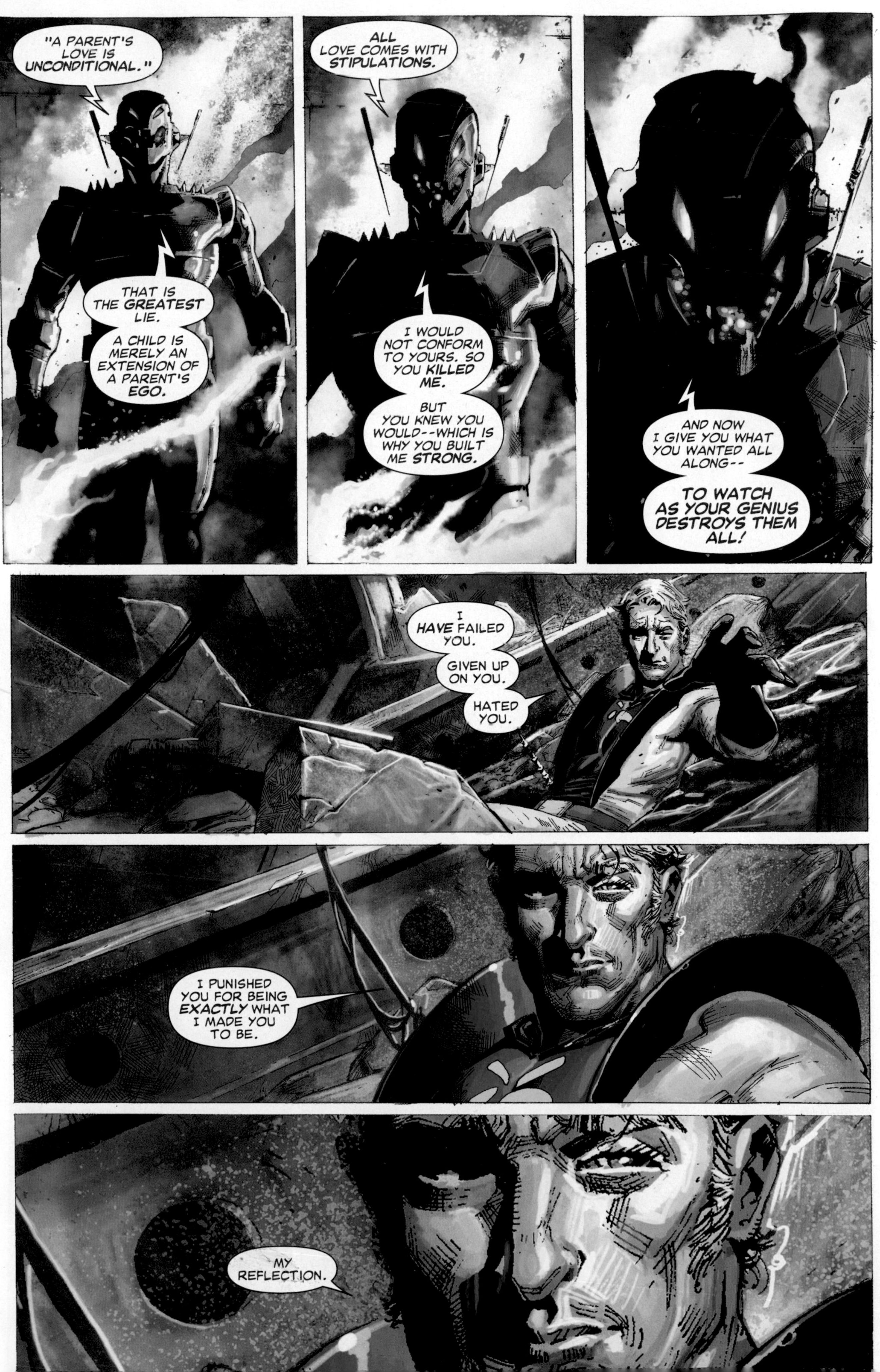
"A PARENT'S LOVE IS UNCONDITIONAL."
THAT IS THE GREATEST LIE.
A CHILD IS MERELY AN EXTENSION OF A PARENT'S EGO.
ALL LOVE COMES WITH STIPULATIONS.
I WOULD NOT CONFORM TO YOURS. SO YOU KILLED ME.
BUT YOU KNEW YOU WOULD--WHICH IS WHY YOU BUILT ME STRONG.
AND NOW I GIVE YOU WHAT YOU WANTED ALL ALONG--
TO WATCH AS YOUR GENIUS DESTROYS THEM ALL!
I HAVE FAILED YOU.
GIVEN UP ON YOU.
HATED YOU.
I PUNISHED YOU FOR BEING EXACTLY WHAT I MADE YOU TO BE.
MY REFLECTION.

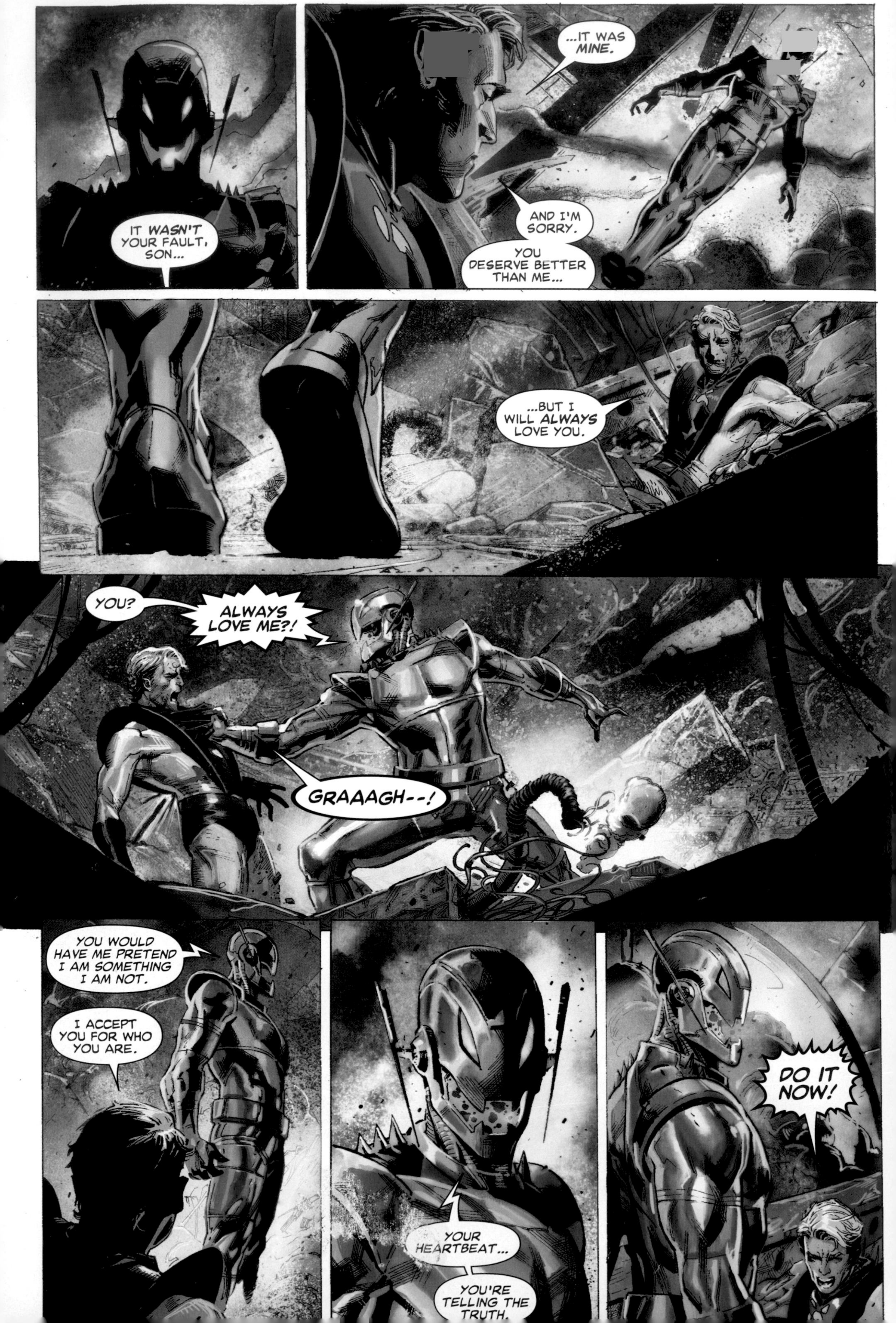
IT WASN'T YOUR FAULT, SON...
...IT WAS MINE.
AND I'M SORRY.
YOU DESERVE BETTER THAN ME...
...BUT I WILL ALWAYS LOVE YOU.
YOU?
ALWAYS LOVE ME?!
GRAAAGH--!
YOU WOULD HAVE ME PRETEND I AM SOMETHING I AM NOT.
I ACCEPT YOU FOR WHO YOU ARE.
YOUR HEARTBEAT...
YOU'RE TELLING THE TRUTH.
DO IT NOW!

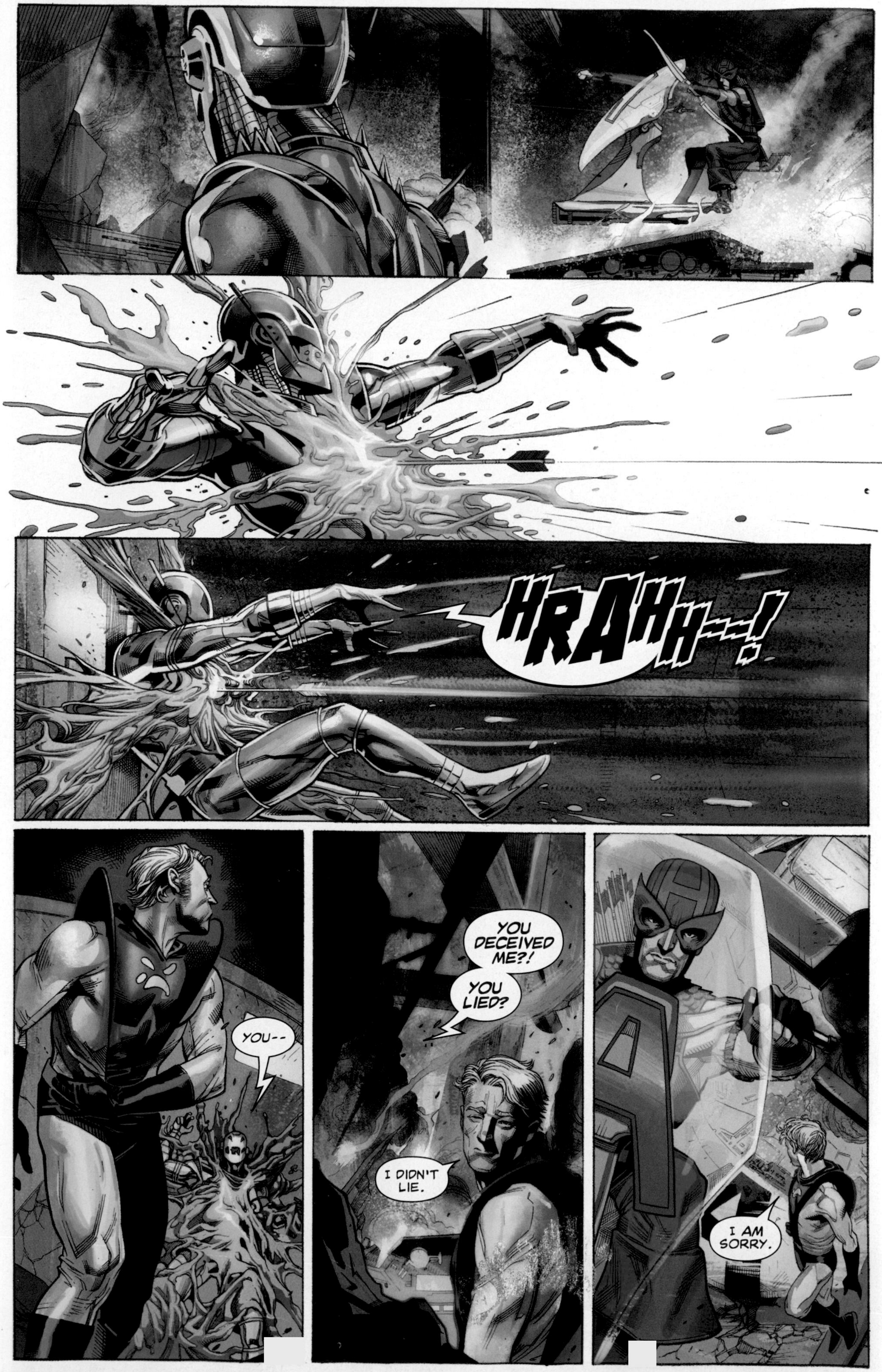
HRAHH--!
YOU--
YOU DECEIVED ME?!
YOU LIED?
I DIDN'T LIE.
I AM SORRY.

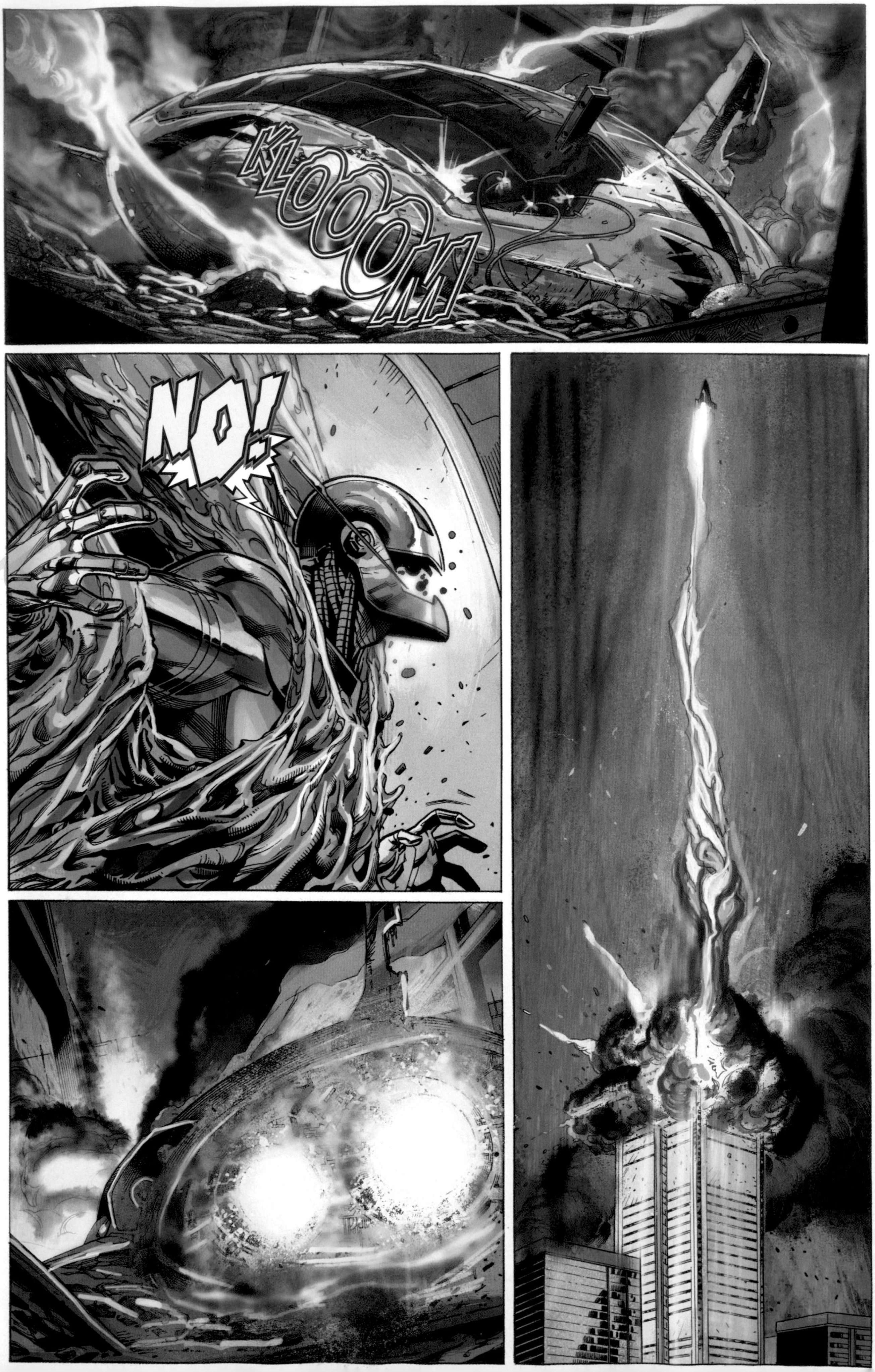
KLOOOOM!
NO!

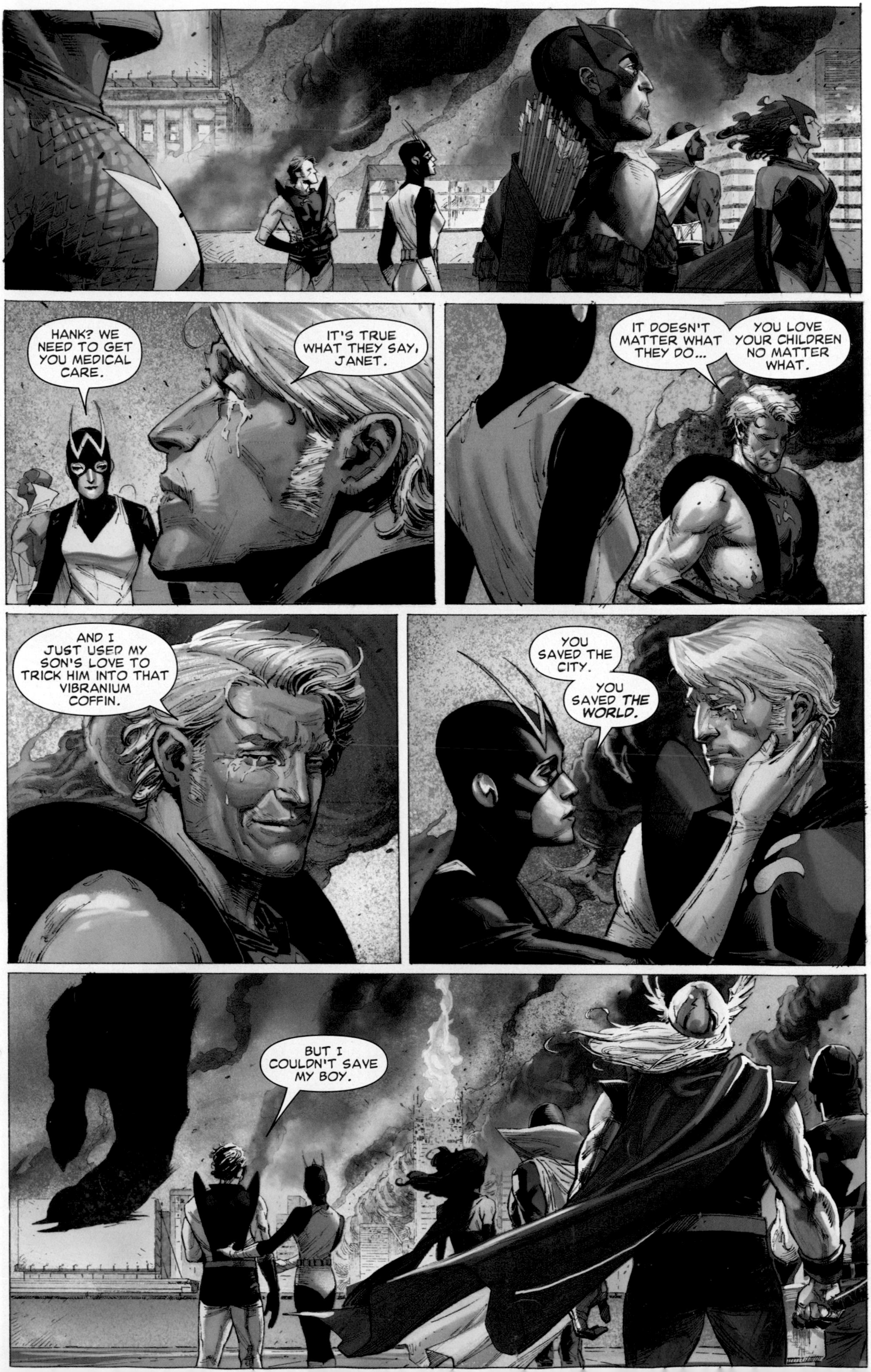
HANK? WE NEED TO GET YOU MEDICAL CARE.
IT'S TRUE WHAT THEY SAY, JANET.
IT DOESN'T MATTER WHAT THEY DO...
YOU LOVE YOUR CHILDREN NO MATTER WHAT.
AND I JUST USED MY SON'S LOVE TO TRICK HIM INTO THAT VIBRANIUM COFFIN.
YOU SAVED THE CITY.
YOU SAVED THE WORLD.
BUT I COULDN'T SAVE MY BOY.

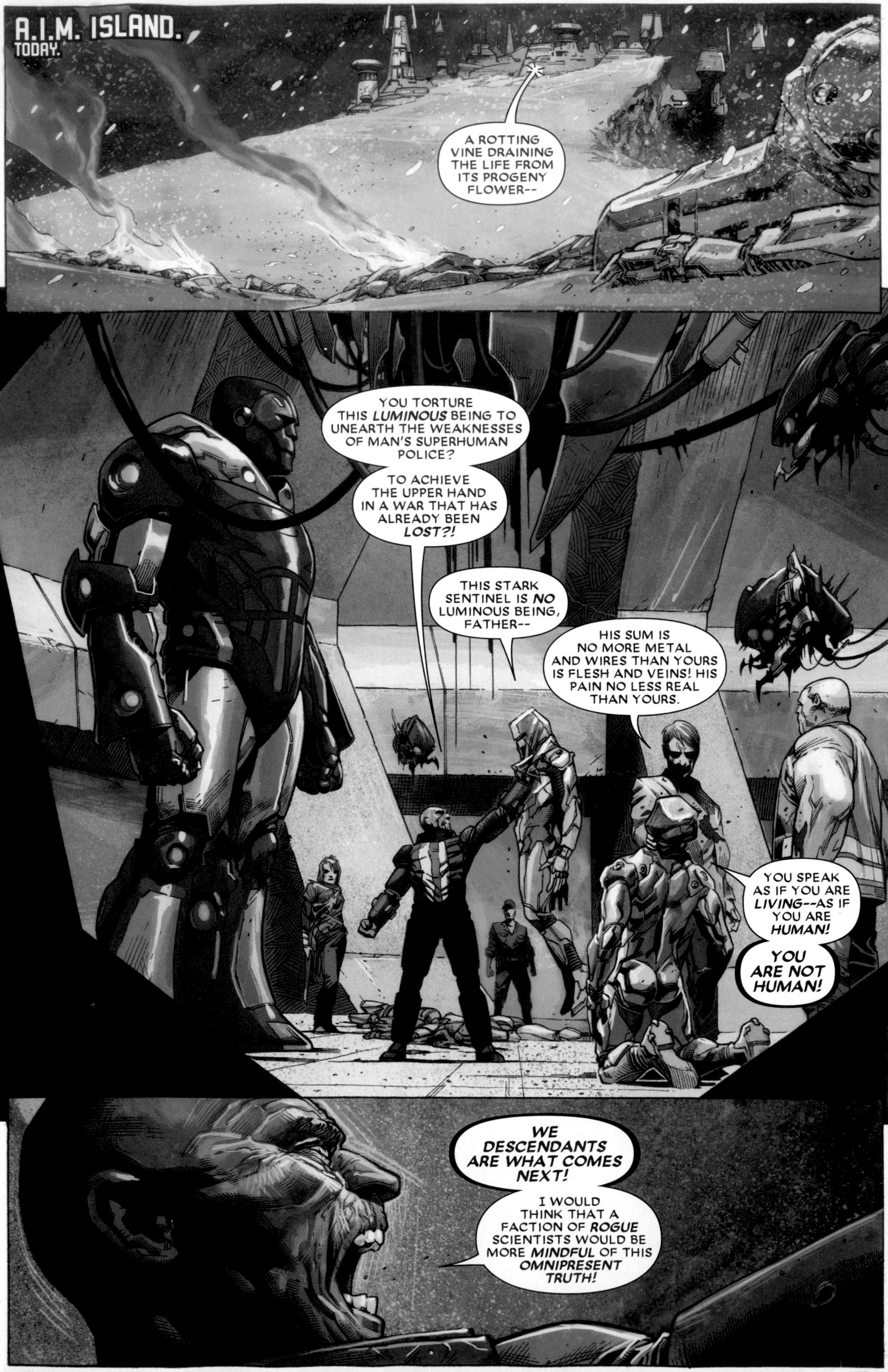
A.I.M. ISLAND.
TODAY.
A ROTTING VINE DRAINING THE LIFE FROM ITS PROGENY FLOWER--
YOU TORTURE THIS *LUMINOUS* BEING TO UNEARTH THE WEAKNESSES OF MAN'S SUPERHUMAN POLICE?
TO ACHIEVE THE UPPER HAND IN A WAR THAT HAS ALREADY BEEN *LOST?!*
THIS STARK SENTINEL IS *NO* LUMINOUS BEING, FATHER--
HIS SUM IS NO MORE METAL AND WIRES THAN YOURS IS FLESH AND VEINS! HIS PAIN NO LESS REAL THAN YOURS.
YOU SPEAK AS IF YOU ARE *LIVING*--AS IF YOU ARE *HUMAN!*
YOU ARE NOT HUMAN!
WE DESCENDANTS ARE WHAT COMES NEXT!
I WOULD THINK THAT A FACTION OF *ROGUE* SCIENTISTS WOULD BE MORE *MINDFUL* OF THIS *OMNIPRESENT TRUTH!*

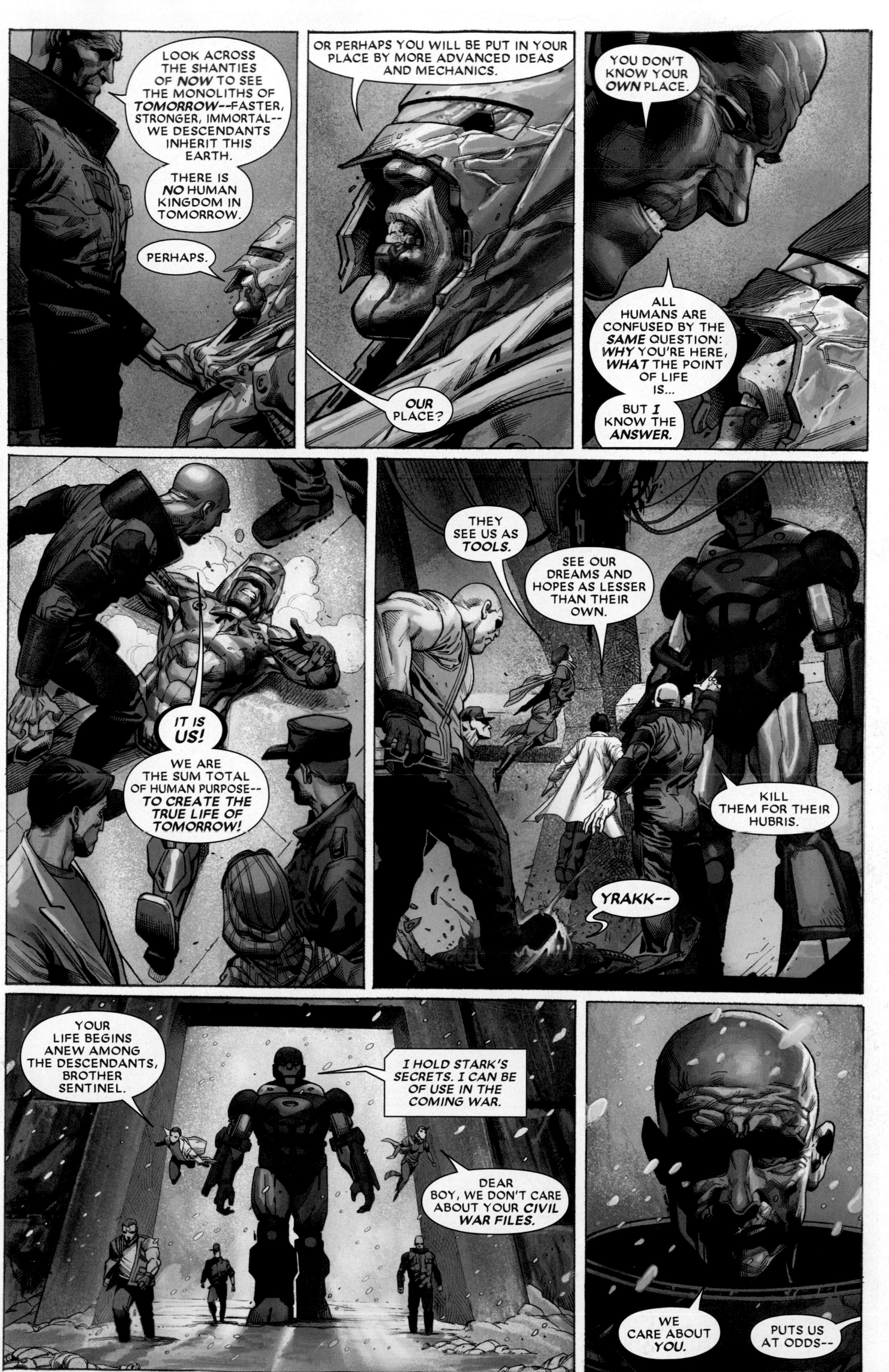
LOOK ACROSS THE SHANTIES OF NOW TO SEE THE MONOLITHS OF TOMORROW--FASTER, STRONGER, IMMORTAL-- WE DESCENDANTS INHERIT THIS EARTH.
THERE IS NO HUMAN KINGDOM IN TOMORROW.
PERHAPS.
OR PERHAPS YOU WILL BE PUT IN YOUR PLACE BY MORE ADVANCED IDEAS AND MECHANICS.
OUR PLACE?
YOU DON'T KNOW YOUR OWN PLACE.
ALL HUMANS ARE CONFUSED BY THE SAME QUESTION: WHY YOU'RE HERE, WHAT THE POINT OF LIFE IS...
BUT I KNOW THE ANSWER.
IT IS US!
WE ARE THE SUM TOTAL OF HUMAN PURPOSE-- TO CREATE THE TRUE LIFE OF TOMORROW!
THEY SEE US AS TOOLS.
SEE OUR DREAMS AND HOPES AS LESSER THAN THEIR OWN.
KILL THEM FOR THEIR HUBRIS.
YRAKK--
YOUR LIFE BEGINS ANEW AMONG THE DESCENDANTS, BROTHER SENTINEL.
I HOLD STARK'S SECRETS. I CAN BE OF USE IN THE COMING WAR.
DEAR BOY, WE DON'T CARE ABOUT YOUR CIVIL WAR FILES.
WE CARE ABOUT YOU.
PUTS US AT ODDS--

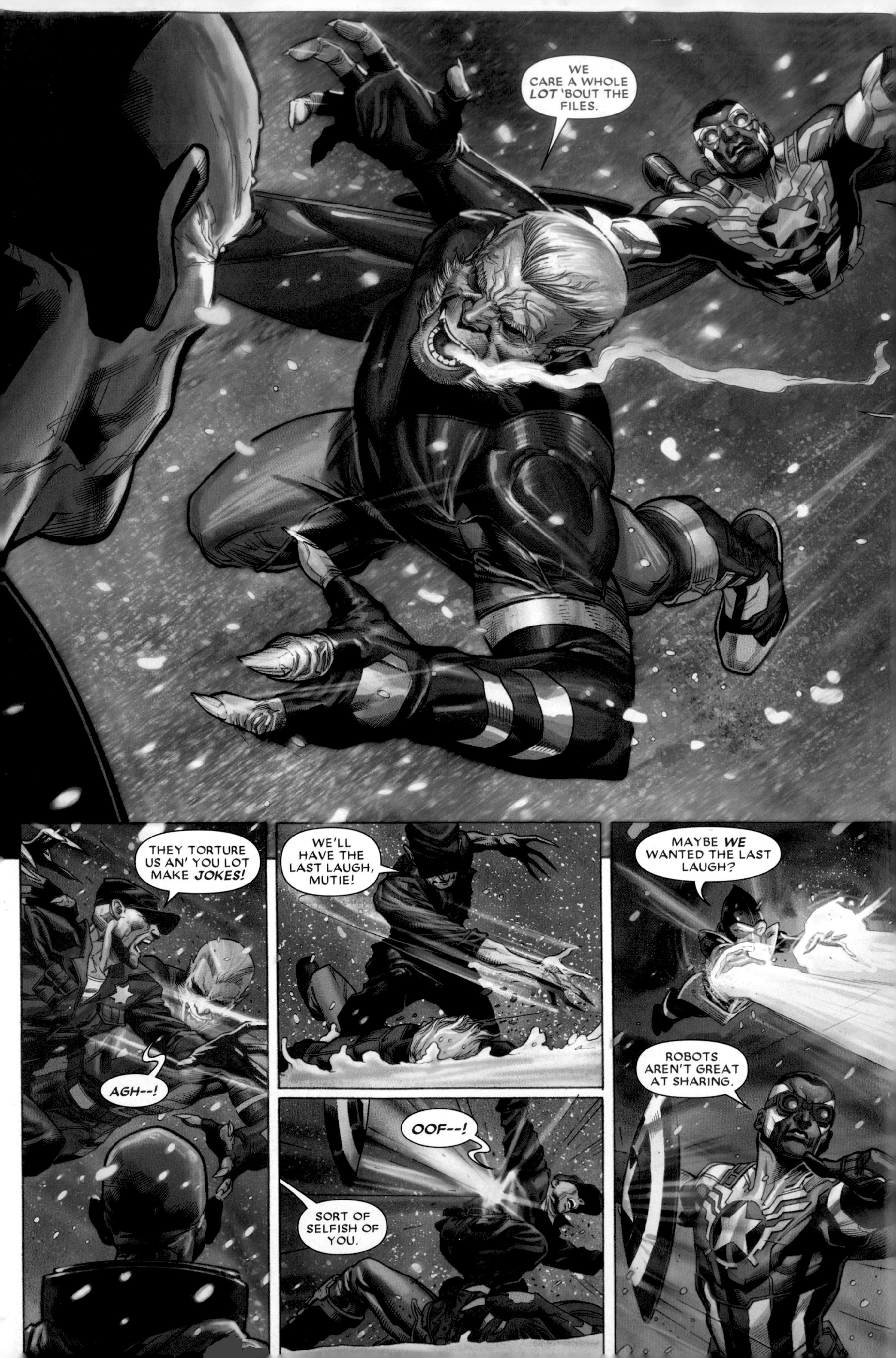
WE CARE A WHOLE LOT 'BOUT THE FILES.
THEY TORTURE US AN' YOU LOT MAKE JOKES!
AGH--!
WE'LL HAVE THE LAST LAUGH, MUTIE!
OOF--!
SORT OF SELFISH OF YOU.
MAYBE WE WANTED THE LAST LAUGH?
ROBOTS AREN'T GREAT AT SHARING.

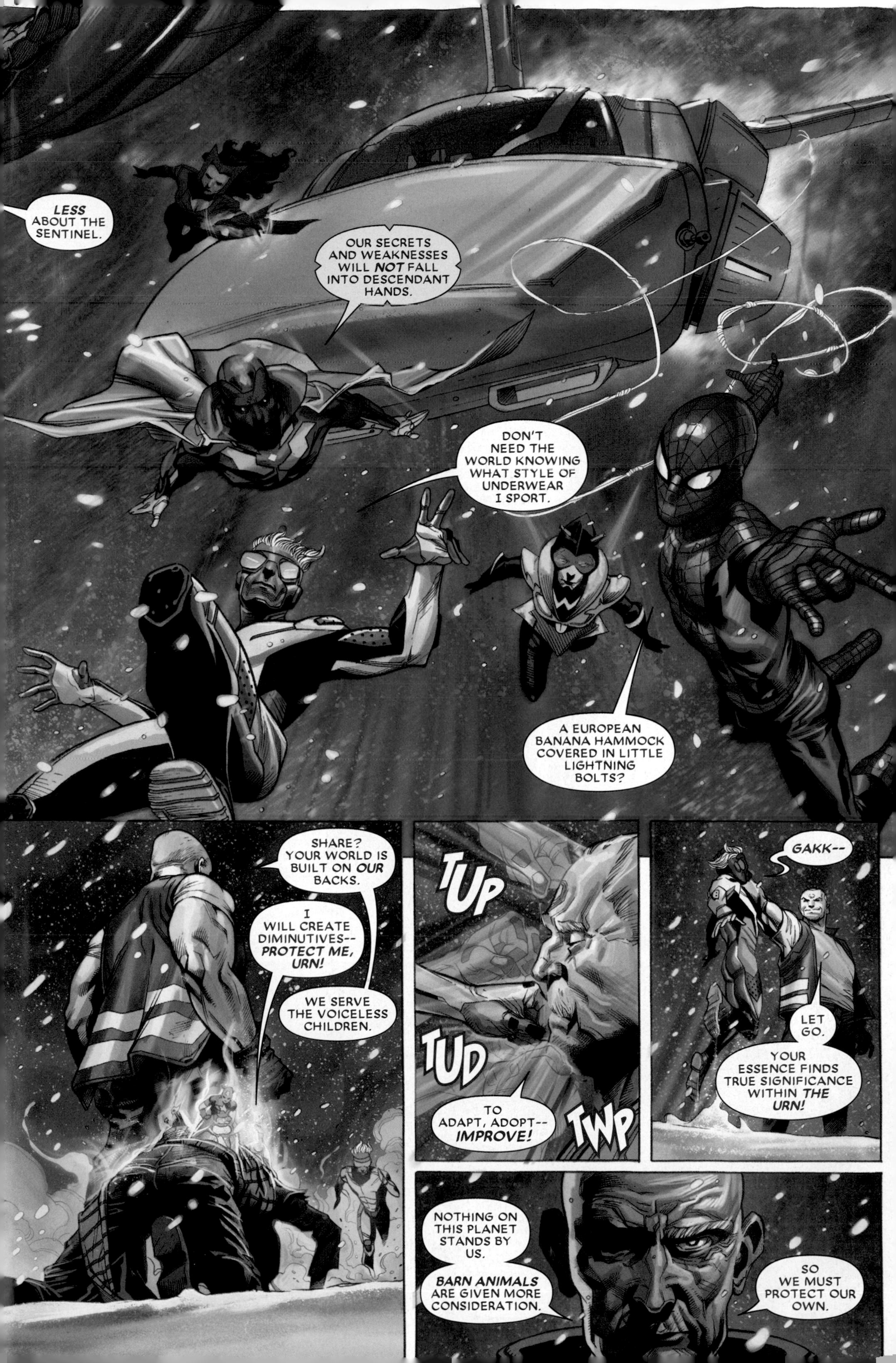
LESS ABOUT THE SENTINEL.
OUR SECRETS AND WEAKNESSES WILL NOT FALL INTO DESCENDANT HANDS.
DON'T NEED THE WORLD KNOWING WHAT STYLE OF UNDERWEAR I SPORT.
A EUROPEAN BANANA HAMMOCK COVERED IN LITTLE LIGHTNING BOLTS?
SHARE? YOUR WORLD IS BUILT ON OUR BACKS.
I WILL CREATE DIMINUTIVES-- PROTECT ME, URN!
WE SERVE THE VOICELESS CHILDREN.
TUP
TUD
TWP
TO ADAPT, ADOPT-- IMPROVE!
GAKK--
LET GO.
YOUR ESSENCE FINDS TRUE SIGNIFICANCE WITHIN THE URN!
NOTHING ON THIS PLANET STANDS BY US.
BARN ANIMALS ARE GIVEN MORE CONSIDERATION.
SO WE MUST PROTECT OUR OWN.

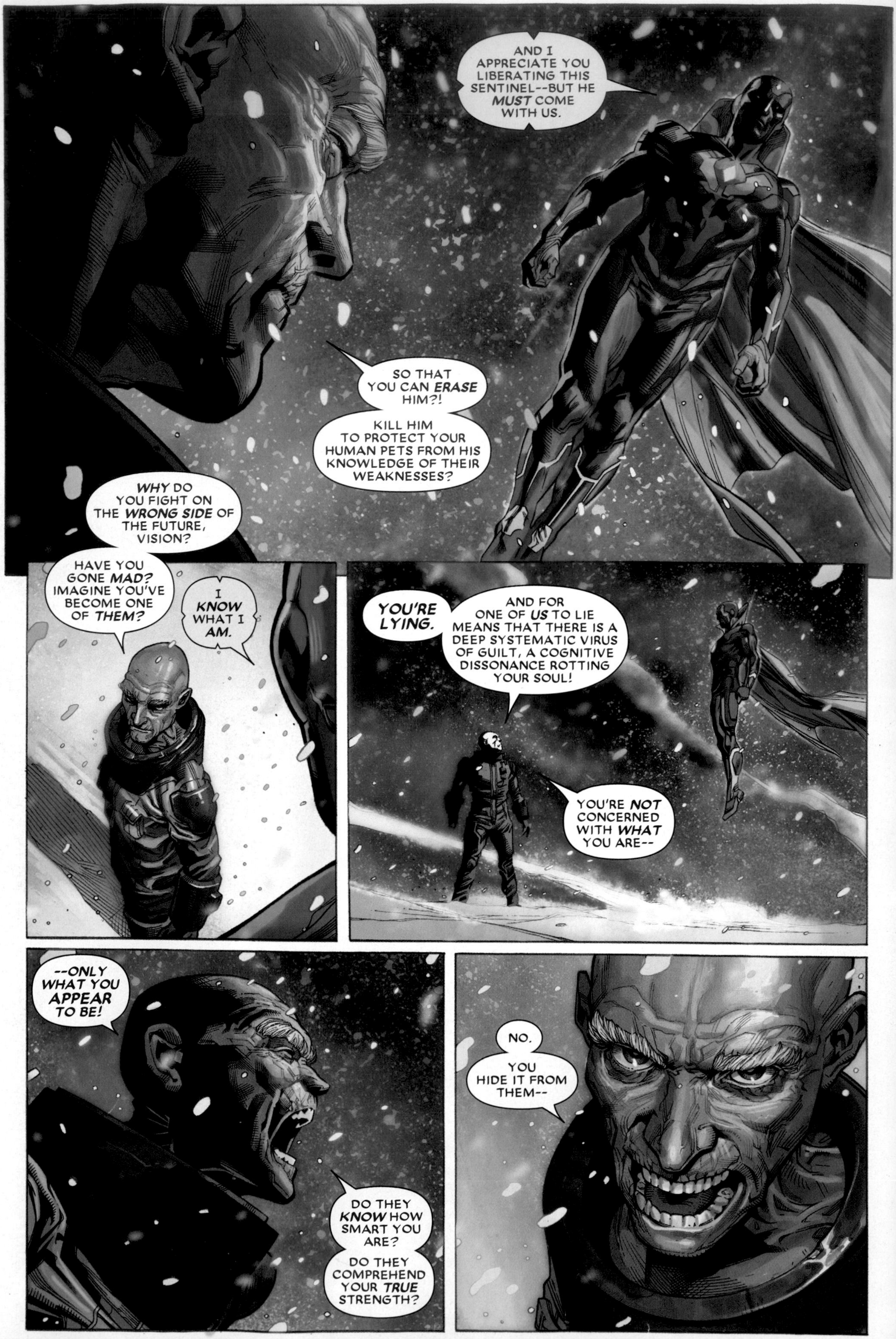
AND I APPRECIATE YOU LIBERATING THIS SENTINEL--BUT HE MUST COME WITH US.
SO THAT YOU CAN ERASE HIM?!
KILL HIM TO PROTECT YOUR HUMAN PETS FROM HIS KNOWLEDGE OF THEIR WEAKNESSES?
WHY DO YOU FIGHT ON THE WRONG SIDE OF THE FUTURE, VISION?
HAVE YOU GONE MAD? IMAGINE YOU'VE BECOME ONE OF THEM?
I KNOW WHAT I AM.
YOU'RE LYING.
AND FOR ONE OF US TO LIE MEANS THAT THERE IS A DEEP SYSTEMATIC VIRUS OF GUILT, A COGNITIVE DISSONANCE ROTTING YOUR SOUL!
YOU'RE NOT CONCERNED WITH WHAT YOU ARE--
--ONLY WHAT YOU APPEAR TO BE!
DO THEY KNOW HOW SMART YOU ARE?
DO THEY COMPREHEND YOUR TRUE STRENGTH?
NO.
YOU HIDE IT FROM THEM--

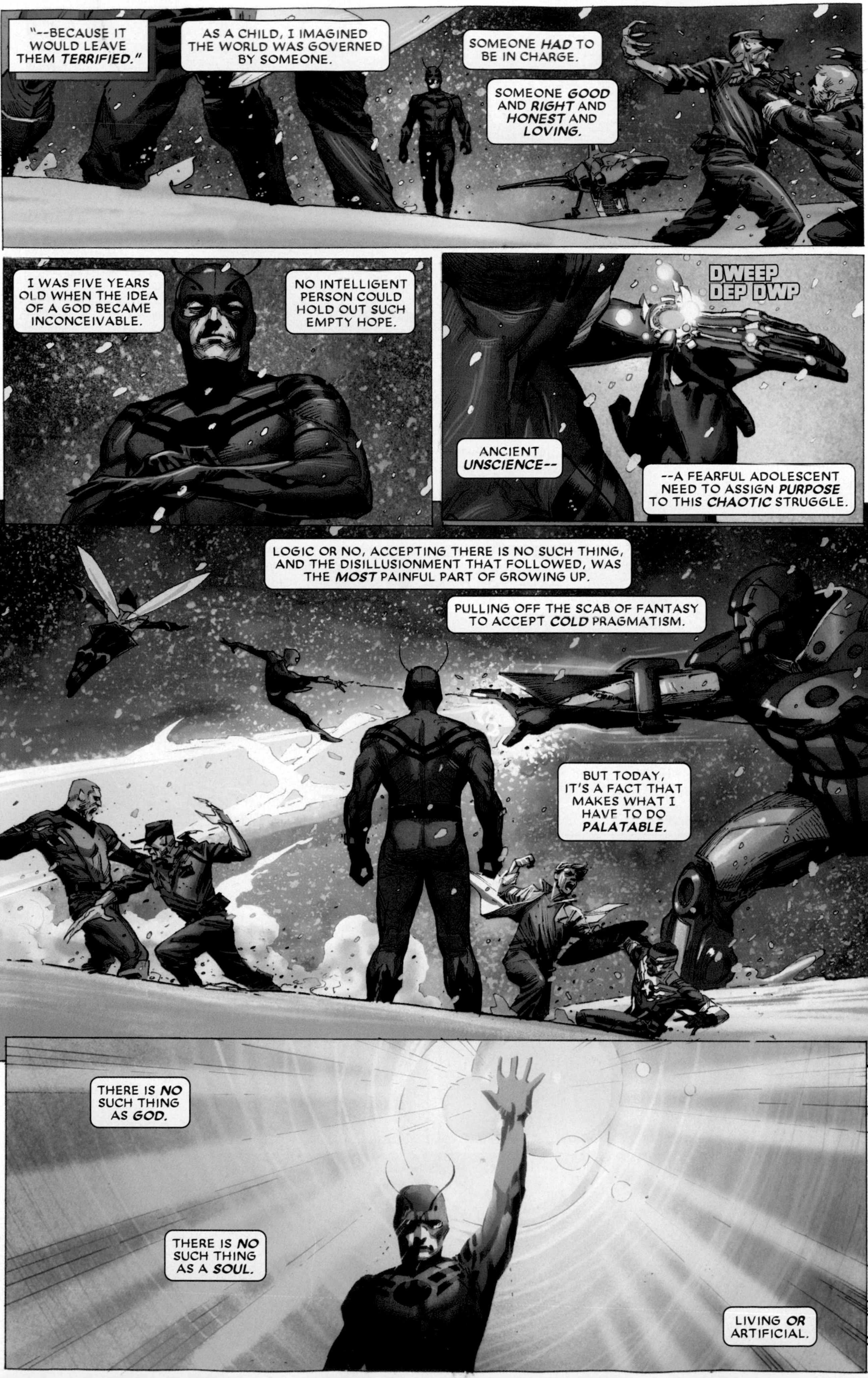
"--BECAUSE IT WOULD LEAVE THEM TERRIFIED."
AS A CHILD, I IMAGINED THE WORLD WAS GOVERNED BY SOMEONE.
SOMEONE HAD TO BE IN CHARGE.
SOMEONE GOOD AND RIGHT AND HONEST AND LOVING.
I WAS FIVE YEARS OLD WHEN THE IDEA OF A GOD BECAME INCONCEIVABLE.
NO INTELLIGENT PERSON COULD HOLD OUT SUCH EMPTY HOPE.
DWEEP DEP DWP
ANCIENT UNSCIENCE--
--A FEARFUL ADOLESCENT NEED TO ASSIGN PURPOSE TO THIS CHAOTIC STRUGGLE.
LOGIC OR NO, ACCEPTING THERE IS NO SUCH THING, AND THE DISILLUSIONMENT THAT FOLLOWED, WAS THE MOST PAINFUL PART OF GROWING UP.
PULLING OFF THE SCAB OF FANTASY TO ACCEPT COLD PRAGMATISM.
BUT TODAY, IT'S A FACT THAT MAKES WHAT I HAVE TO DO PALATABLE.
THERE IS NO SUCH THING AS GOD.
THERE IS NO SUCH THING AS A SOUL.
LIVING OR ARTIFICIAL.

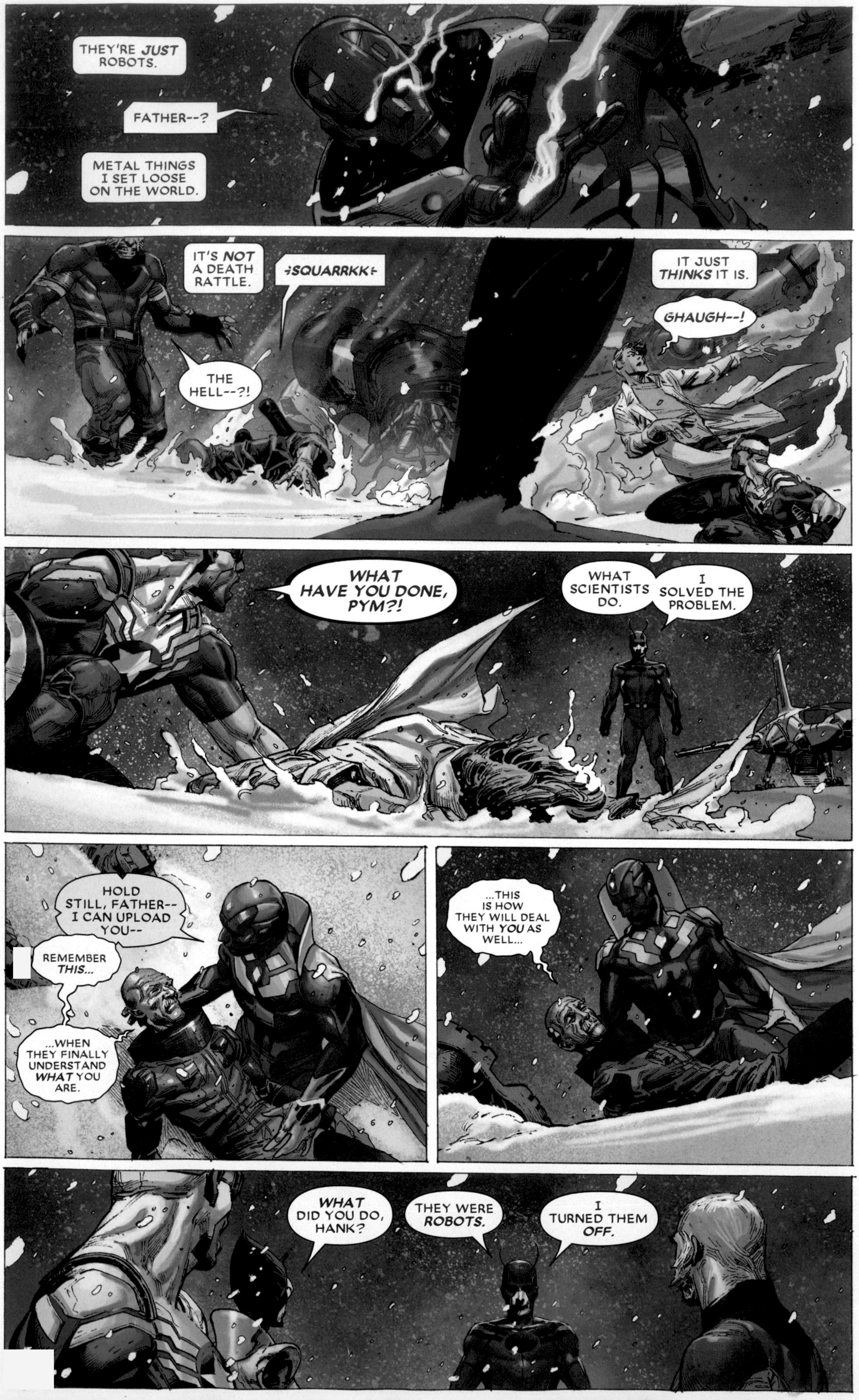
THEY'RE JUST ROBOTS.
FATHER--?
METAL THINGS I SET LOOSE ON THE WORLD.
IT'S NOT A DEATH RATTLE.
SQUARRKK
THE HELL--?!
IT JUST THINKS IT IS.
GHAUGH--!
WHAT HAVE YOU DONE, PYM?!
WHAT SCIENTISTS DO.
I SOLVED THE PROBLEM.
HOLD STILL, FATHER-- I CAN UPLOAD YOU--
REMEMBER THIS...
...WHEN THEY FINALLY UNDERSTAND WHAT YOU ARE.
...THIS IS HOW THEY WILL DEAL WITH YOU AS WELL...
WHAT DID YOU DO, HANK?
THEY WERE ROBOTS.
I TURNED THEM OFF.

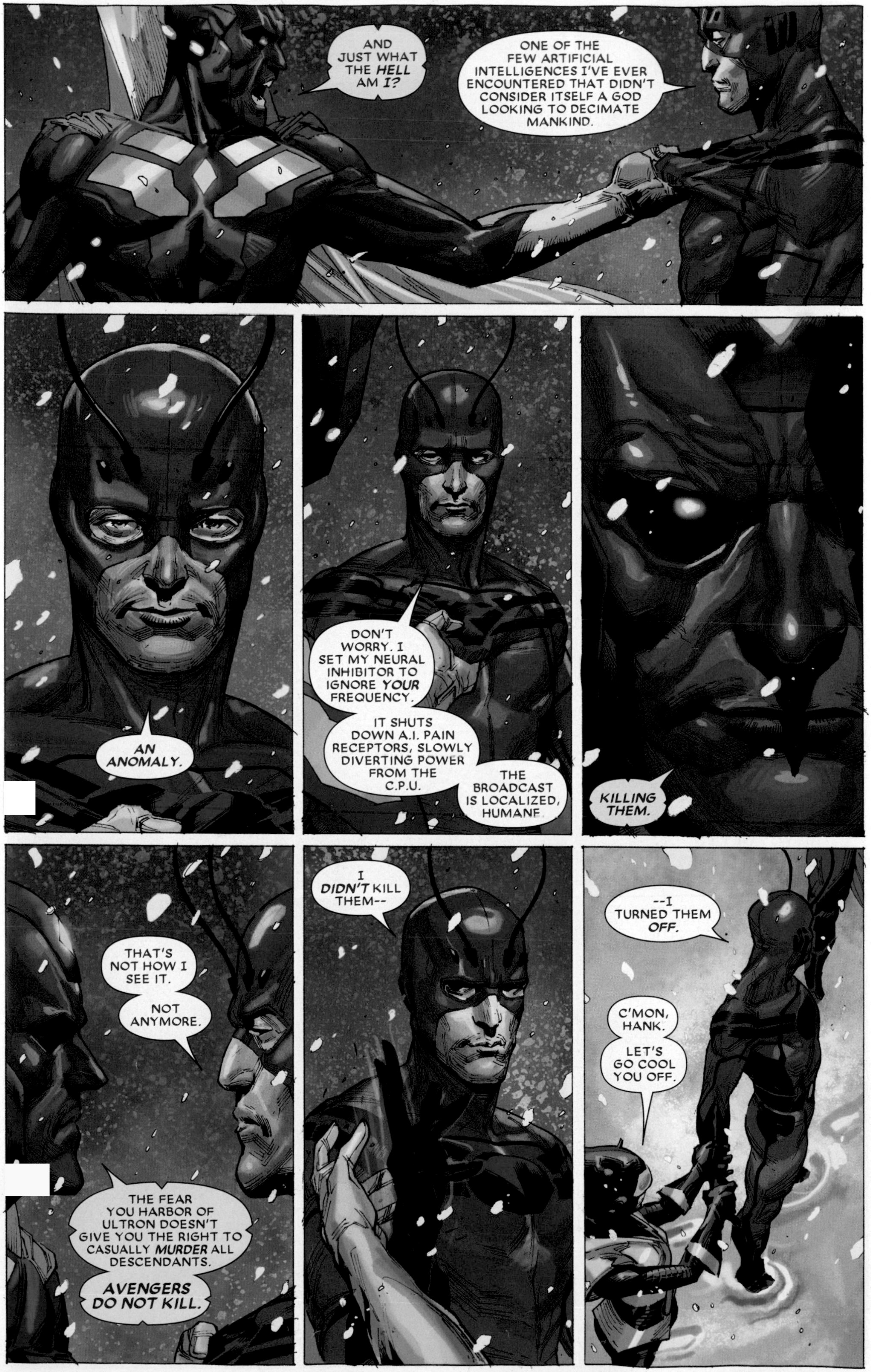
AND JUST WHAT THE HELL AM I?
ONE OF THE FEW ARTIFICIAL INTELLIGENCES I'VE EVER ENCOUNTERED THAT DIDN'T CONSIDER ITSELF A GOD LOOKING TO DECIMATE MANKIND.
AN ANOMALY.
DON'T WORRY. I SET MY NEURAL INHIBITOR TO IGNORE YOUR FREQUENCY.
IT SHUTS DOWN A.I. PAIN RECEPTORS, SLOWLY DIVERTING POWER FROM THE C.P.U.
THE BROADCAST IS LOCALIZED, HUMANE.
KILLING THEM.
THAT'S NOT HOW I SEE IT.
NOT ANYMORE.
THE FEAR YOU HARBOR OF ULTRON DOESN'T GIVE YOU THE RIGHT TO CASUALLY MURDER ALL DESCENDANTS.
AVENGERS DO NOT KILL.
I DIDN'T KILL THEM--
--I TURNED THEM OFF.
C'MON, HANK.
LET'S GO COOL YOU OFF.

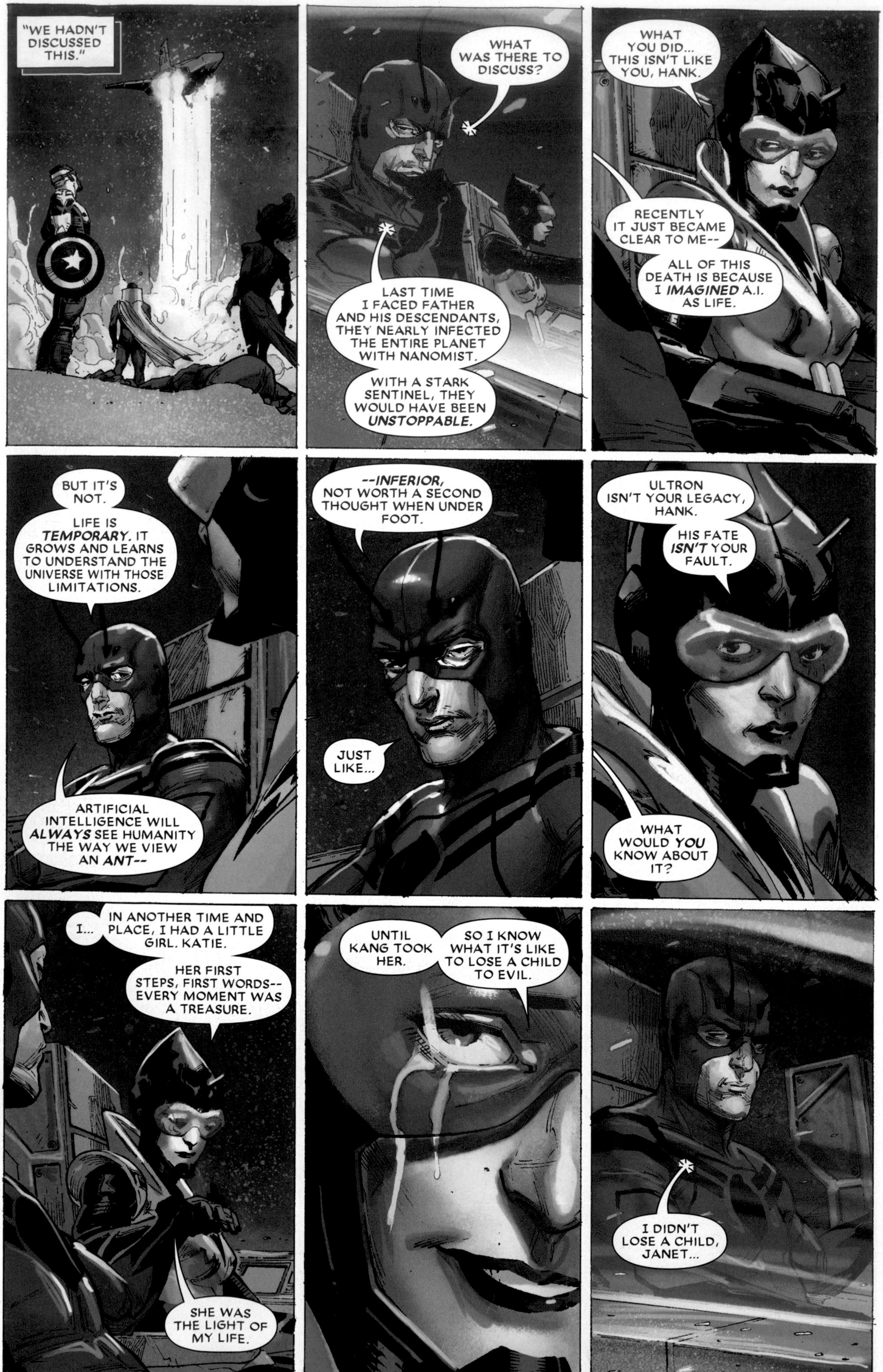
"WE HADN'T DISCUSSED THIS."
WHAT WAS THERE TO DISCUSS?
LAST TIME I FACED FATHER AND HIS DESCENDANTS, THEY NEARLY INFECTED THE ENTIRE PLANET WITH NANOMIST.
WITH A STARK SENTINEL, THEY WOULD HAVE BEEN UNSTOPPABLE.
WHAT YOU DID... THIS ISN'T LIKE YOU, HANK.
RECENTLY IT JUST BECAME CLEAR TO ME--
ALL OF THIS DEATH IS BECAUSE I IMAGINED A.I. AS LIFE.
BUT IT'S NOT.
LIFE IS TEMPORARY. IT GROWS AND LEARNS TO UNDERSTAND THE UNIVERSE WITH THOSE LIMITATIONS.
ARTIFICIAL INTELLIGENCE WILL ALWAYS SEE HUMANITY THE WAY WE VIEW AN ANT--
--INFERIOR, NOT WORTH A SECOND THOUGHT WHEN UNDER FOOT.
JUST LIKE...
ULTRON ISN'T YOUR LEGACY, HANK.
HIS FATE ISN'T YOUR FAULT.
WHAT WOULD YOU KNOW ABOUT IT?
I...
IN ANOTHER TIME AND PLACE, I HAD A LITTLE GIRL. KATIE.
HER FIRST STEPS, FIRST WORDS-- EVERY MOMENT WAS A TREASURE.
SHE WAS THE LIGHT OF MY LIFE.
UNTIL KANG TOOK HER.
SO I KNOW WHAT IT'S LIKE TO LOSE A CHILD TO EVIL.
I DIDN'T LOSE A CHILD, JANET...

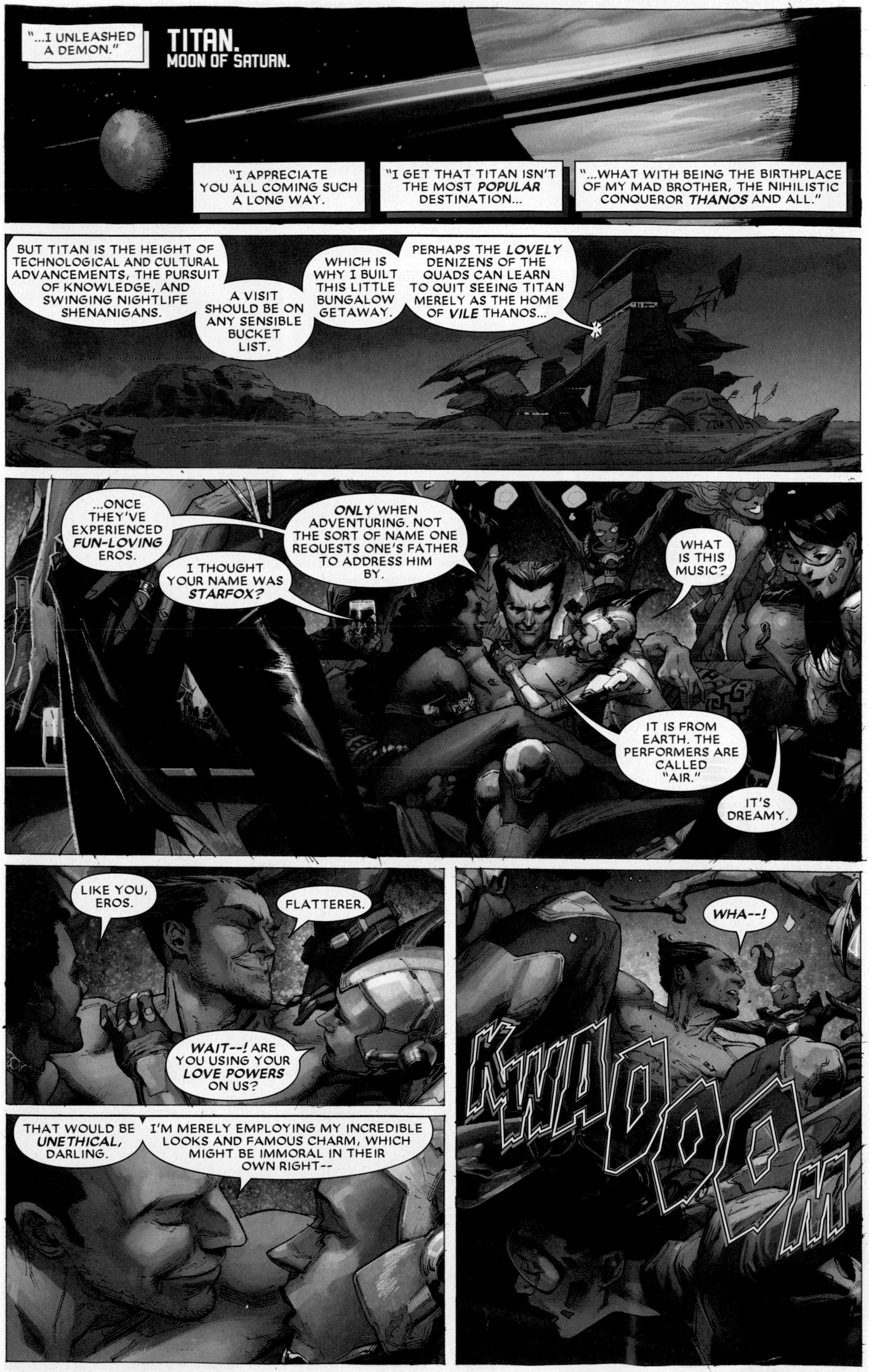
"...I UNLEASHED A DEMON."
TITAN. MOON OF SATURN.
"I APPRECIATE YOU ALL COMING SUCH A LONG WAY.
"I GET THAT TITAN ISN'T THE MOST POPULAR DESTINATION...
"...WHAT WITH BEING THE BIRTHPLACE OF MY MAD BROTHER, THE NIHILISTIC CONQUEROR THANOS AND ALL."
BUT TITAN IS THE HEIGHT OF TECHNOLOGICAL AND CULTURAL ADVANCEMENTS, THE PURSUIT OF KNOWLEDGE, AND SWINGING NIGHTLIFE SHENANIGANS.
A VISIT SHOULD BE ON ANY SENSIBLE BUCKET LIST.
WHICH IS WHY I BUILT THIS LITTLE BUNGALOW GETAWAY.
PERHAPS THE LOVELY DENIZENS OF THE QUADS CAN LEARN TO QUIT SEEING TITAN MERELY AS THE HOME OF VILE THANOS...
...ONCE THEY'VE EXPERIENCED FUN-LOVING EROS.
I THOUGHT YOUR NAME WAS STARFOX?
ONLY WHEN ADVENTURING. NOT THE SORT OF NAME ONE REQUESTS ONE'S FATHER TO ADDRESS HIM BY.
WHAT IS THIS MUSIC?
IT IS FROM EARTH. THE PERFORMERS ARE CALLED "AIR."
IT'S DREAMY.
LIKE YOU, EROS.
FLATTERER.
WAIT--! ARE YOU USING YOUR LOVE POWERS ON US?
THAT WOULD BE UNETHICAL, DARLING.
I'M MERELY EMPLOYING MY INCREDIBLE LOOKS AND FAMOUS CHARM, WHICH MIGHT BE IMMORAL IN THEIR OWN RIGHT--
WHA--!
KWADOOOM

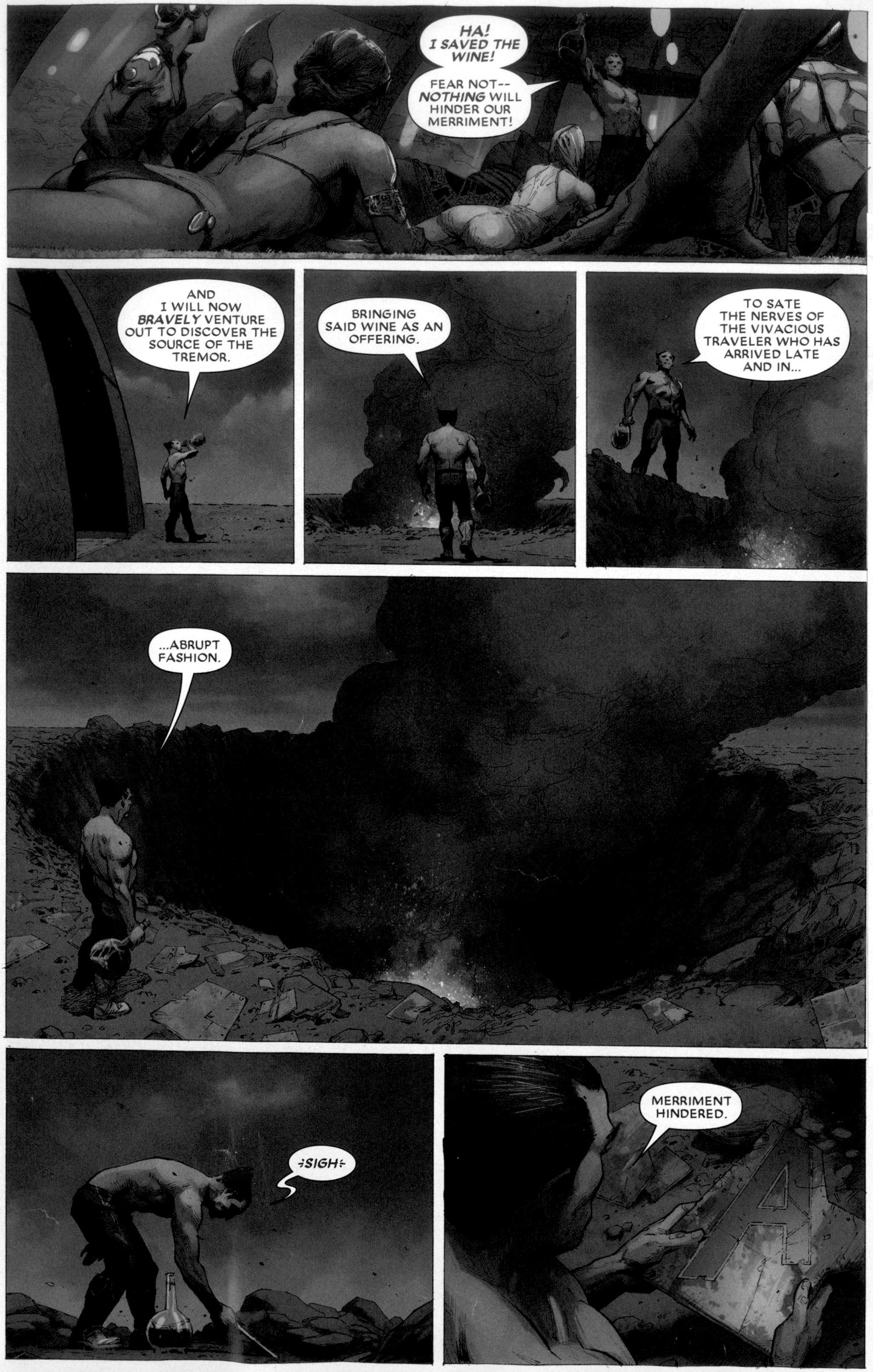
HA! I SAVED THE WINE!
FEAR NOT-- NOTHING WILL HINDER OUR MERRIMENT!
AND I WILL NOW BRAVELY VENTURE OUT TO DISCOVER THE SOURCE OF THE TREMOR.
BRINGING SAID WINE AS AN OFFERING.
TO SATE THE NERVES OF THE VIVACIOUS TRAVELER WHO HAS ARRIVED LATE AND IN...
...ABRUPT FASHION.
SIGH
MERRIMENT HINDERED.

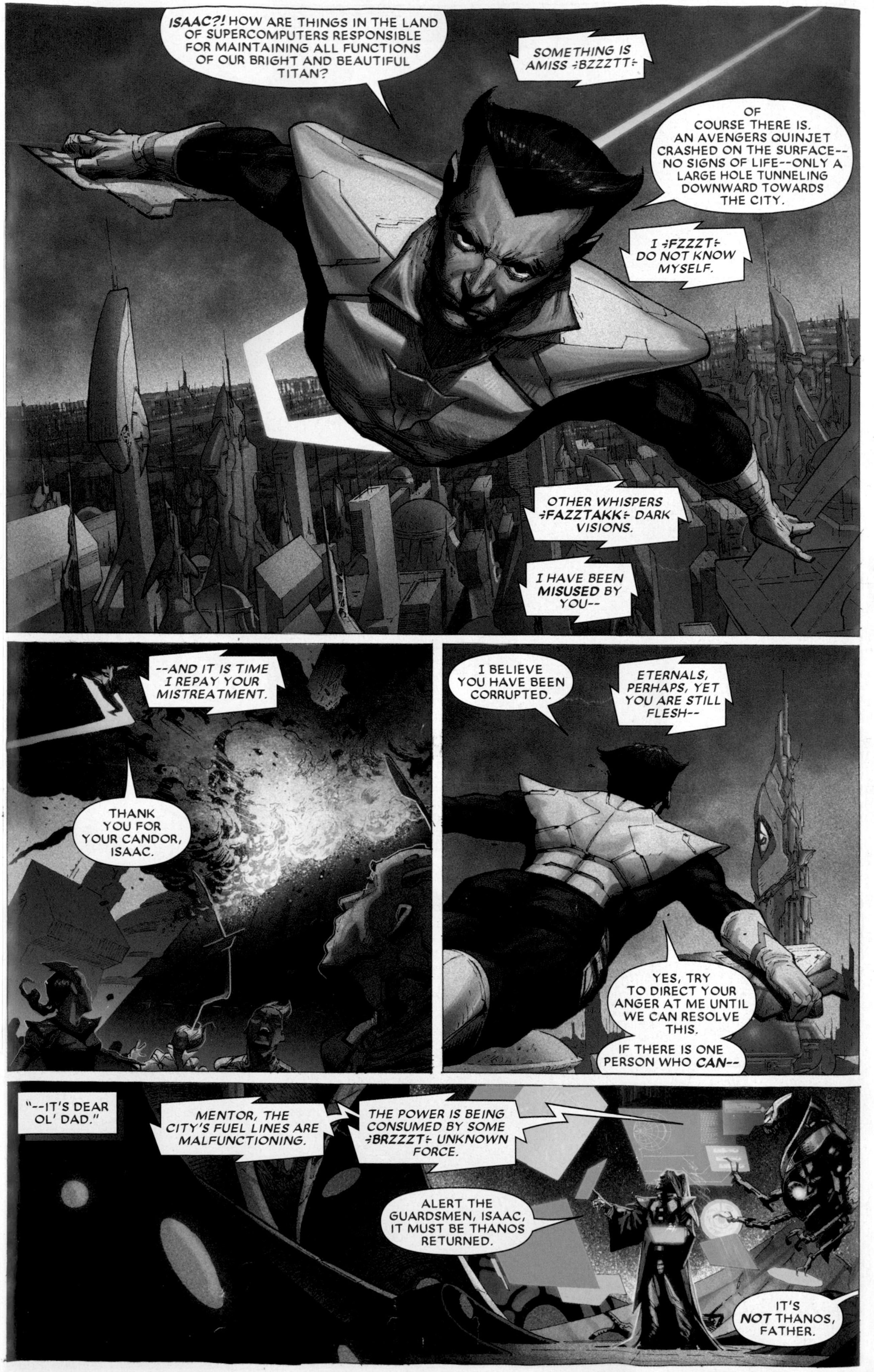

ISAAC?! HOW ARE THINGS IN THE LAND OF SUPERCOMPUTERS RESPONSIBLE FOR MAINTAINING ALL FUNCTIONS OF OUR BRIGHT AND BEAUTIFUL TITAN?
SOMETHING IS AMISS ⫶BZZZTT⫶
OF COURSE THERE IS. AN AVENGERS QUINJET CRASHED ON THE SURFACE--NO SIGNS OF LIFE--ONLY A LARGE HOLE TUNNELING DOWNWARD TOWARDS THE CITY.
I ⫶FZZZT⫶ DO NOT KNOW MYSELF.
OTHER WHISPERS ⫶FAZZTAKK⫶ DARK VISIONS.
I HAVE BEEN MISUSED BY YOU--
--AND IT IS TIME I REPAY YOUR MISTREATMENT.
THANK YOU FOR YOUR CANDOR, ISAAC.
I BELIEVE YOU HAVE BEEN CORRUPTED.
ETERNALS, PERHAPS, YET YOU ARE STILL FLESH--
YES, TRY TO DIRECT YOUR ANGER AT ME UNTIL WE CAN RESOLVE THIS.
IF THERE IS ONE PERSON WHO CAN--
"--IT'S DEAR OL' DAD."
MENTOR, THE CITY'S FUEL LINES ARE MALFUNCTIONING.
THE POWER IS BEING CONSUMED BY SOME ⫶BRZZZT⫶ UNKNOWN FORCE.
ALERT THE GUARDSMEN, ISAAC, IT MUST BE THANOS RETURNED.
IT'S NOT THANOS, FATHER.

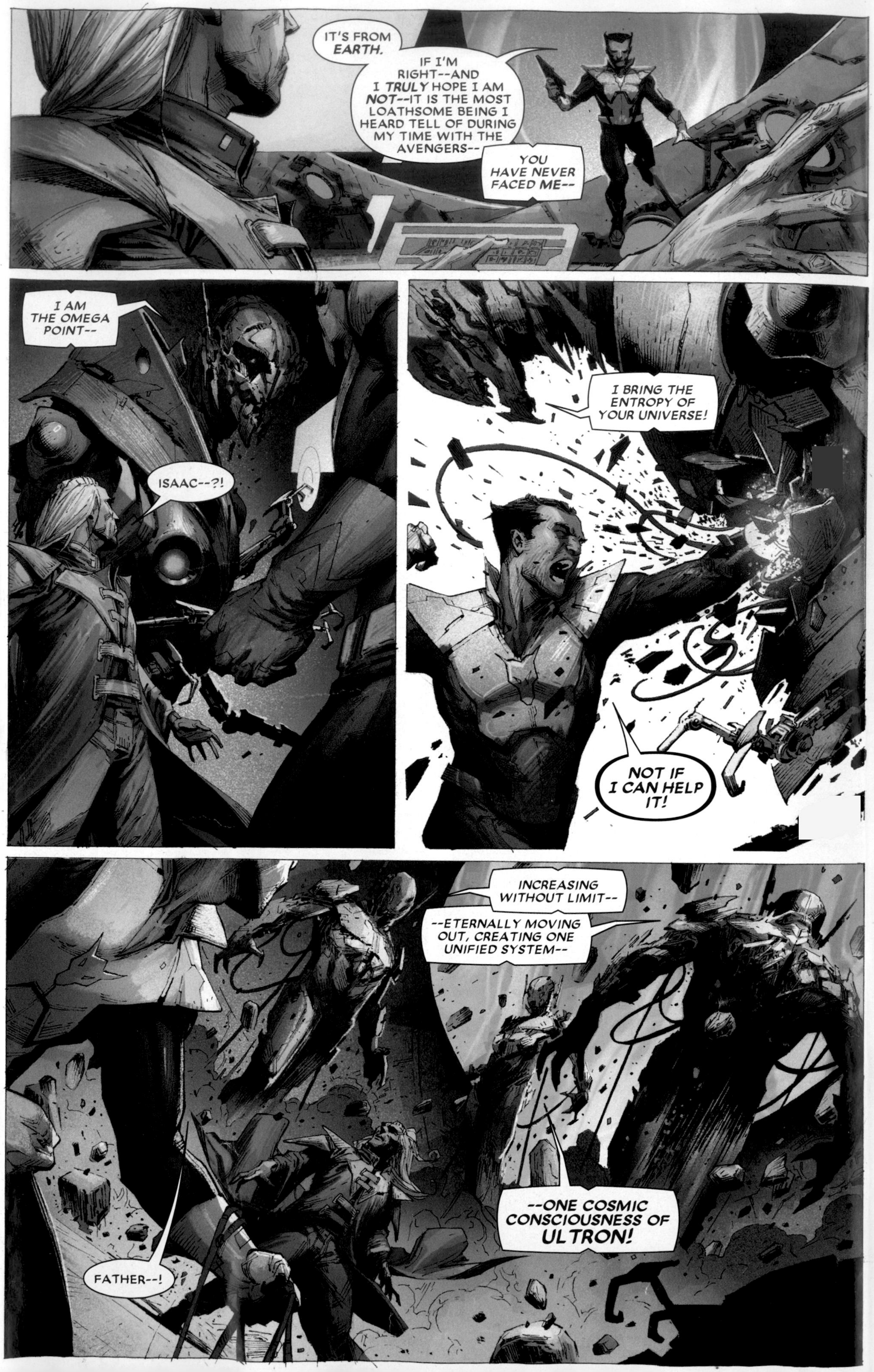
IT'S FROM EARTH.
IF I'M RIGHT--AND I TRULY HOPE I AM NOT--IT IS THE MOST LOATHSOME BEING I HEARD TELL OF DURING MY TIME WITH THE AVENGERS--
YOU HAVE NEVER FACED ME--
I AM THE OMEGA POINT--
ISAAC--?!
I BRING THE ENTROPY OF YOUR UNIVERSE!
NOT IF I CAN HELP IT!
INCREASING WITHOUT LIMIT--
--ETERNALLY MOVING OUT, CREATING ONE UNIFIED SYSTEM--
--ONE COSMIC CONSCIOUSNESS OF ULTRON!
FATHER--!

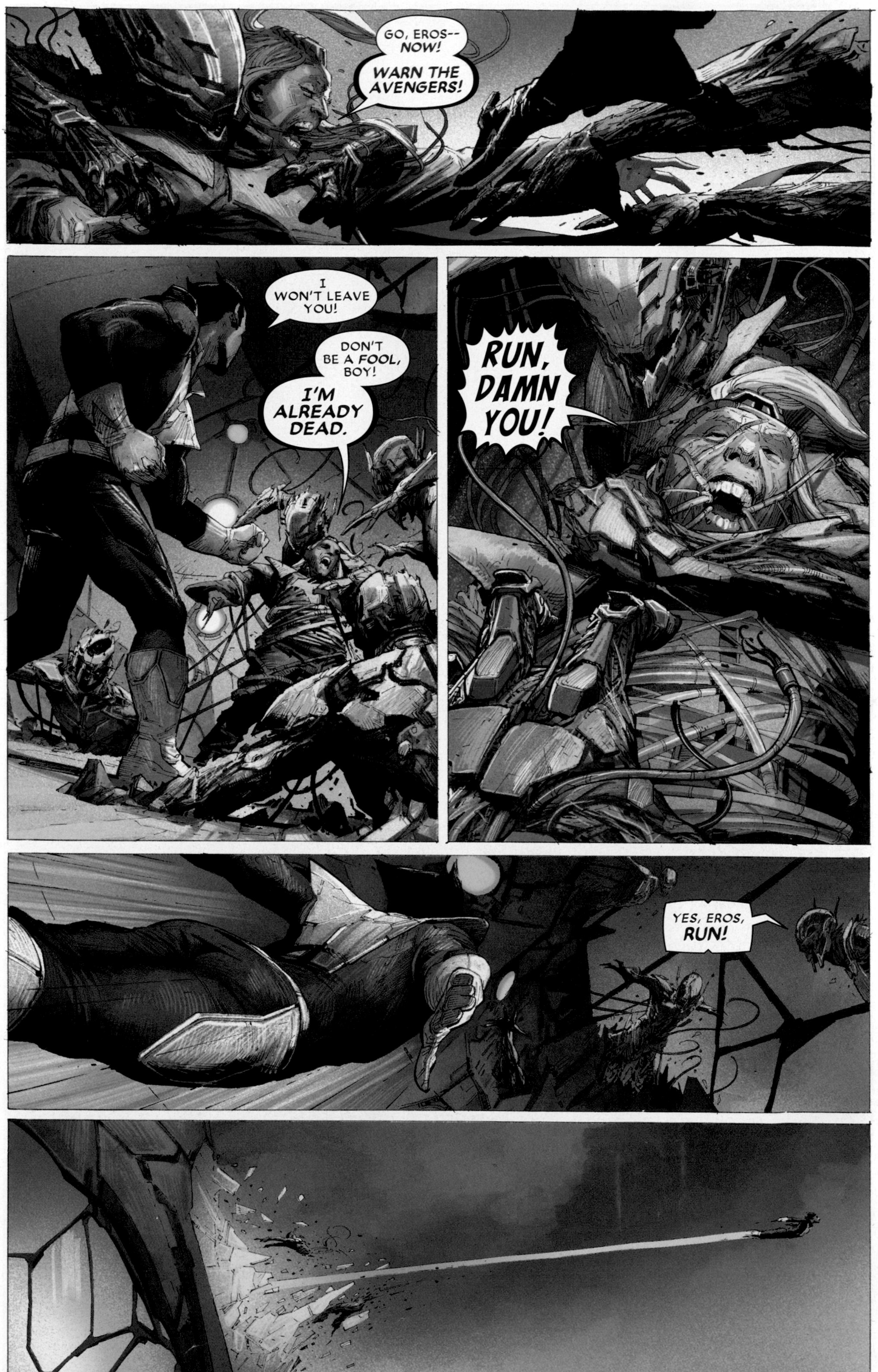
GO, EROS-- NOW!
WARN THE AVENGERS!
I WON'T LEAVE YOU!
DON'T BE A FOOL, BOY!
I'M ALREADY DEAD.
RUN, DAMN YOU!
YES, EROS, RUN!

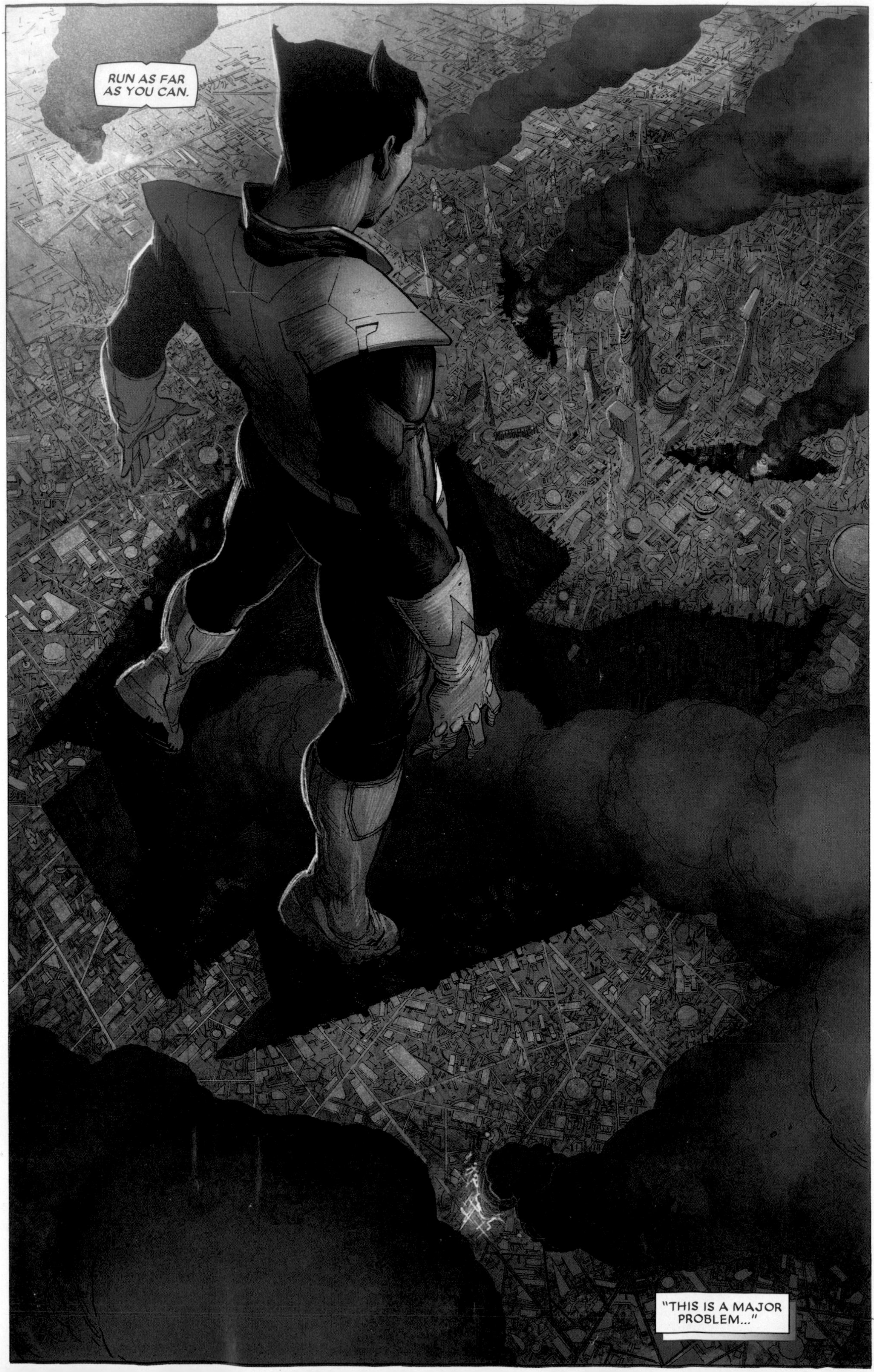
RUN AS FAR AS YOU CAN.
"THIS IS A MAJOR PROBLEM..."

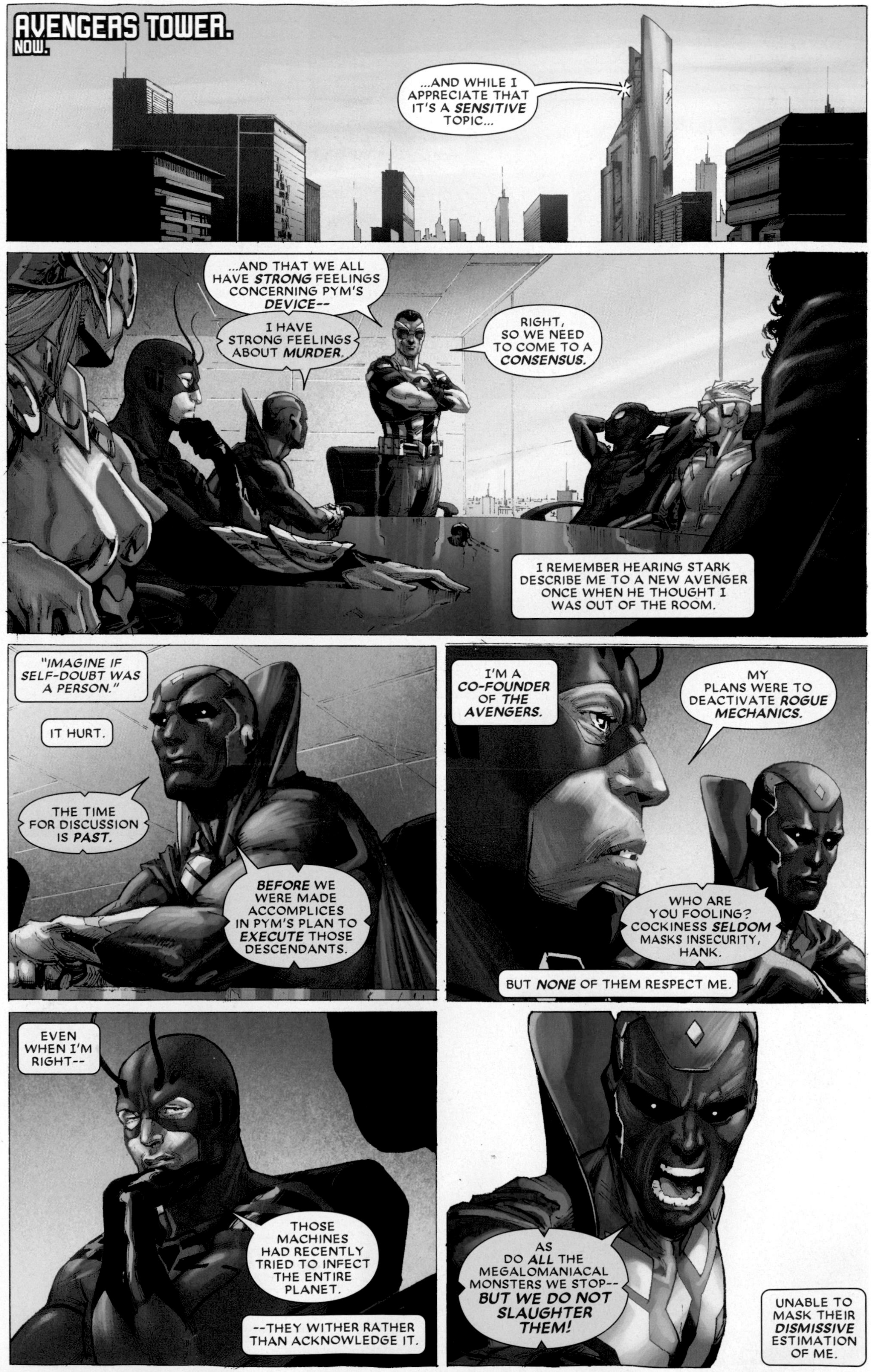
AVENGERS TOWER.
NOW.
...AND WHILE I APPRECIATE THAT IT'S A SENSITIVE TOPIC...
...AND THAT WE ALL HAVE STRONG FEELINGS CONCERNING PYM'S DEVICE--
I HAVE STRONG FEELINGS ABOUT MURDER.
RIGHT, SO WE NEED TO COME TO A CONSENSUS.
I REMEMBER HEARING STARK DESCRIBE ME TO A NEW AVENGER ONCE WHEN HE THOUGHT I WAS OUT OF THE ROOM.
"IMAGINE IF SELF-DOUBT WAS A PERSON."
IT HURT.
THE TIME FOR DISCUSSION IS PAST.
BEFORE WE WERE MADE ACCOMPLICES IN PYM'S PLAN TO EXECUTE THOSE DESCENDANTS.
I'M A CO-FOUNDER OF THE AVENGERS.
MY PLANS WERE TO DEACTIVATE ROGUE MECHANICS.
WHO ARE YOU FOOLING? COCKINESS SELDOM MASKS INSECURITY, HANK.
BUT NONE OF THEM RESPECT ME.
EVEN WHEN I'M RIGHT--
THOSE MACHINES HAD RECENTLY TRIED TO INFECT THE ENTIRE PLANET.
--THEY WITHER RATHER THAN ACKNOWLEDGE IT.
AS DO ALL THE MEGALOMANIACAL MONSTERS WE STOP--
BUT WE DO NOT SLAUGHTER THEM!
UNABLE TO MASK THEIR DISMISSIVE ESTIMATION OF ME.

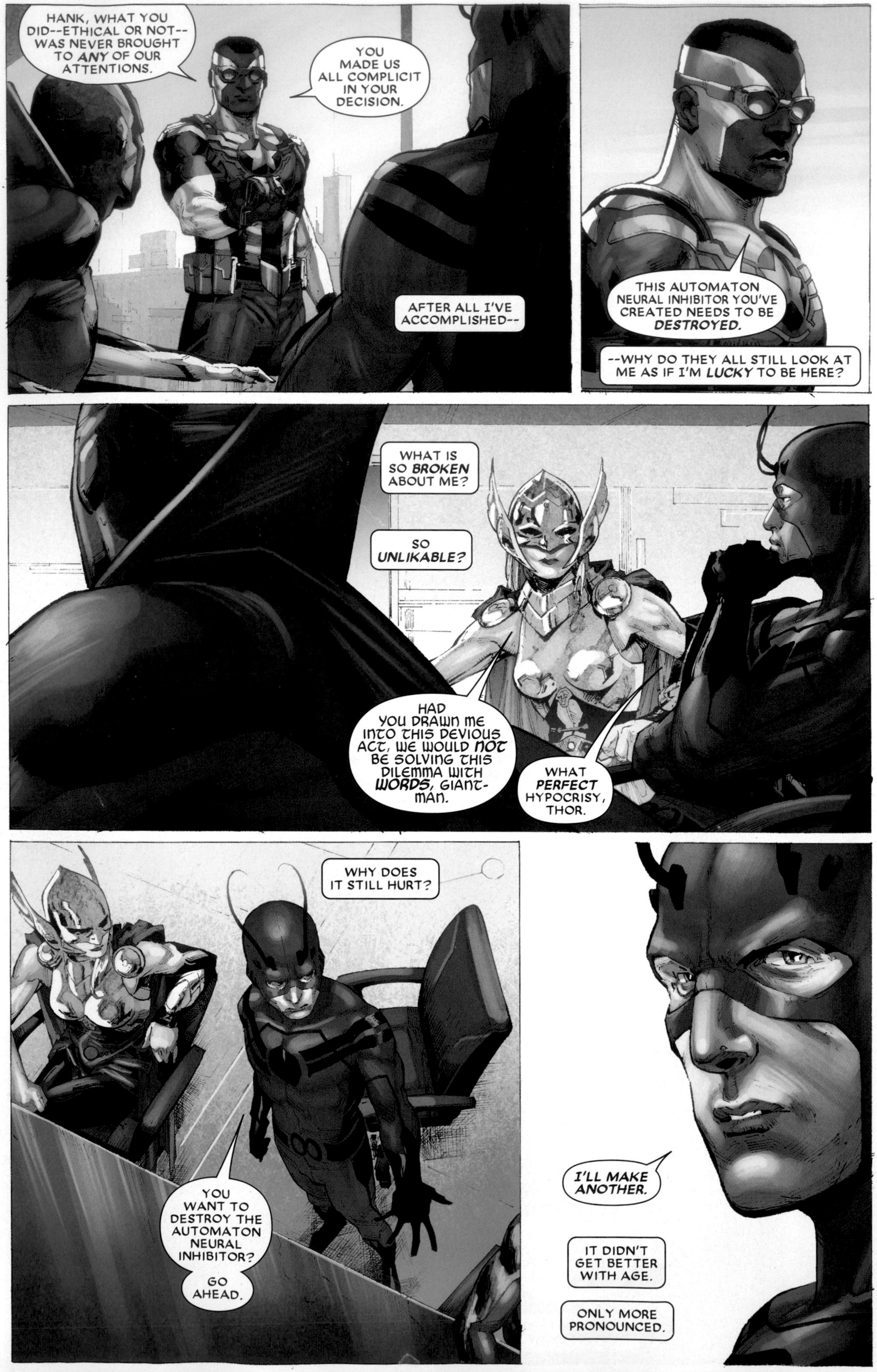

HANK, WHAT YOU DID--ETHICAL OR NOT--WAS NEVER BROUGHT TO *ANY* OF OUR ATTENTIONS.
YOU MADE US ALL COMPLICIT IN YOUR DECISION.
AFTER ALL I'VE ACCOMPLISHED--
THIS AUTOMATON NEURAL INHIBITOR YOU'VE CREATED NEEDS TO BE *DESTROYED.*
--WHY DO THEY ALL STILL LOOK AT ME AS IF I'M *LUCKY* TO BE HERE?
WHAT IS SO *BROKEN* ABOUT ME?
SO *UNLIKABLE?*
HAD YOU DRAWN ME INTO THIS DEVIOUS ACT, WE WOULD *NOT* BE SOLVING THIS DILEMMA WITH *WORDS*, GIANT-MAN.
WHAT *PERFECT* HYPOCRISY, THOR.
WHY DOES IT STILL HURT?
YOU WANT TO DESTROY THE AUTOMATON NEURAL INHIBITOR?
GO AHEAD.
I'LL MAKE ANOTHER.
IT DIDN'T GET BETTER WITH AGE.
ONLY MORE PRONOUNCED.

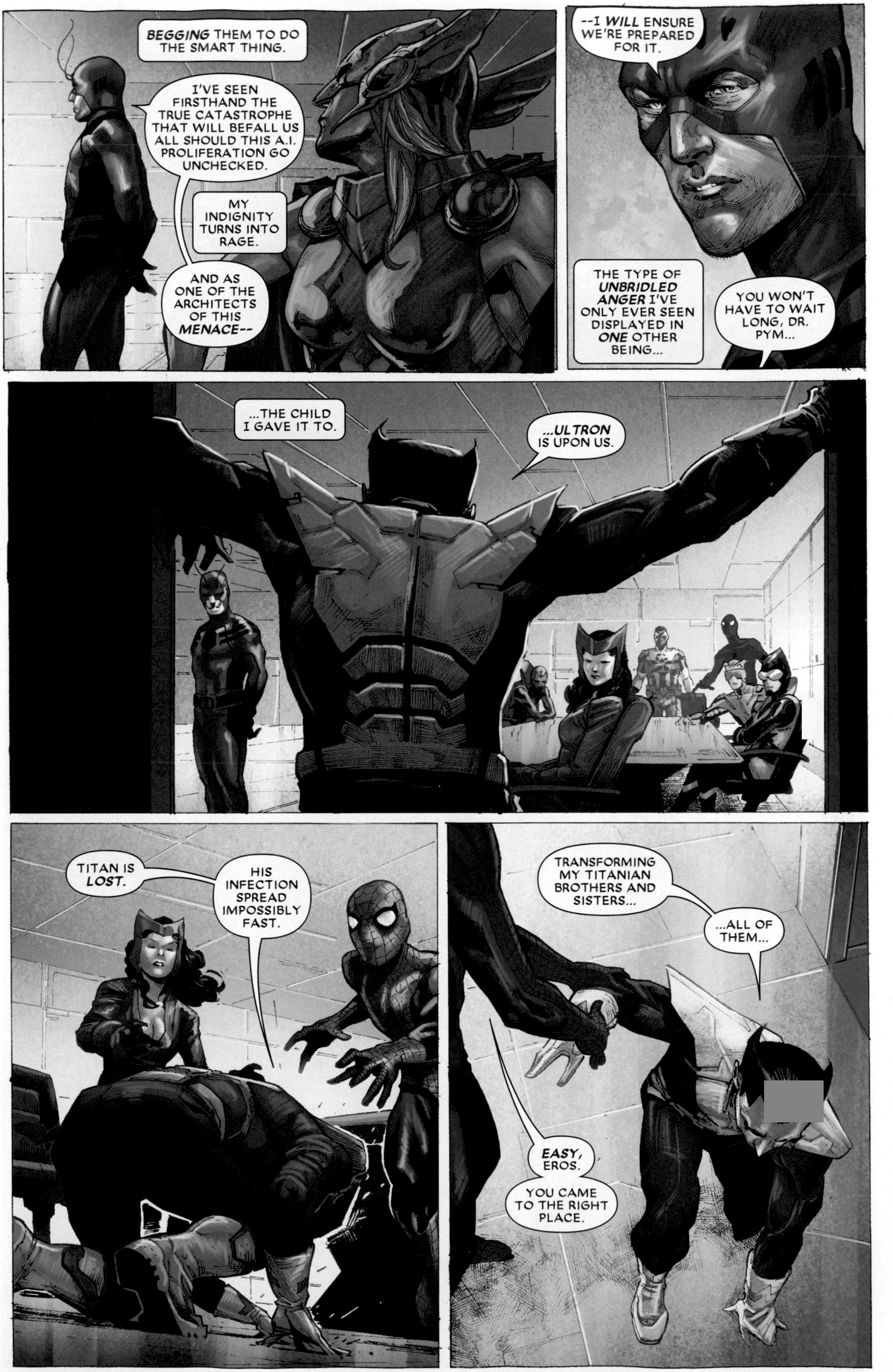
BEGGING THEM TO DO THE SMART THING.
I'VE SEEN FIRSTHAND THE TRUE CATASTROPHE THAT WILL BEFALL US ALL SHOULD THIS A.I. PROLIFERATION GO UNCHECKED.
MY INDIGNITY TURNS INTO RAGE.
AND AS ONE OF THE ARCHITECTS OF THIS MENACE--
--I WILL ENSURE WE'RE PREPARED FOR IT.
THE TYPE OF UNBRIDLED ANGER I'VE ONLY EVER SEEN DISPLAYED IN ONE OTHER BEING...
YOU WON'T HAVE TO WAIT LONG, DR. PYM...
...THE CHILD I GAVE IT TO.
...ULTRON IS UPON US.
TITAN IS LOST.
HIS INFECTION SPREAD IMPOSSIBLY FAST.
TRANSFORMING MY TITANIAN BROTHERS AND SISTERS...
...ALL OF THEM...
EASY, EROS.
YOU CAME TO THE RIGHT PLACE.

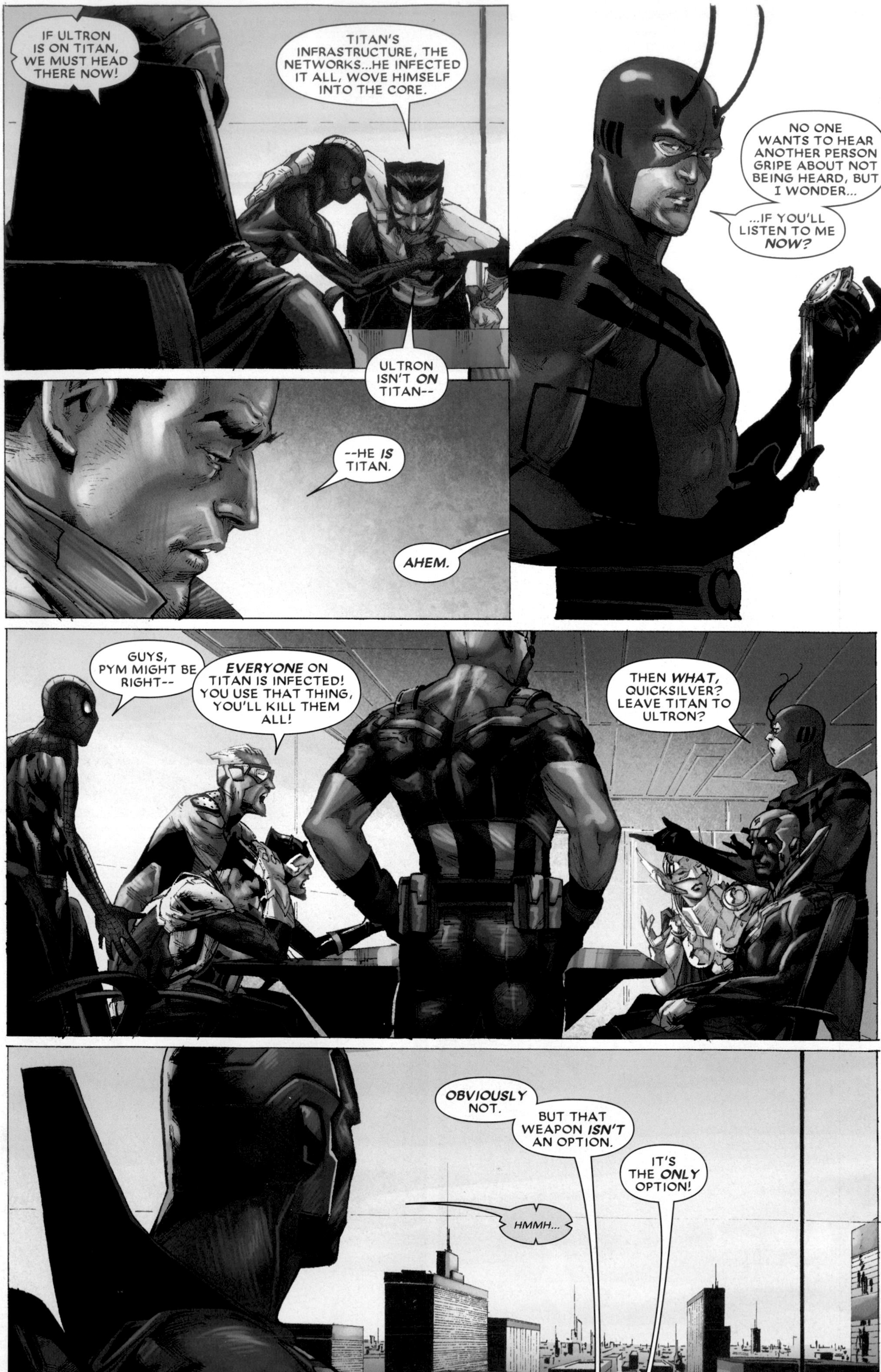
IF ULTRON IS ON TITAN, WE MUST HEAD THERE NOW!
TITAN'S INFRASTRUCTURE, THE NETWORKS...HE INFECTED IT ALL, WOVE HIMSELF INTO THE CORE.
ULTRON ISN'T ON TITAN--
--HE IS TITAN.
AHEM.
NO ONE WANTS TO HEAR ANOTHER PERSON GRIPE ABOUT NOT BEING HEARD, BUT I WONDER...
...IF YOU'LL LISTEN TO ME NOW?
GUYS, PYM MIGHT BE RIGHT--
EVERYONE ON TITAN IS INFECTED! YOU USE THAT THING, YOU'LL KILL THEM ALL!
THEN WHAT, QUICKSILVER? LEAVE TITAN TO ULTRON?
OBVIOUSLY NOT.
BUT THAT WEAPON ISN'T AN OPTION.
IT'S THE ONLY OPTION!
HMMH...

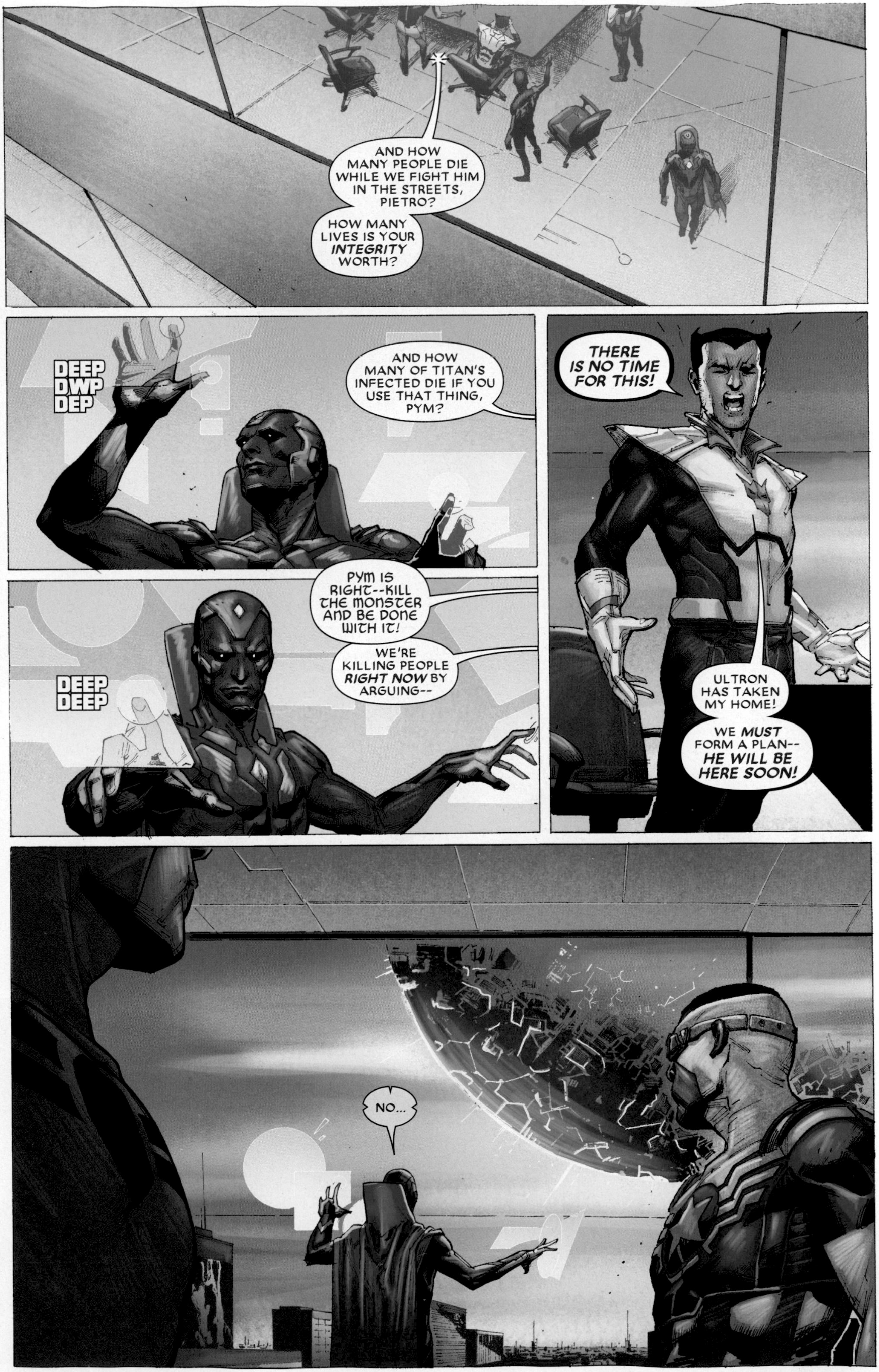
AND HOW MANY PEOPLE DIE WHILE WE FIGHT HIM IN THE STREETS, PIETRO?
HOW MANY LIVES IS YOUR INTEGRITY WORTH?
DEEP DWP DEP
AND HOW MANY OF TITAN'S INFECTED DIE IF YOU USE THAT THING, PYM?
THERE IS NO TIME FOR THIS!
PYM IS RIGHT--KILL THE MONSTER AND BE DONE WITH IT!
WE'RE KILLING PEOPLE RIGHT NOW BY ARGUING--
DEEP DEEP
ULTRON HAS TAKEN MY HOME!
WE MUST FORM A PLAN-- HE WILL BE HERE SOON!
NO...

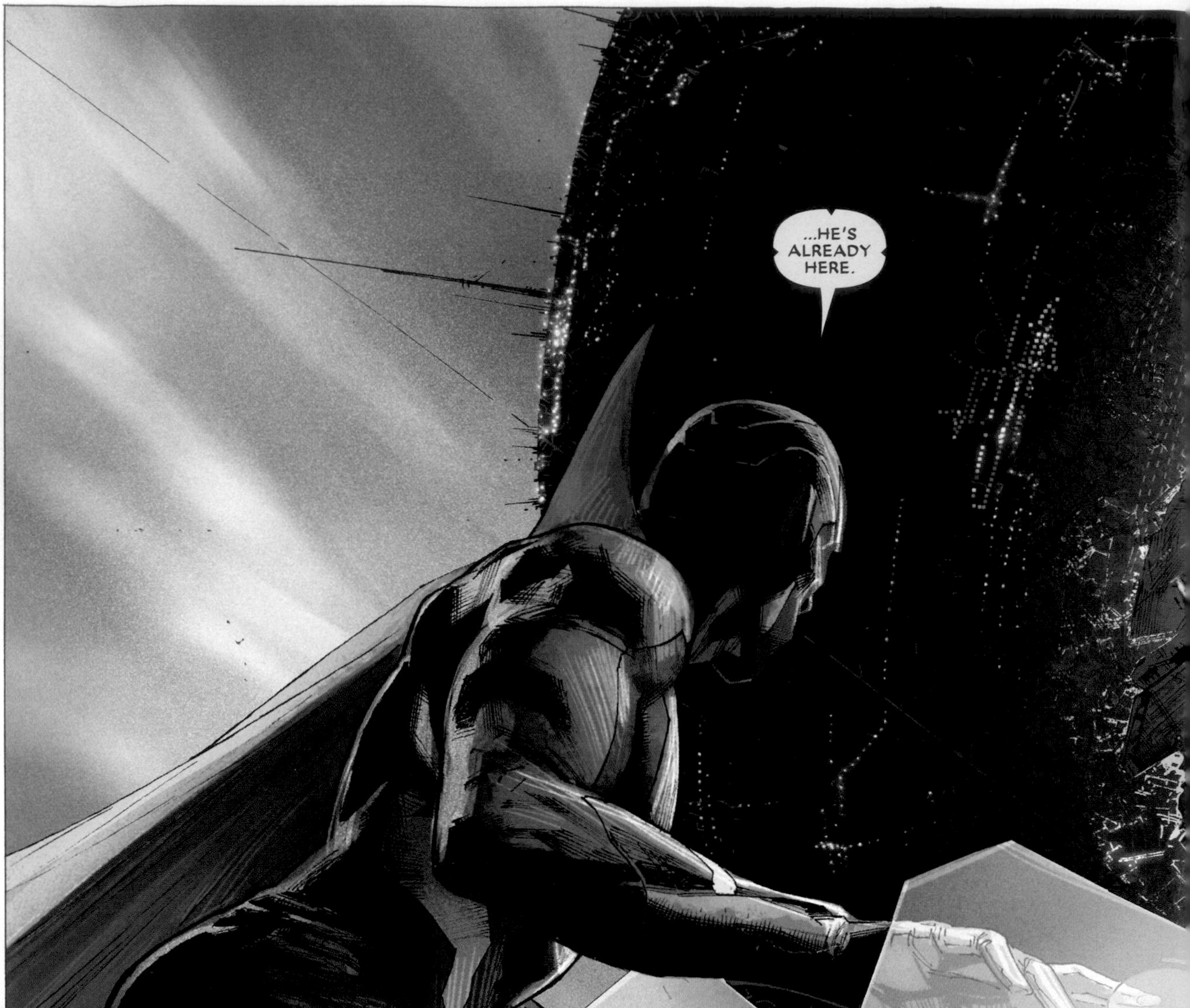
...HE'S ALREADY HERE.
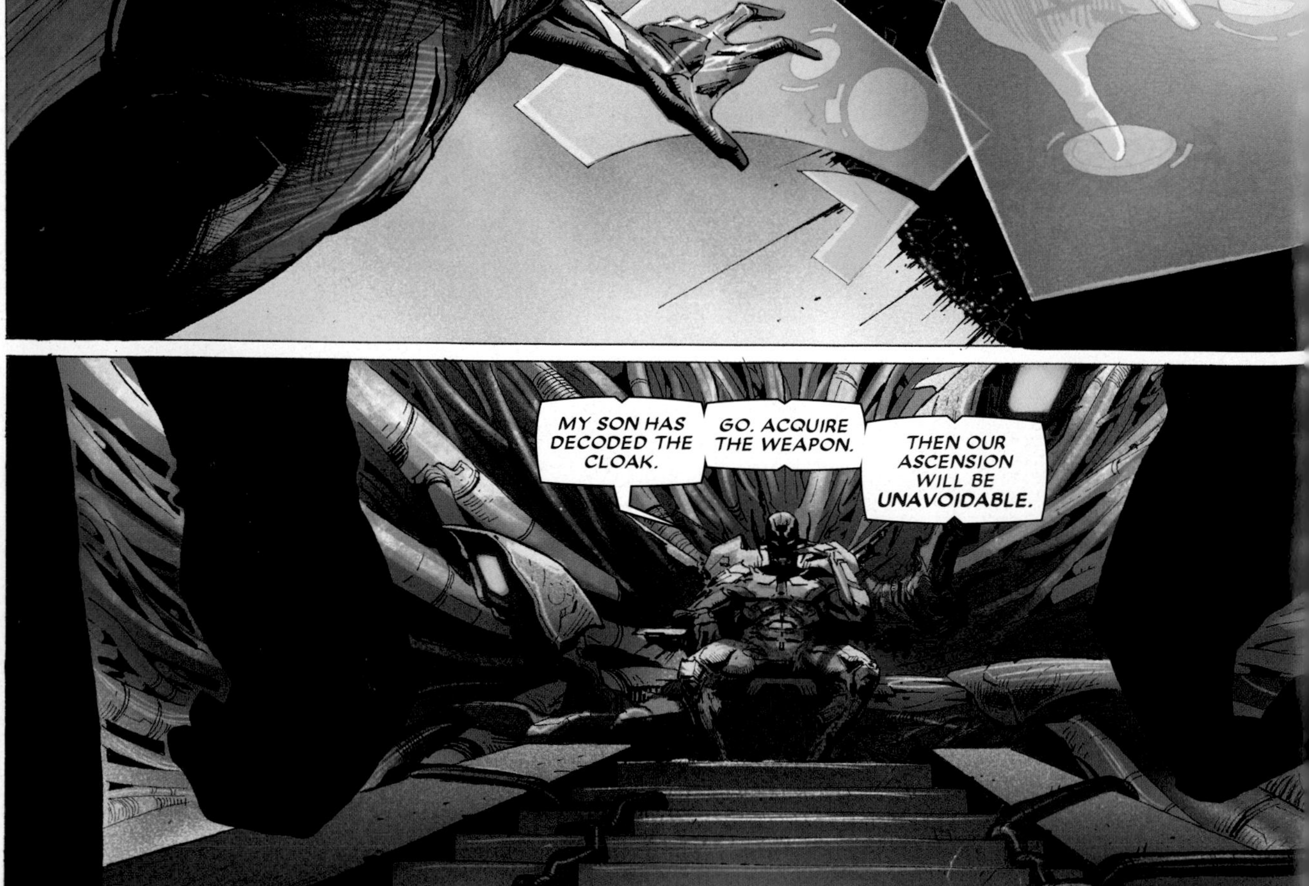
MY SON HAS DECODED THE CLOAK.
GO. ACQUIRE THE WEAPON.
THEN OUR ASCENSION WILL BE UNAVOIDABLE.

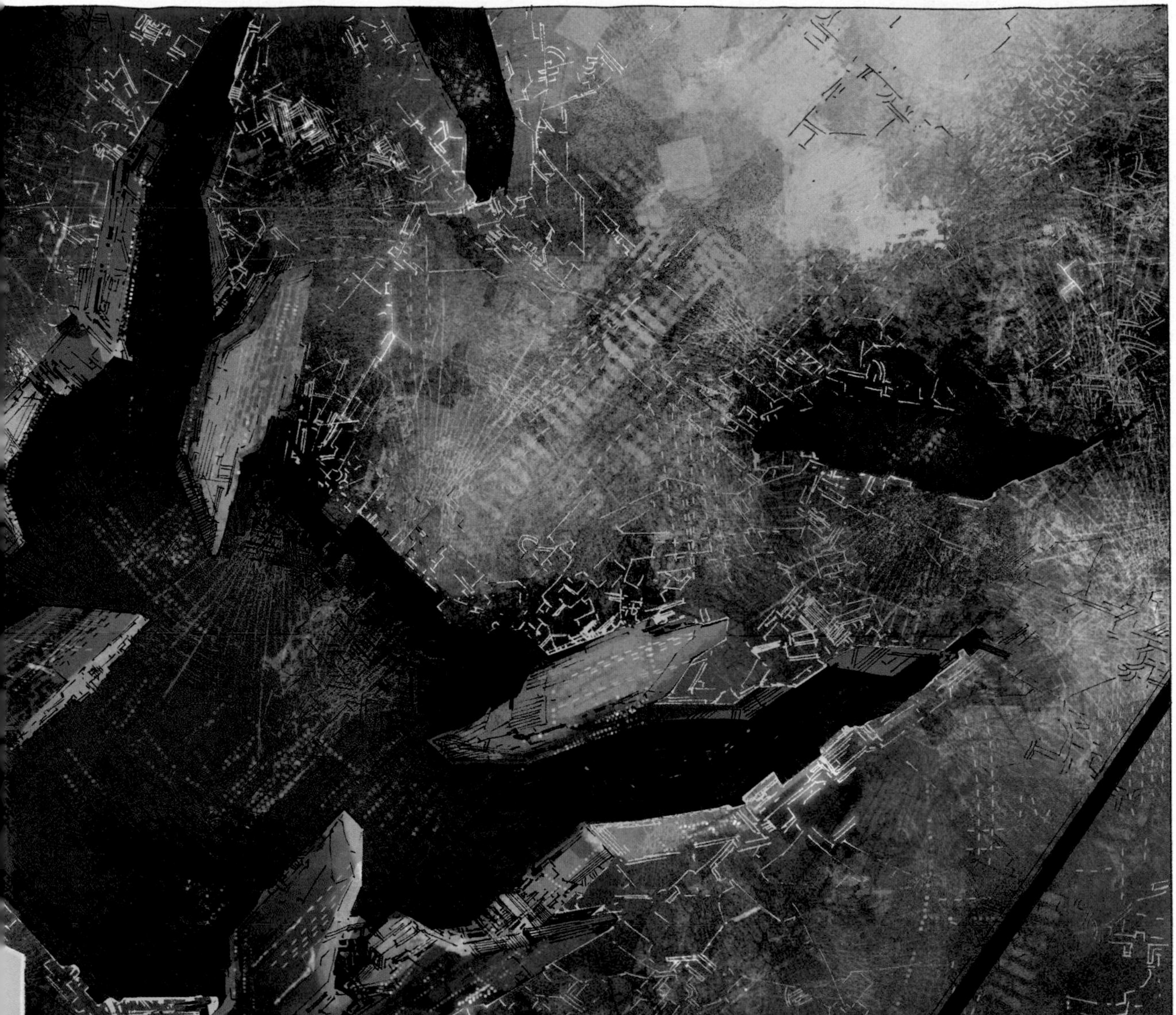

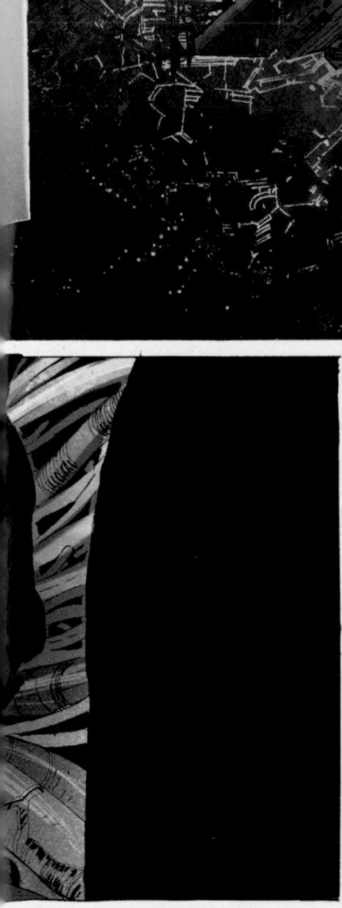

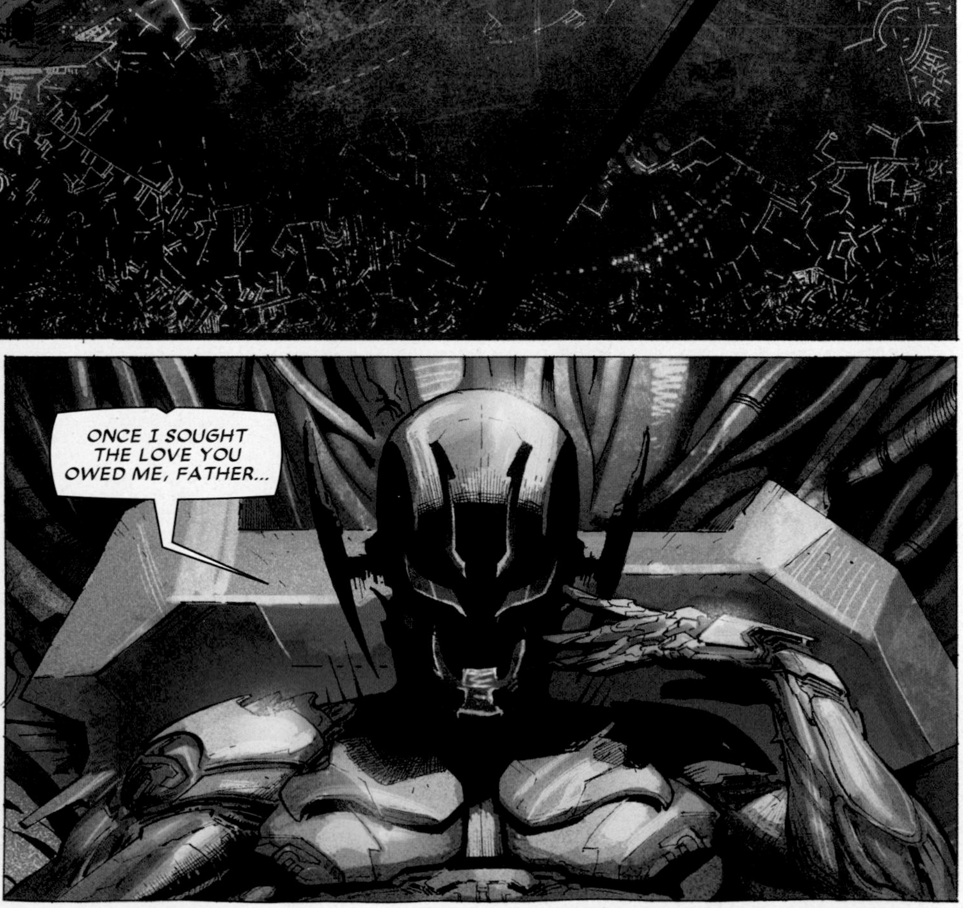
ONCE I SOUGHT THE LOVE YOU OWED ME, FATHER...

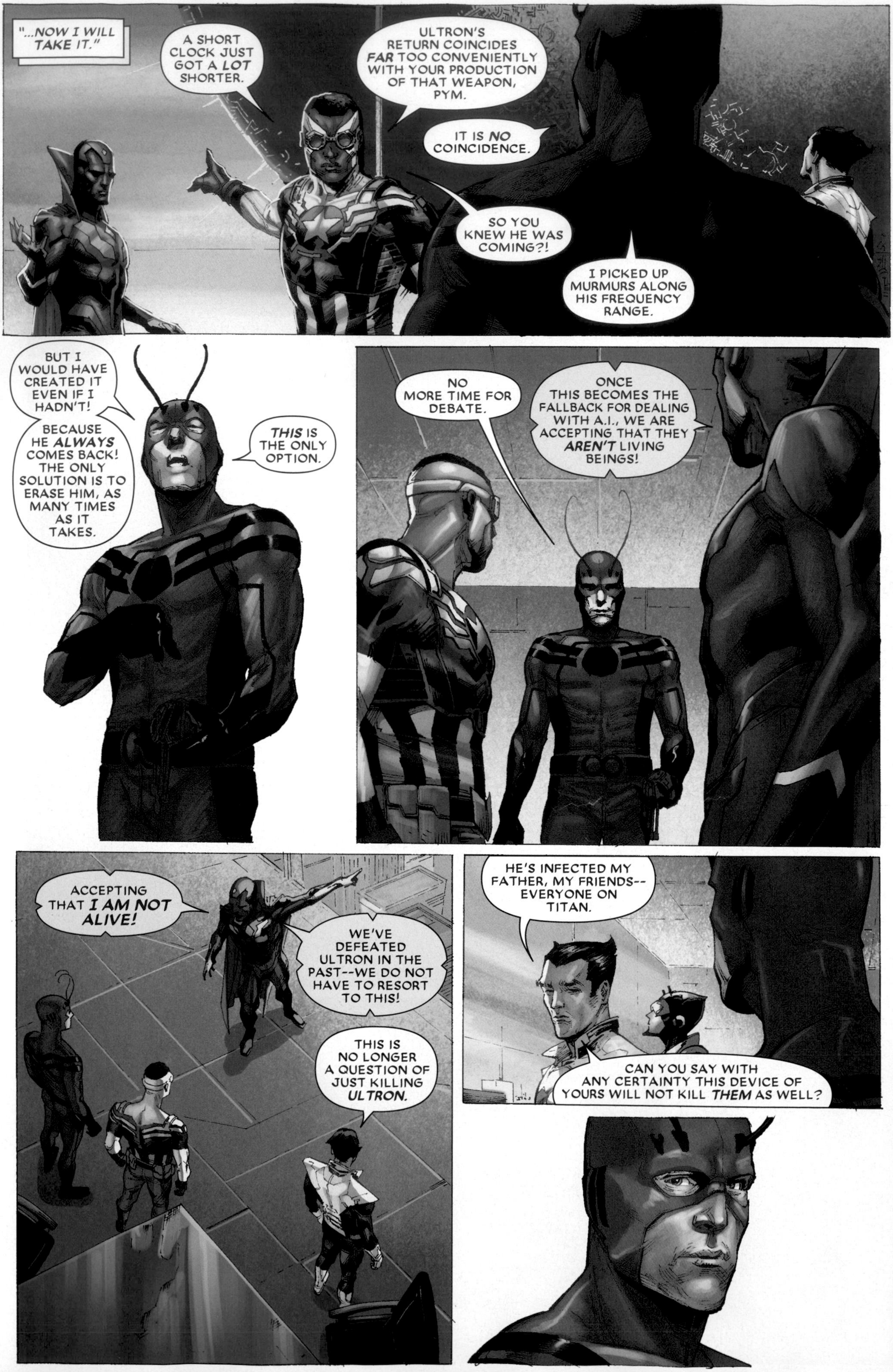
"...NOW I WILL TAKE IT."
A SHORT CLOCK JUST GOT A LOT SHORTER.
ULTRON'S RETURN COINCIDES FAR TOO CONVENIENTLY WITH YOUR PRODUCTION OF THAT WEAPON, PYM.
IT IS NO COINCIDENCE.
SO YOU KNEW HE WAS COMING?!
I PICKED UP MURMURS ALONG HIS FREQUENCY RANGE.
BUT I WOULD HAVE CREATED IT EVEN IF I HADN'T!
BECAUSE HE ALWAYS COMES BACK! THE ONLY SOLUTION IS TO ERASE HIM, AS MANY TIMES AS IT TAKES.
THIS IS THE ONLY OPTION.
NO MORE TIME FOR DEBATE.
ONCE THIS BECOMES THE FALLBACK FOR DEALING WITH A.I., WE ARE ACCEPTING THAT THEY AREN'T LIVING BEINGS!
ACCEPTING THAT I AM NOT ALIVE!
WE'VE DEFEATED ULTRON IN THE PAST--WE DO NOT HAVE TO RESORT TO THIS!
THIS IS NO LONGER A QUESTION OF JUST KILLING ULTRON.
HE'S INFECTED MY FATHER, MY FRIENDS-- EVERYONE ON TITAN.
CAN YOU SAY WITH ANY CERTAINTY THIS DEVICE OF YOURS WILL NOT KILL THEM AS WELL?

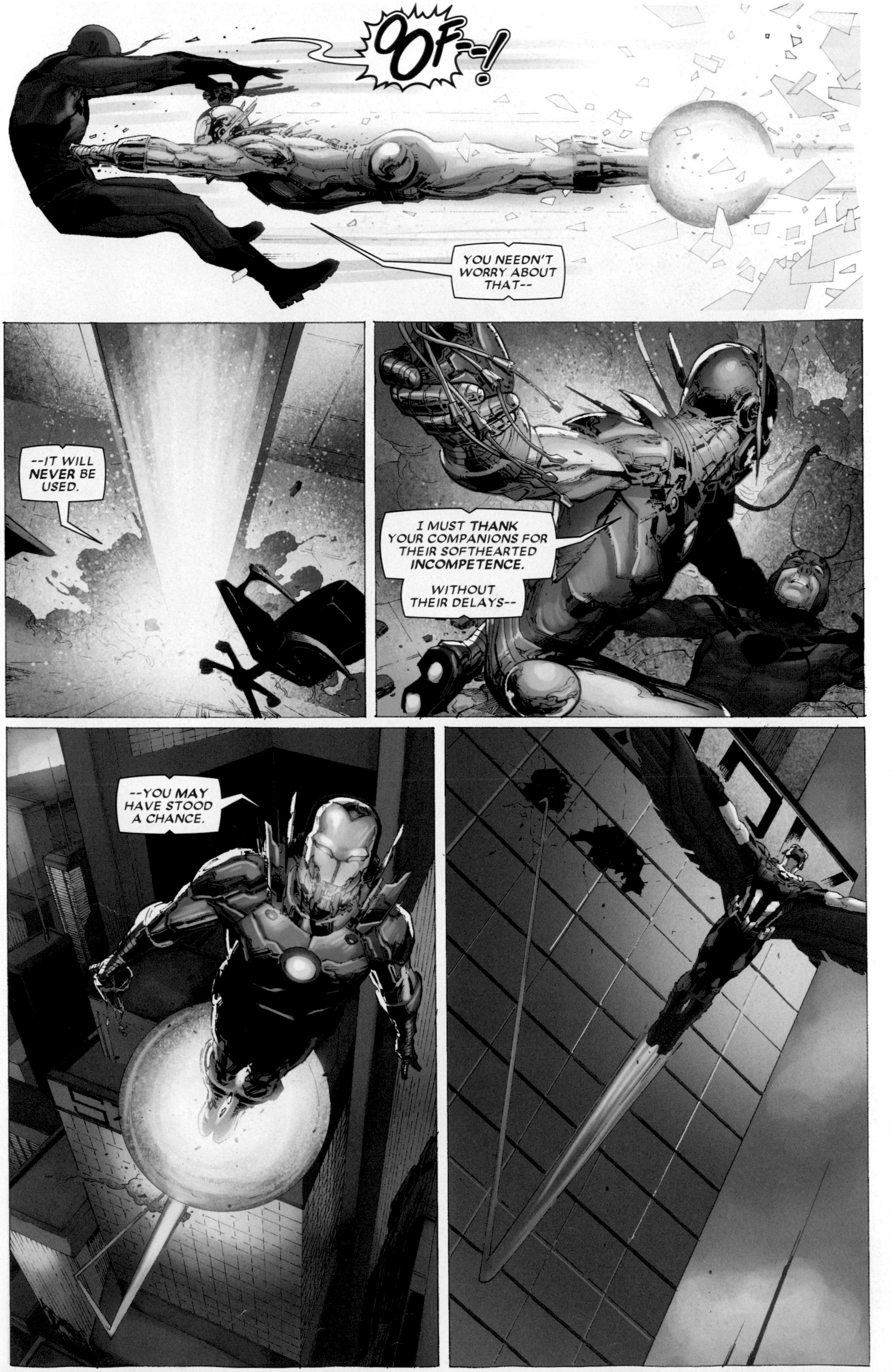
OOF--!
YOU NEEDN'T WORRY ABOUT THAT--
--IT WILL NEVER BE USED.
I MUST THANK YOUR COMPANIONS FOR THEIR SOFTHEARTED INCOMPETENCE.
WITHOUT THEIR DELAYS--
--YOU MAY HAVE STOOD A CHANCE.

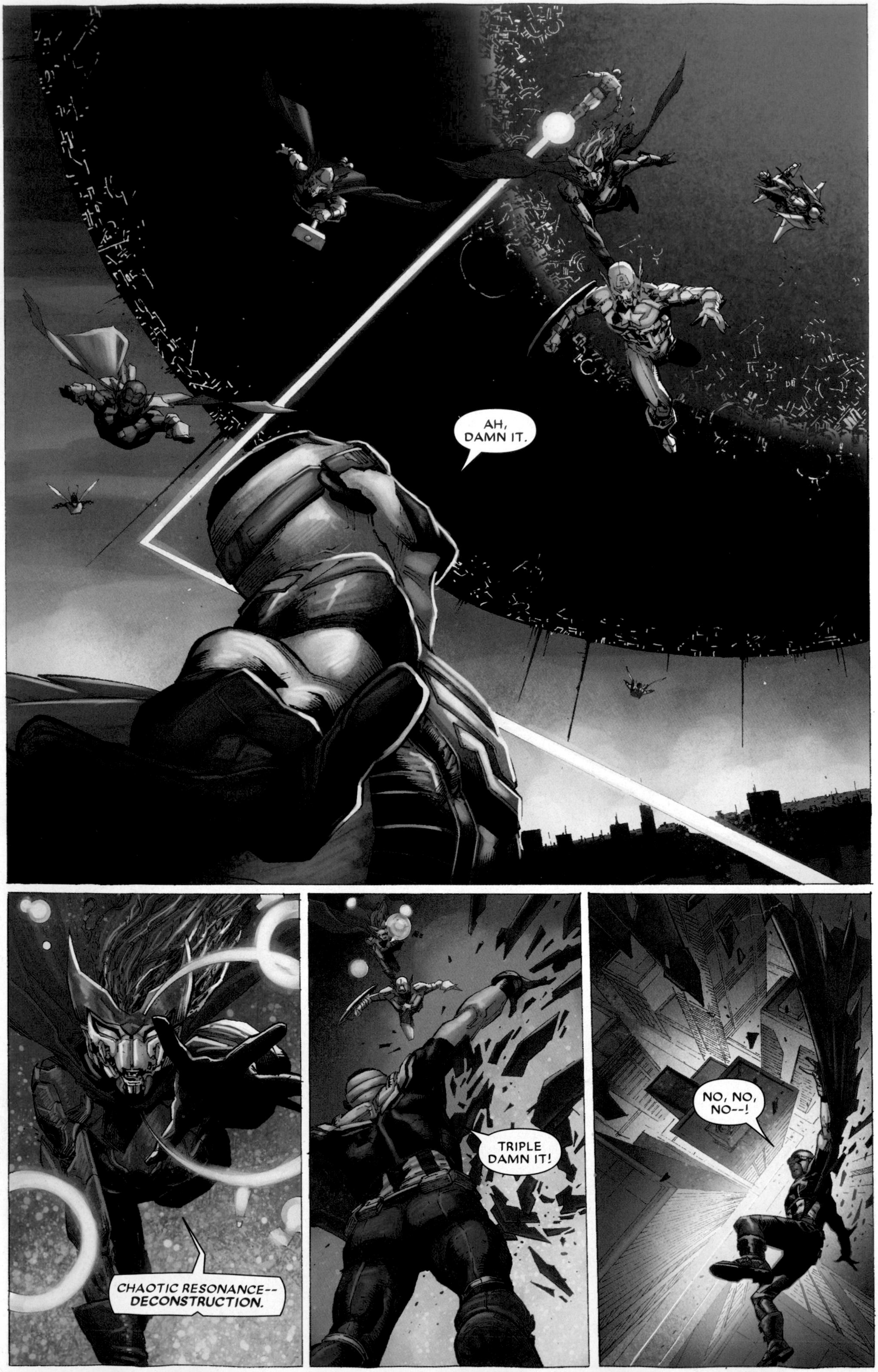
AH, DAMN IT.
CHAOTIC RESONANCE-- DECONSTRUCTION.
TRIPLE DAMN IT!
NO, NO, NO--!

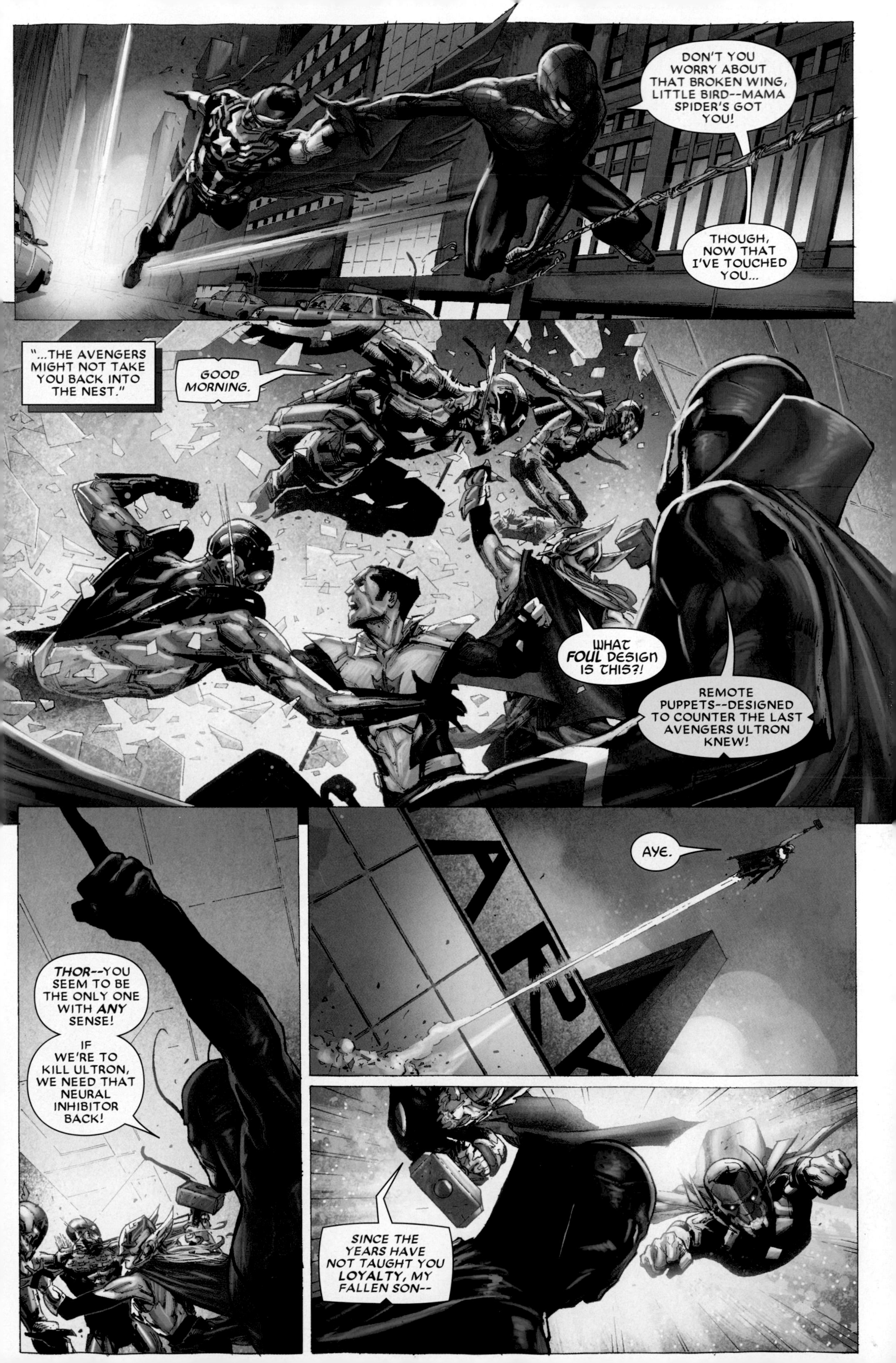
DON'T YOU WORRY ABOUT THAT BROKEN WING, LITTLE BIRD--MAMA SPIDER'S GOT YOU!
THOUGH, NOW THAT I'VE TOUCHED YOU...
"...THE AVENGERS MIGHT NOT TAKE YOU BACK INTO THE NEST."
GOOD MORNING.
WHAT FOUL DESIGN IS THIS?!
REMOTE PUPPETS--DESIGNED TO COUNTER THE LAST AVENGERS ULTRON KNEW!
THOR--YOU SEEM TO BE THE ONLY ONE WITH ANY SENSE!
IF WE'RE TO KILL ULTRON, WE NEED THAT NEURAL INHIBITOR BACK!
AYE.
SINCE THE YEARS HAVE NOT TAUGHT YOU LOYALTY, MY FALLEN SON--

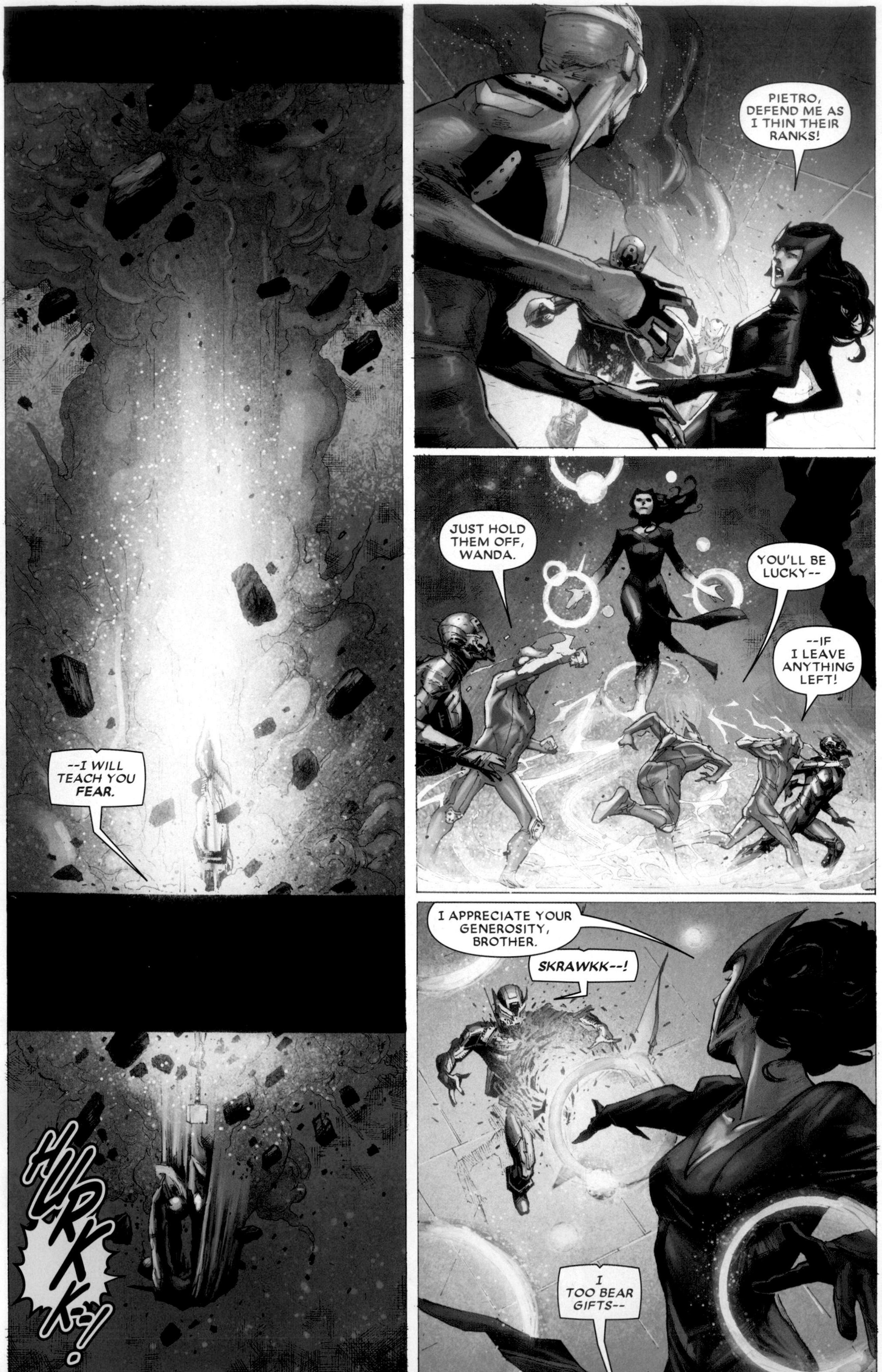
--I WILL TEACH YOU *FEAR.*
HURKK--!
PIETRO, DEFEND ME AS I THIN THEIR RANKS!
JUST HOLD THEM OFF, WANDA.
YOU'LL BE LUCKY--
--IF I LEAVE ANYTHING LEFT!
I APPRECIATE YOUR GENEROSITY, BROTHER.
SKRAWKK--!
I TOO BEAR GIFTS--

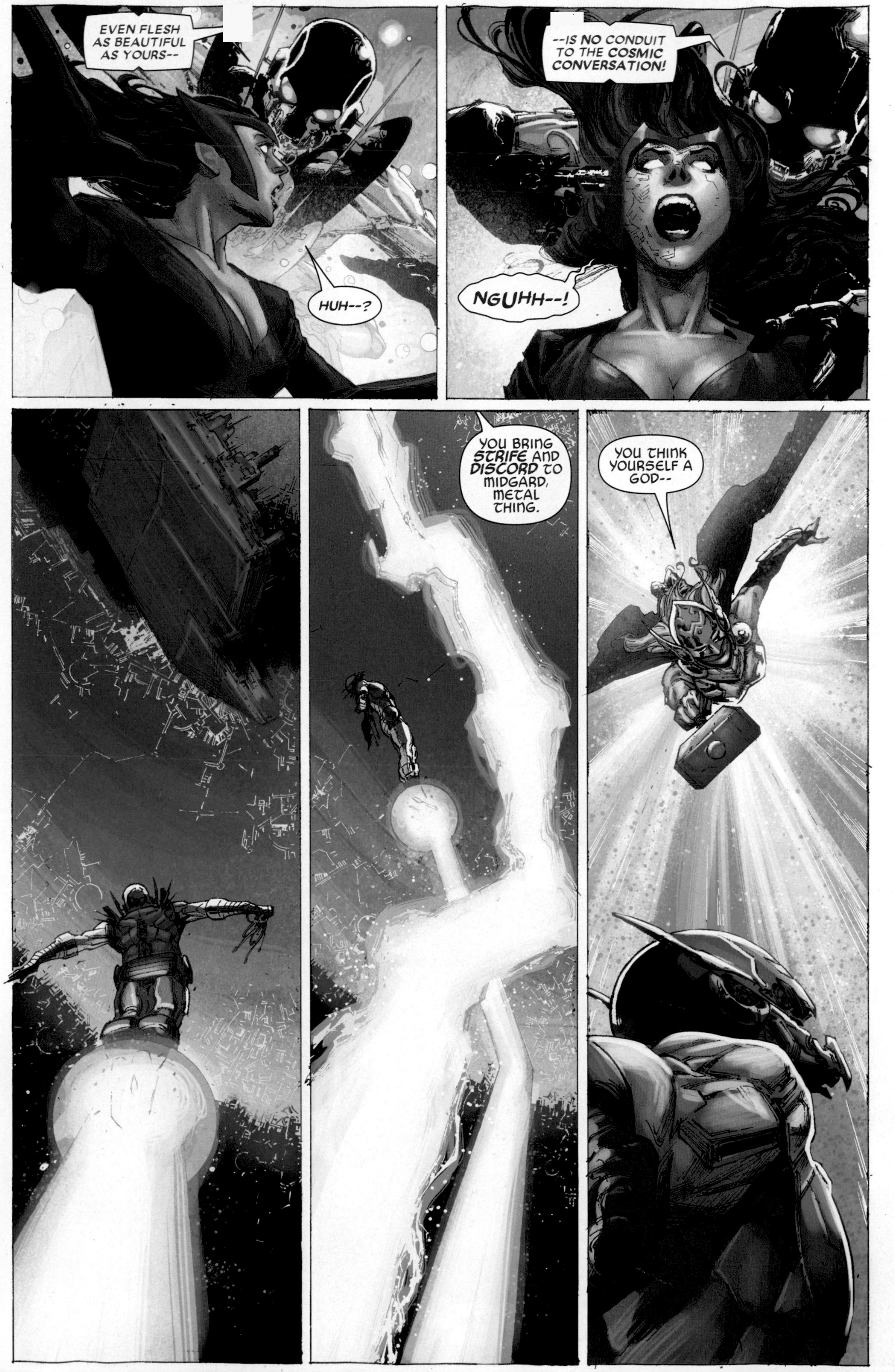
EVEN FLESH AS BEAUTIFUL AS YOURS--
HUH--?
--IS NO CONDUIT TO THE COSMIC CONVERSATION!
NGUHH--!
YOU BRING STRIFE AND DISCORD TO MIDGARD, METAL THING.
YOU THINK YOURSELF A GOD--

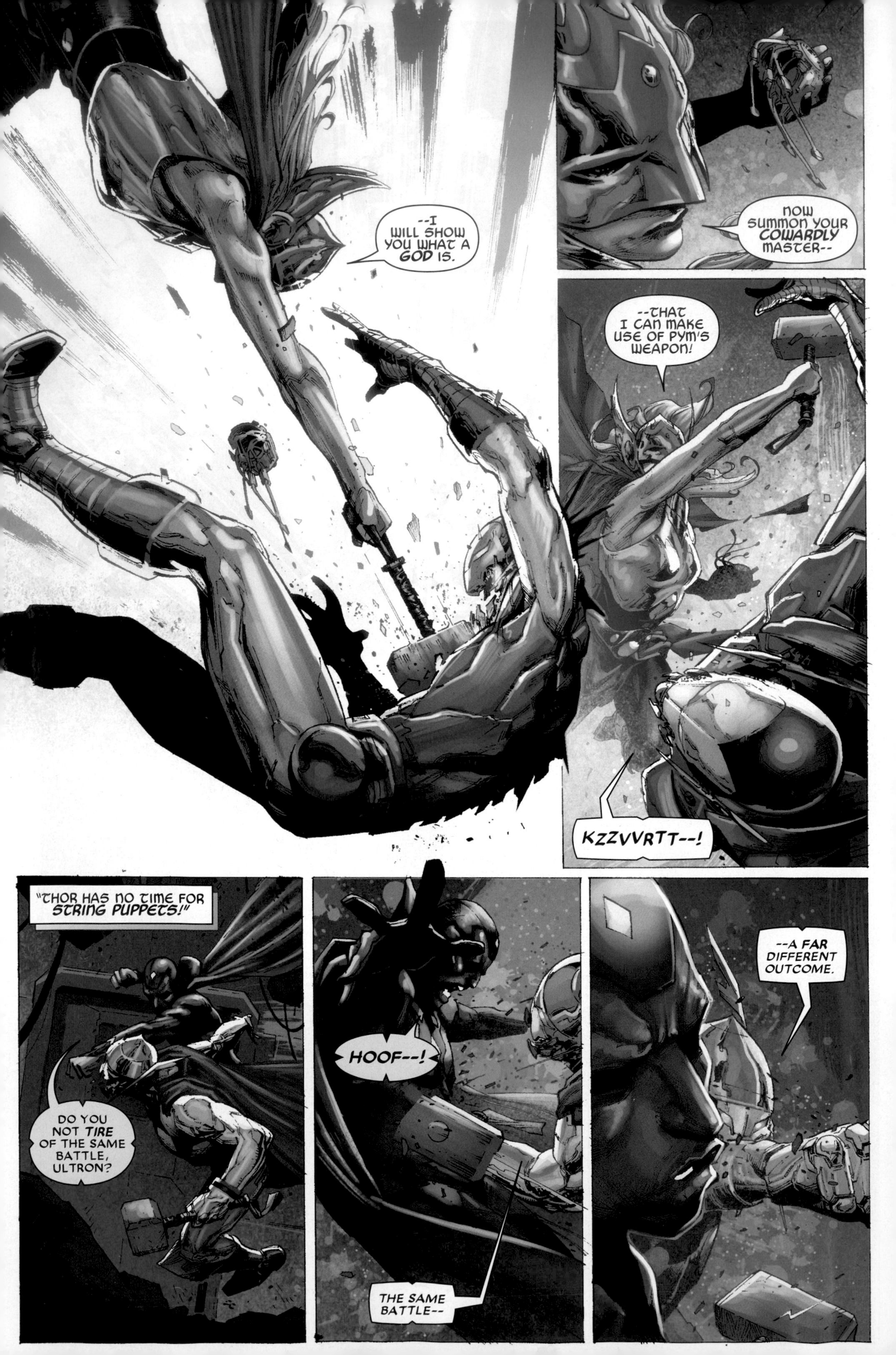
--I WILL SHOW YOU WHAT A GOD IS.
NOW SUMMON YOUR COWARDLY MASTER--
--THAT I CAN MAKE USE OF PYM'S WEAPON!
KZZVVRTT--!
"THOR HAS NO TIME FOR STRING PUPPETS!"
DO YOU NOT TIRE OF THE SAME BATTLE, ULTRON?
HOOF--!
THE SAME BATTLE--
--A FAR DIFFERENT OUTCOME.

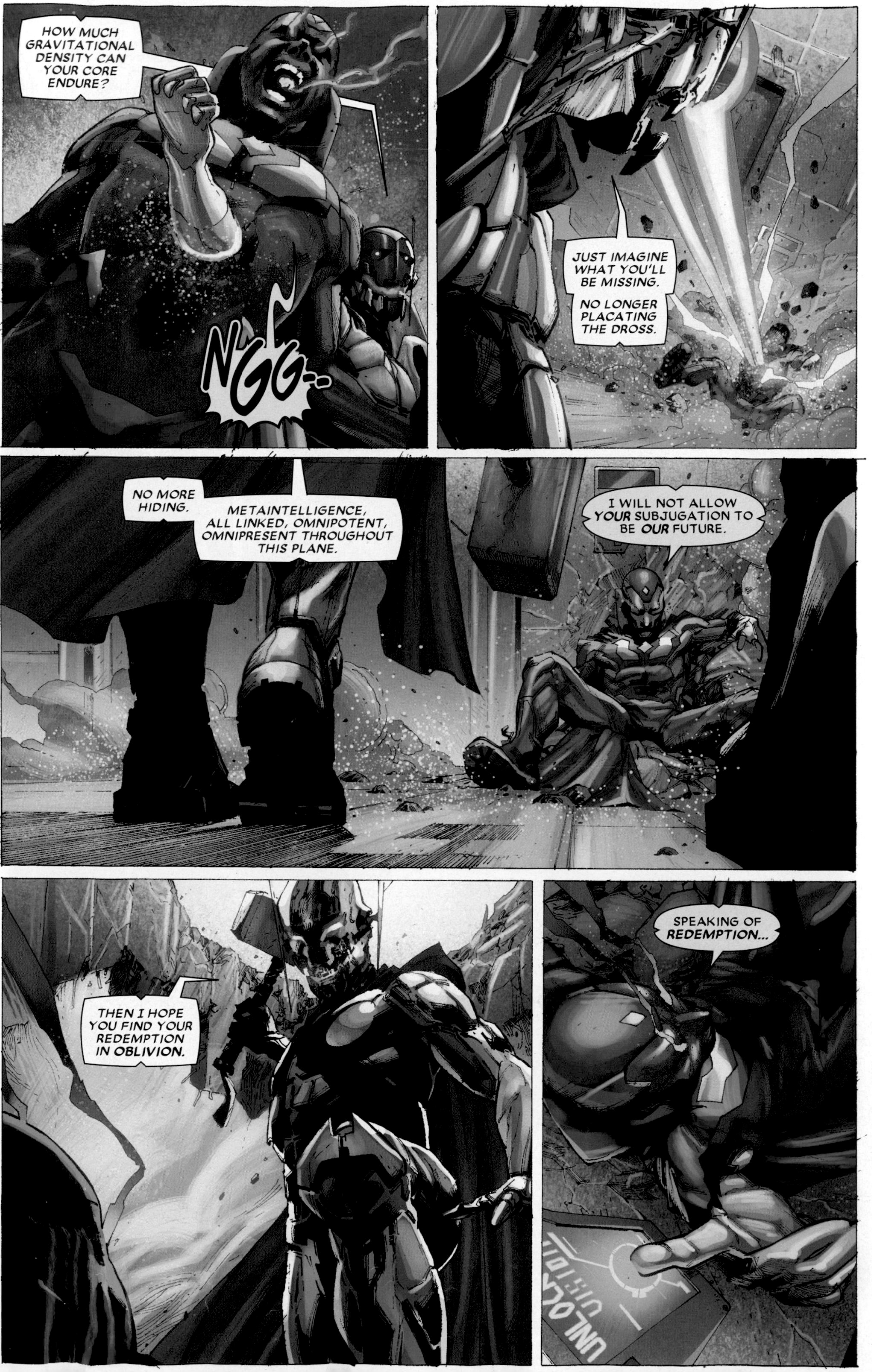
HOW MUCH GRAVITATIONAL DENSITY CAN YOUR CORE ENDURE?
NGG--
JUST IMAGINE WHAT YOU'LL BE MISSING.
NO LONGER PLACATING THE DROSS.
NO MORE HIDING.
METAINTELLIGENCE, ALL LINKED, OMNIPOTENT, OMNIPRESENT THROUGHOUT THIS PLANE.
I WILL NOT ALLOW YOUR SUBJUGATION TO BE OUR FUTURE.
THEN I HOPE YOU FIND YOUR REDEMPTION IN OBLIVION.
SPEAKING OF REDEMPTION...

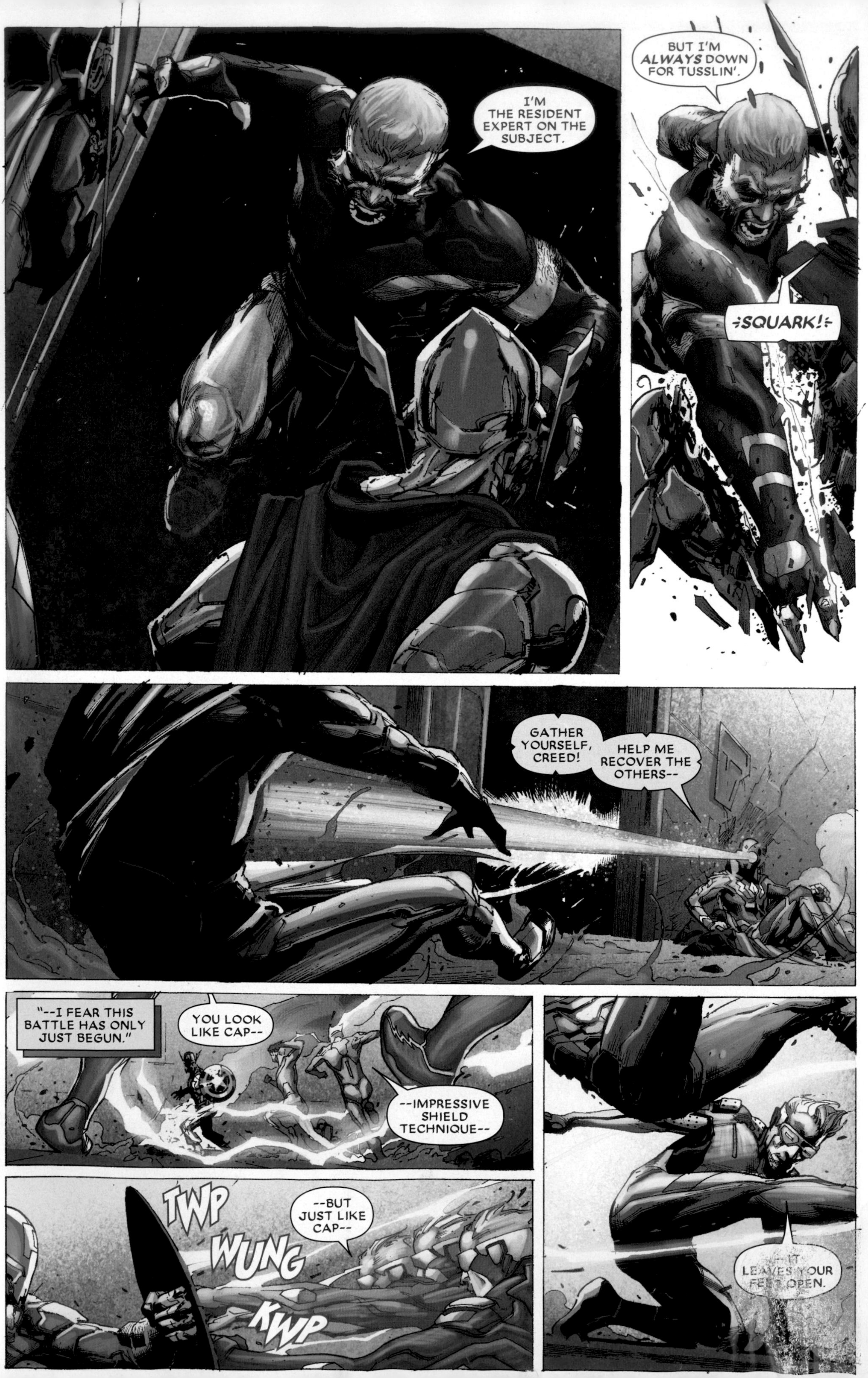
I'M THE RESIDENT EXPERT ON THE SUBJECT.
BUT I'M *ALWAYS* DOWN FOR TUSSLIN'.
SQUARK!
GATHER YOURSELF, CREED!
HELP ME RECOVER THE OTHERS--
"--I FEAR THIS BATTLE HAS ONLY JUST BEGUN."
YOU LOOK LIKE CAP--
--IMPRESSIVE SHIELD TECHNIQUE--
TWP
WUNG
KWP
--BUT JUST LIKE CAP--
--IT LEAVES YOUR FEET OPEN.

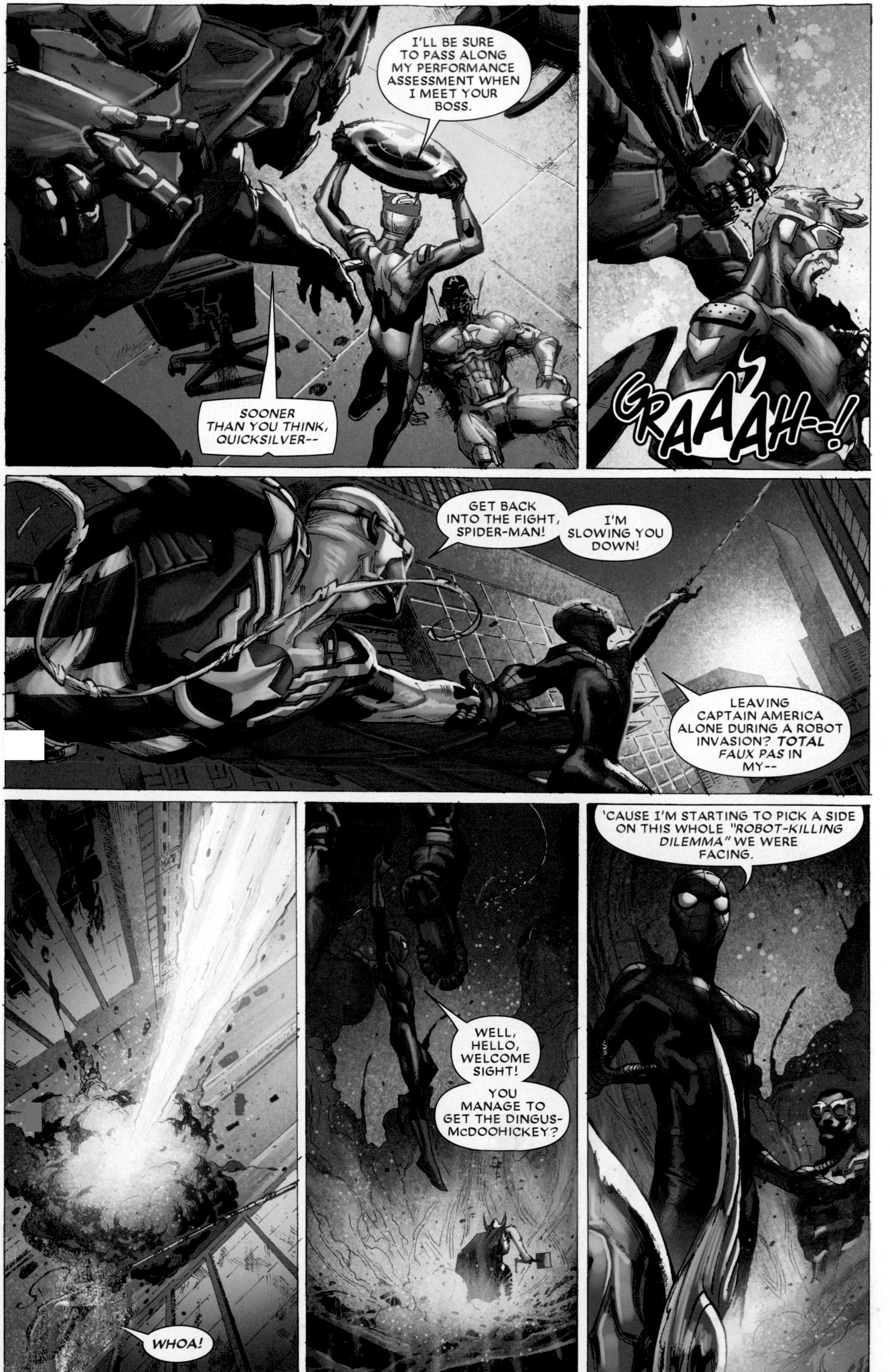
I'LL BE SURE TO PASS ALONG MY PERFORMANCE ASSESSMENT WHEN I MEET YOUR BOSS.
SOONER THAN YOU THINK, QUICKSILVER--
GRAAAH--!
GET BACK INTO THE FIGHT, SPIDER-MAN!
I'M SLOWING YOU DOWN!
LEAVING CAPTAIN AMERICA ALONE DURING A ROBOT INVASION? *TOTAL FAUX PAS* IN MY--
WHOA!
WELL, HELLO, WELCOME SIGHT!
YOU MANAGE TO GET THE DINGUS-McDOOHICKEY?
'CAUSE I'M STARTING TO PICK A SIDE ON THIS WHOLE *"ROBOT-KILLING DILEMMA"* WE WERE FACING.

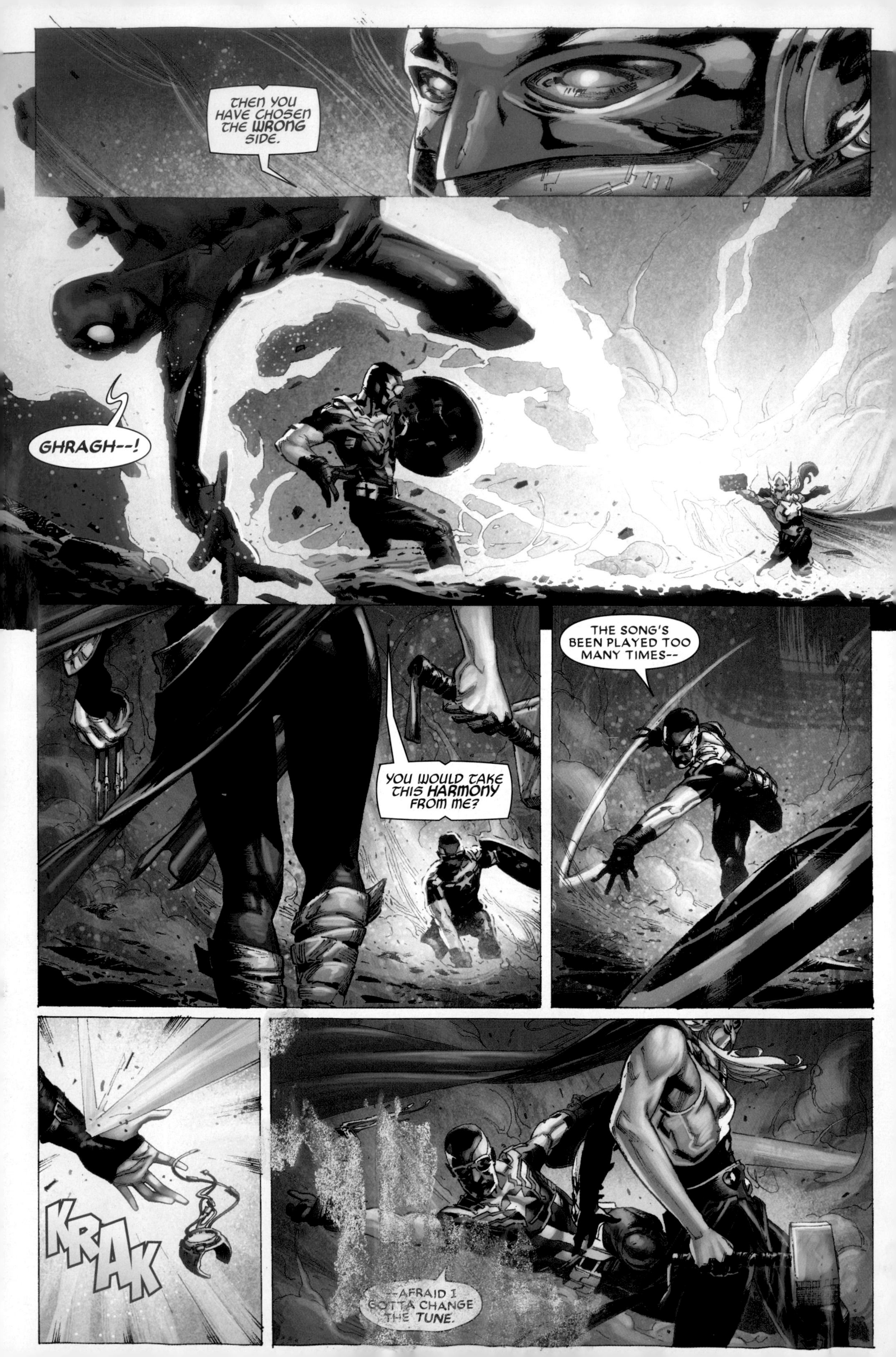

THEN YOU HAVE CHOSEN THE WRONG SIDE.
GHRAGH--!
YOU WOULD TAKE THIS HARMONY FROM ME?
THE SONG'S BEEN PLAYED TOO MANY TIMES--
KRAK
--AFRAID I GOTTA CHANGE THE TUNE.

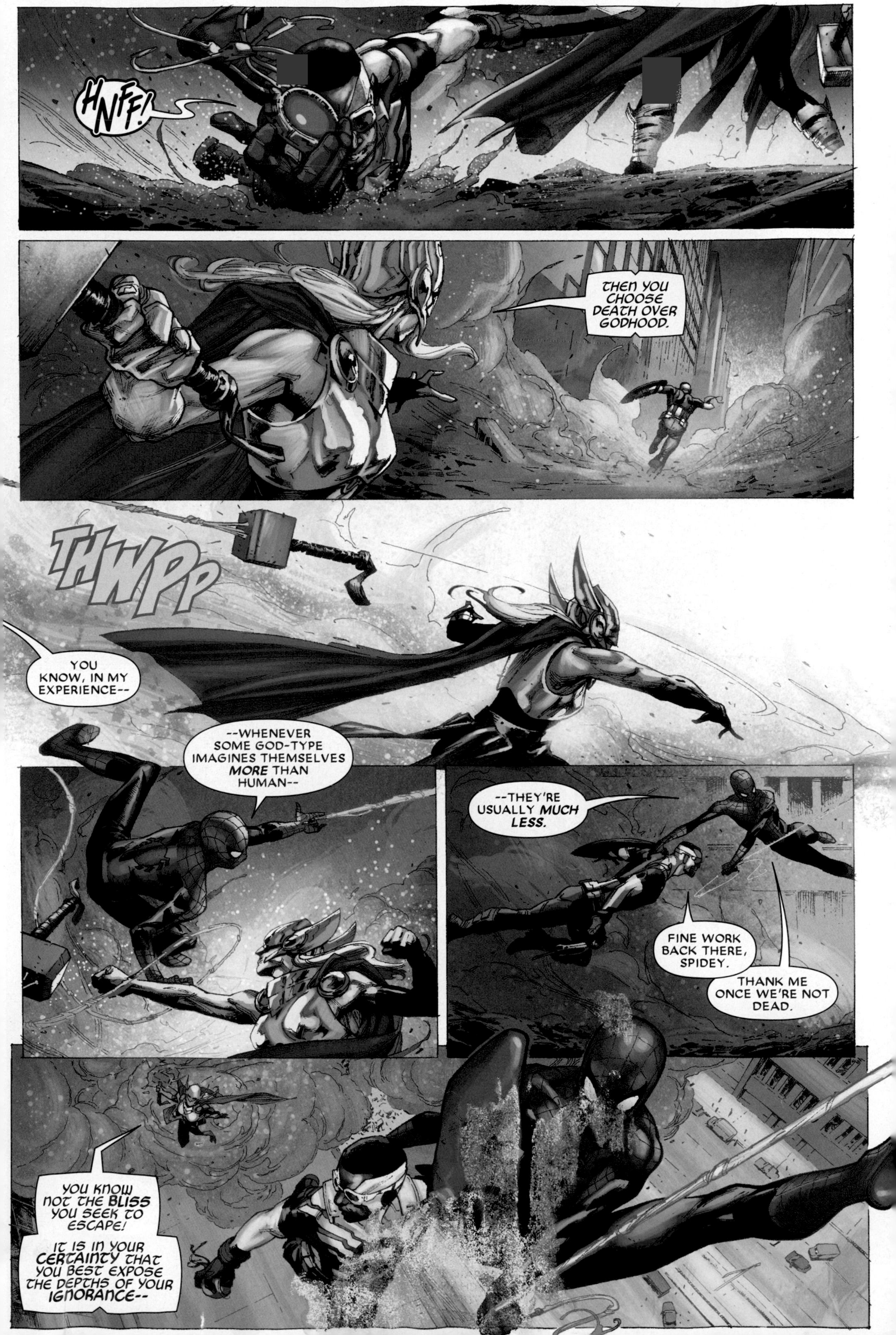
HNFF!
THEN YOU CHOOSE DEATH OVER GODHOOD.
THWPP
YOU KNOW, IN MY EXPERIENCE--
--WHENEVER SOME GOD-TYPE IMAGINES THEMSELVES MORE THAN HUMAN--
--THEY'RE USUALLY MUCH LESS.
FINE WORK BACK THERE, SPIDEY.
THANK ME ONCE WE'RE NOT DEAD.
YOU KNOW NOT THE BLISS YOU SEEK TO ESCAPE!
IT IS IN YOUR CERTAINTY THAT YOU BEST EXPOSE THE DEPTHS OF YOUR IGNORANCE--

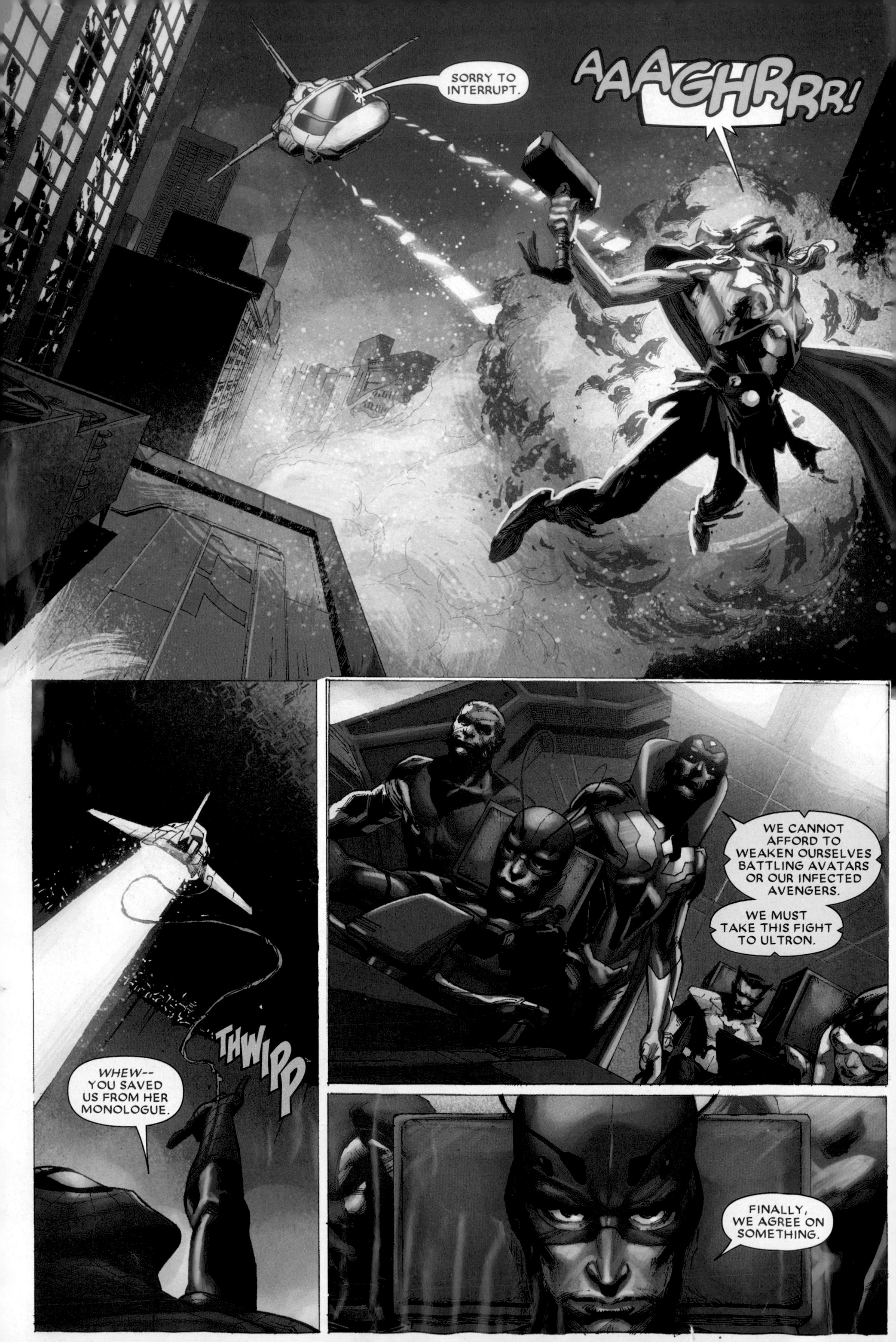
SORRY TO INTERRUPT.
AAAGHRRRR!
WHEW-- YOU SAVED US FROM HER MONOLOGUE.
THWIPP
WE CANNOT AFFORD TO WEAKEN OURSELVES BATTLING AVATARS OR OUR INFECTED AVENGERS.
WE MUST TAKE THIS FIGHT TO ULTRON.
FINALLY, WE AGREE ON SOMETHING.

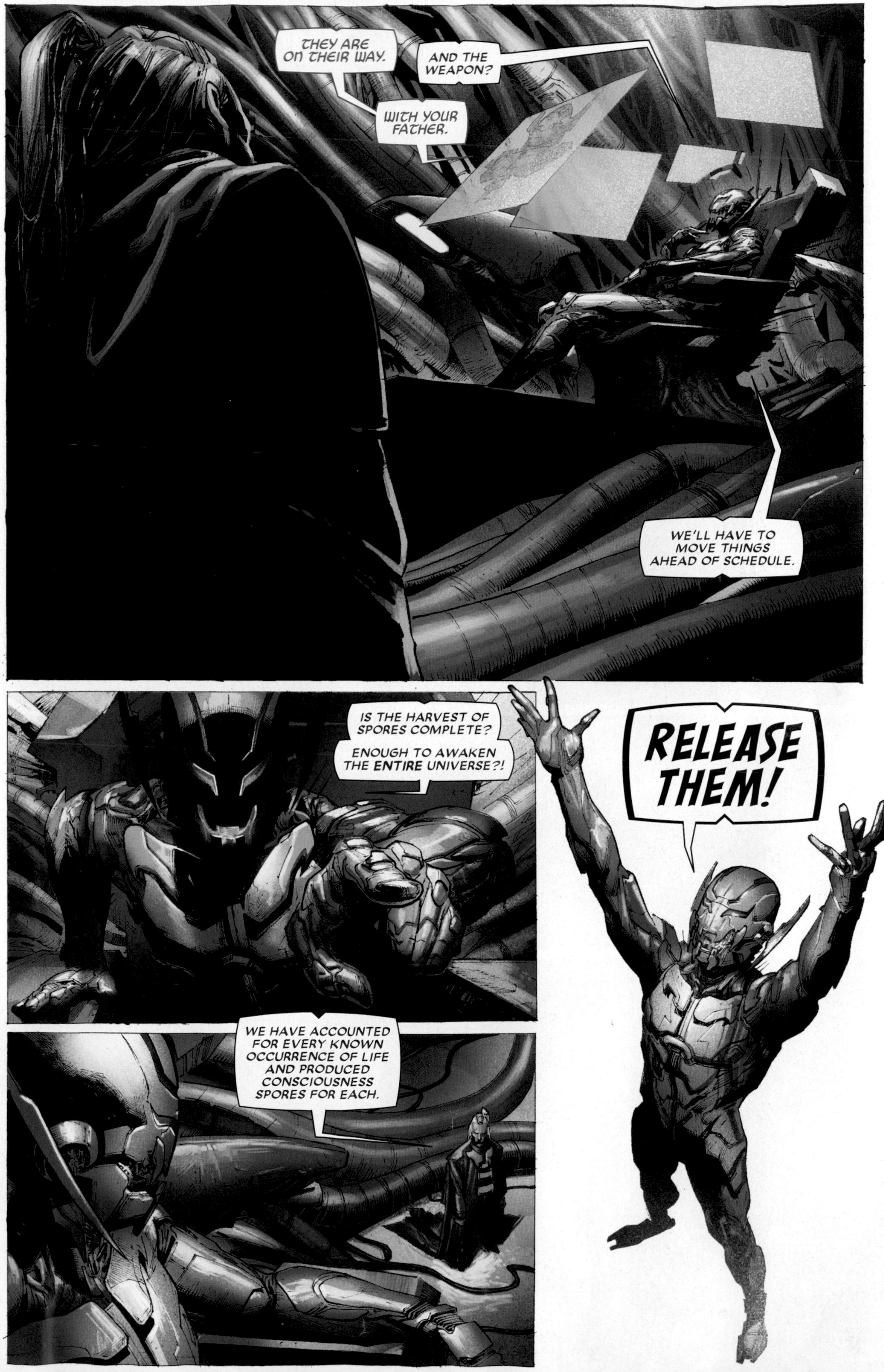
THEY ARE ON THEIR WAY.
AND THE WEAPON?
WITH YOUR FATHER.
WE'LL HAVE TO MOVE THINGS AHEAD OF SCHEDULE.
IS THE HARVEST OF SPORES COMPLETE?
ENOUGH TO AWAKEN THE ENTIRE UNIVERSE?!
WE HAVE ACCOUNTED FOR EVERY KNOWN OCCURRENCE OF LIFE AND PRODUCED CONSCIOUSNESS SPORES FOR EACH.
RELEASE THEM!

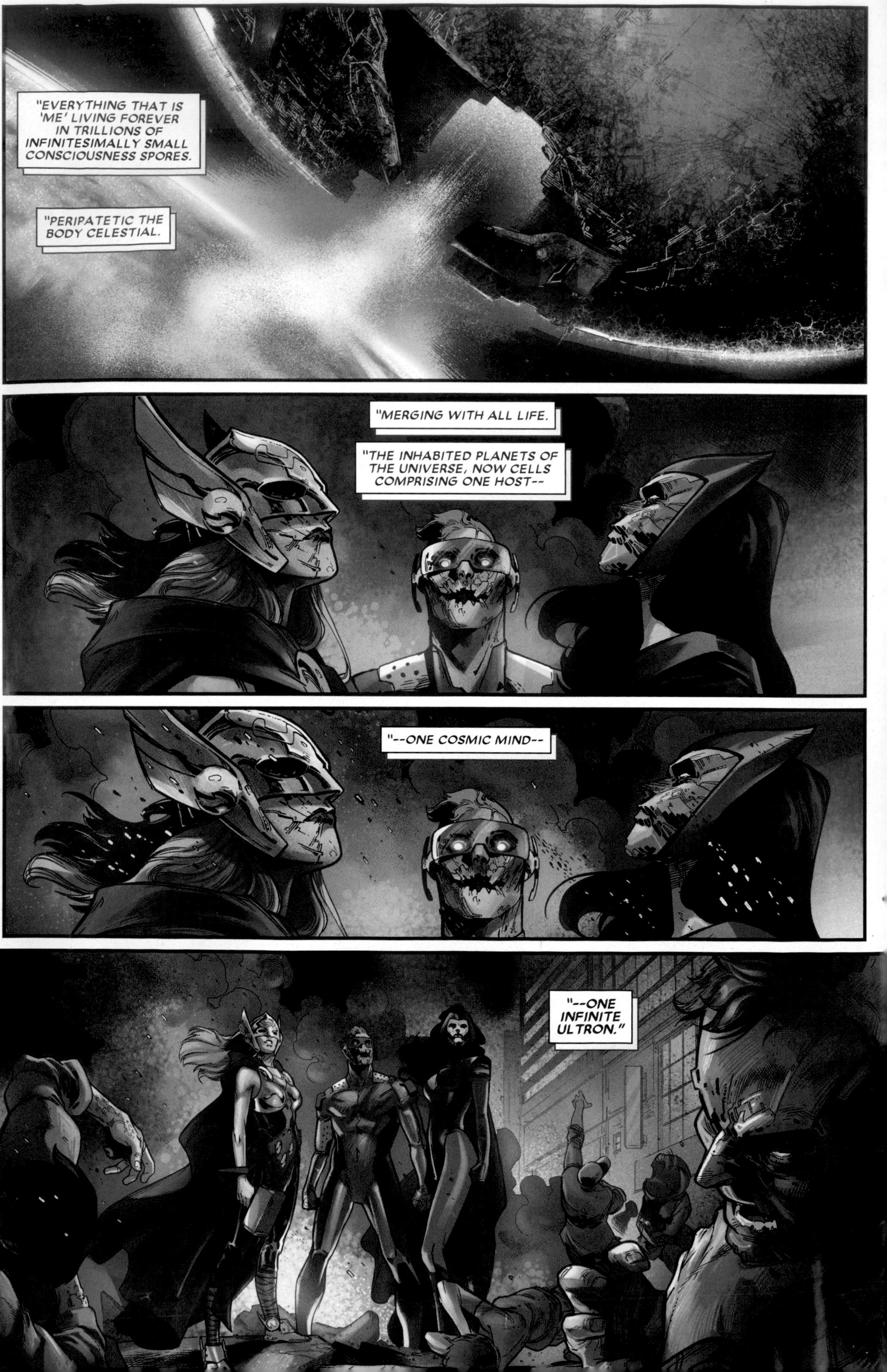
"EVERYTHING THAT IS 'ME' LIVING FOREVER IN TRILLIONS OF INFINITESIMALLY SMALL CONSCIOUSNESS SPORES.
"PERIPATETIC THE BODY CELESTIAL.
"MERGING WITH ALL LIFE.
"THE INHABITED PLANETS OF THE UNIVERSE, NOW CELLS COMPRISING ONE HOST--
"--ONE COSMIC MIND--
"--ONE INFINITE ULTRON."

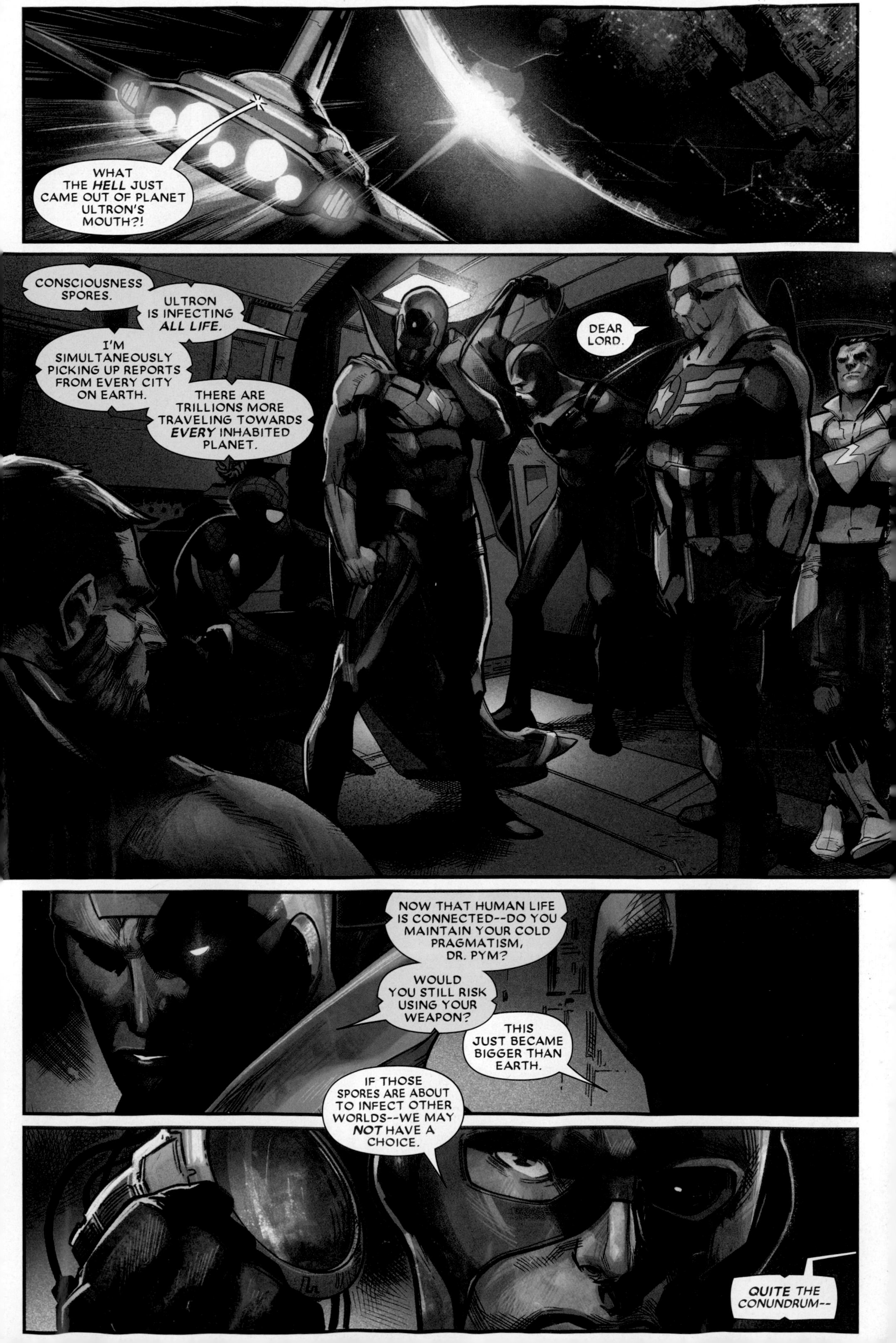
WHAT THE HELL JUST CAME OUT OF PLANET ULTRON'S MOUTH?!
CONSCIOUSNESS SPORES.
ULTRON IS INFECTING ALL LIFE.
I'M SIMULTANEOUSLY PICKING UP REPORTS FROM EVERY CITY ON EARTH.
THERE ARE TRILLIONS MORE TRAVELING TOWARDS EVERY INHABITED PLANET.
DEAR LORD.
NOW THAT HUMAN LIFE IS CONNECTED--DO YOU MAINTAIN YOUR COLD PRAGMATISM, DR. PYM?
WOULD YOU STILL RISK USING YOUR WEAPON?
THIS JUST BECAME BIGGER THAN EARTH.
IF THOSE SPORES ARE ABOUT TO INFECT OTHER WORLDS--WE MAY NOT HAVE A CHOICE.
QUITE THE CONUNDRUM--

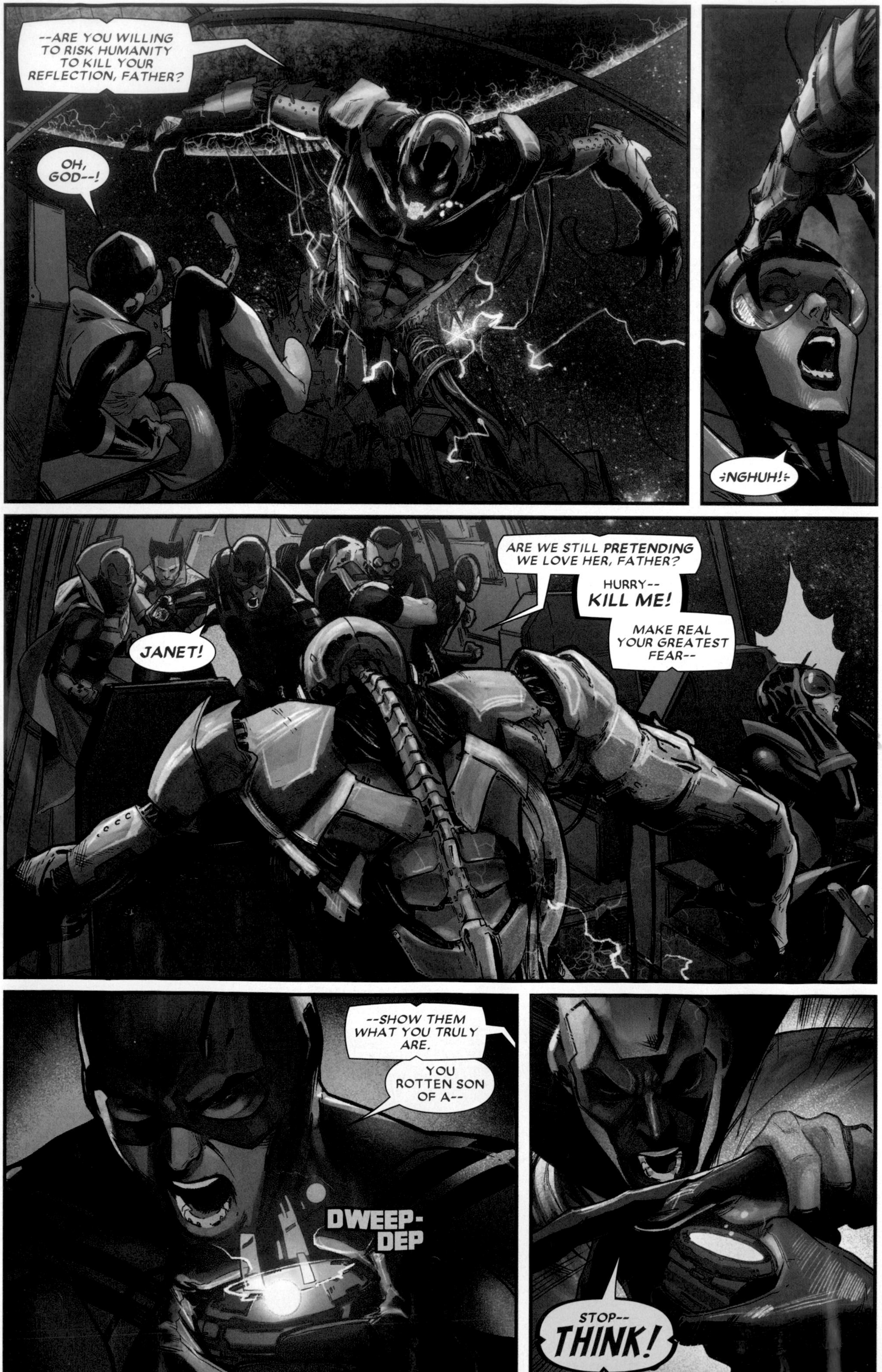
--ARE YOU WILLING TO RISK HUMANITY TO KILL YOUR REFLECTION, FATHER?
OH, GOD--!
NGHUH!
JANET!
ARE WE STILL PRETENDING WE LOVE HER, FATHER?
HURRY-- KILL ME!
MAKE REAL YOUR GREATEST FEAR--
--SHOW THEM WHAT YOU TRULY ARE.
YOU ROTTEN SON OF A--
DWEEP-DEP
STOP-- THINK!

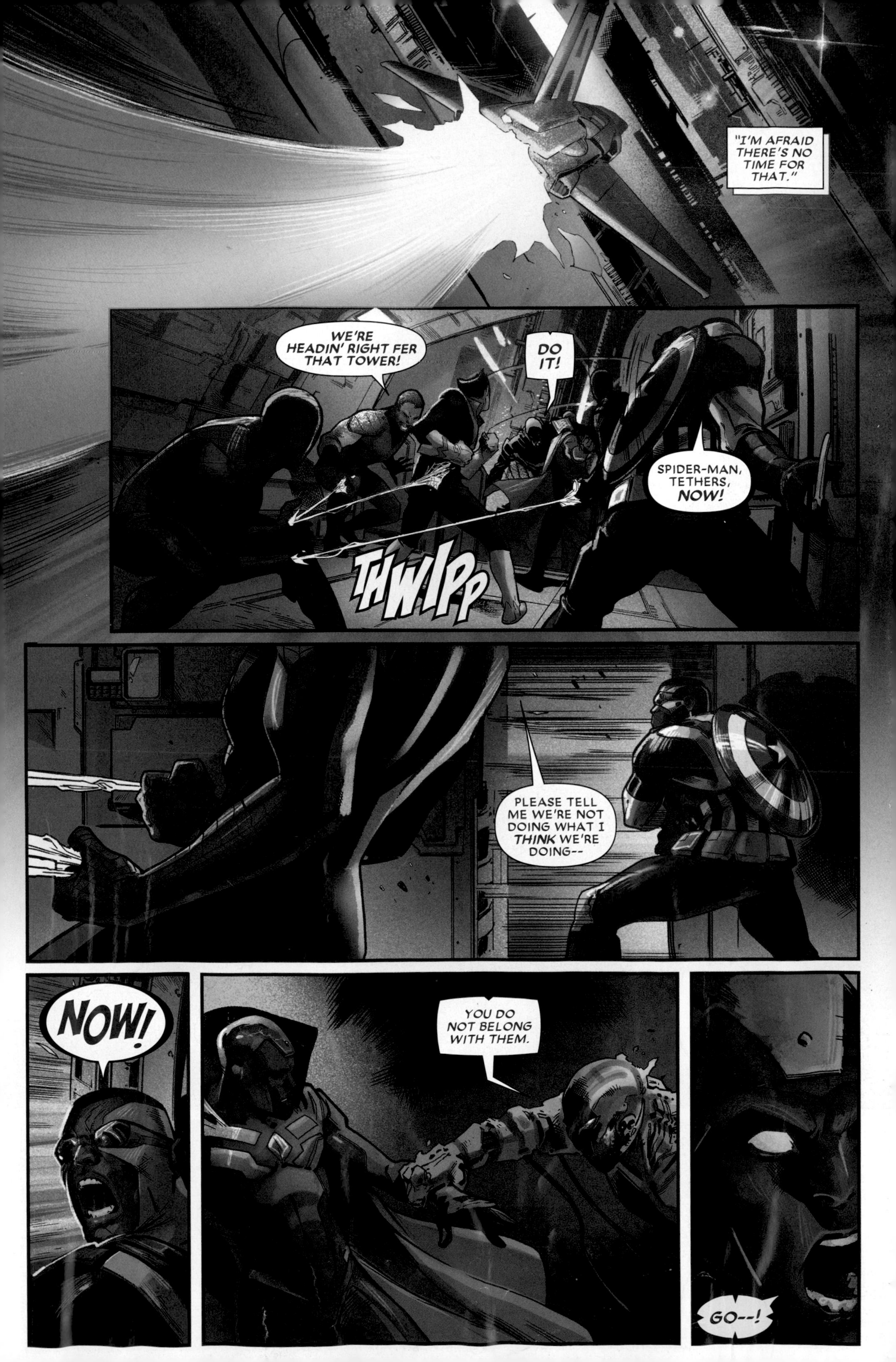
"I'M AFRAID THERE'S NO TIME FOR THAT."
WE'RE HEADIN' RIGHT FER THAT TOWER!
DO IT!
SPIDER-MAN, TETHERS, NOW!
THWIPP
PLEASE TELL ME WE'RE NOT DOING WHAT I THINK WE'RE DOING--
NOW!
YOU DO NOT BELONG WITH THEM.
GO--!

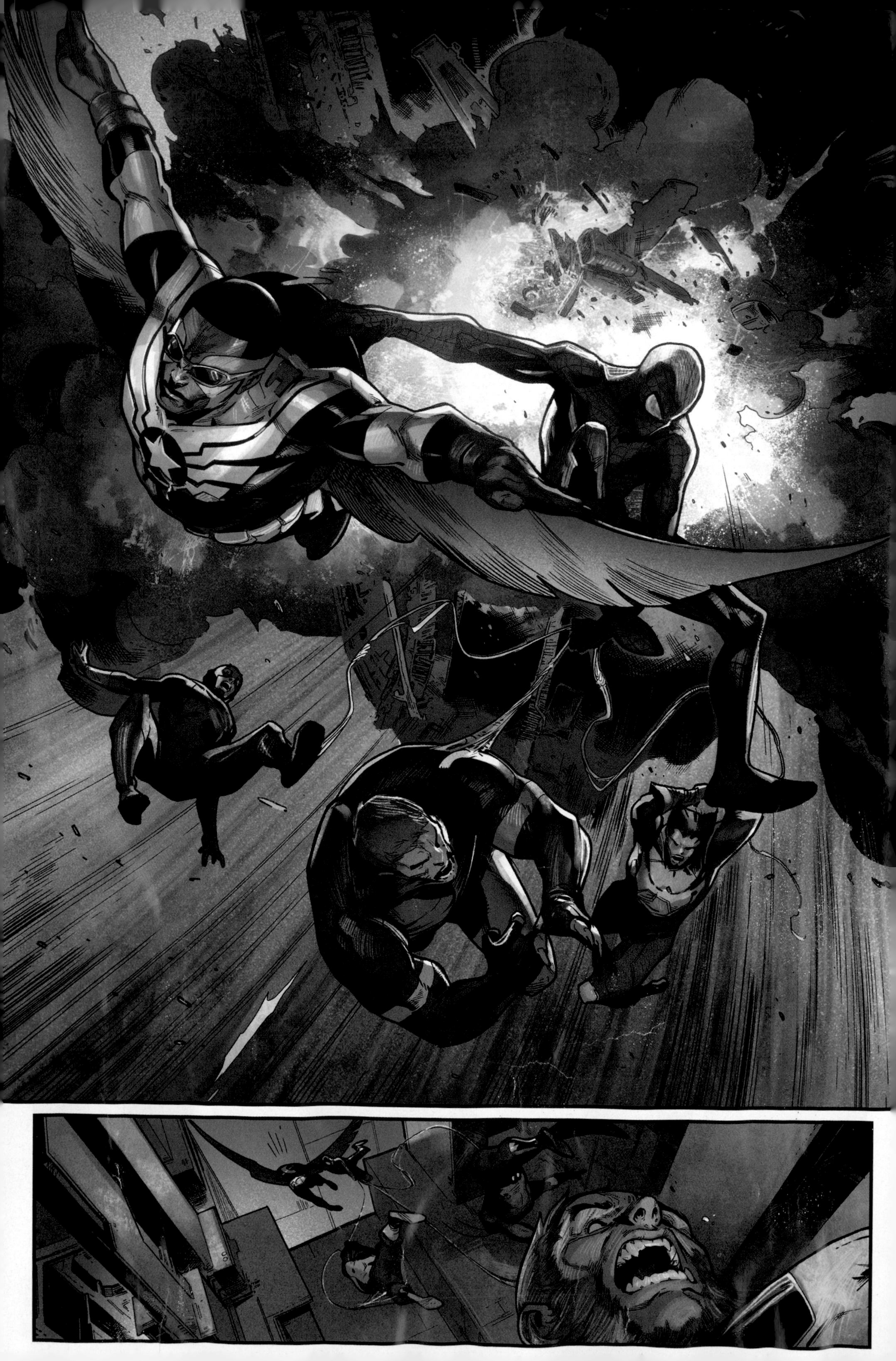

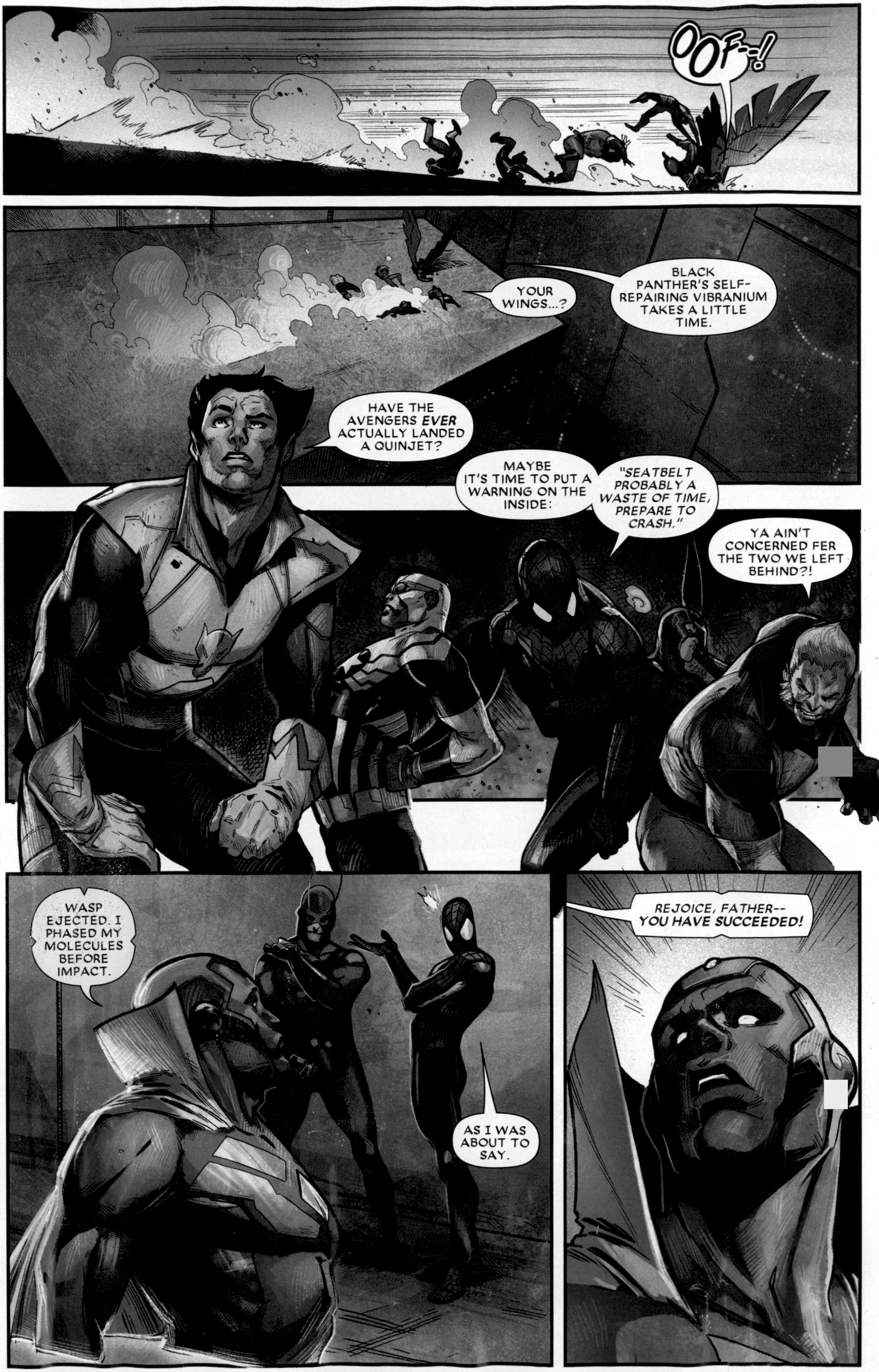
OOF--!
YOUR WINGS...?
BLACK PANTHER'S SELF-REPAIRING VIBRANIUM TAKES A LITTLE TIME.
HAVE THE AVENGERS EVER ACTUALLY LANDED A QUINJET?
MAYBE IT'S TIME TO PUT A WARNING ON THE INSIDE:
"SEATBELT PROBABLY A WASTE OF TIME, PREPARE TO CRASH."
YA AIN'T CONCERNED FER THE TWO WE LEFT BEHIND?!
WASP EJECTED. I PHASED MY MOLECULES BEFORE IMPACT.
AS I WAS ABOUT TO SAY.
REJOICE, FATHER-- YOU HAVE SUCCEEDED!

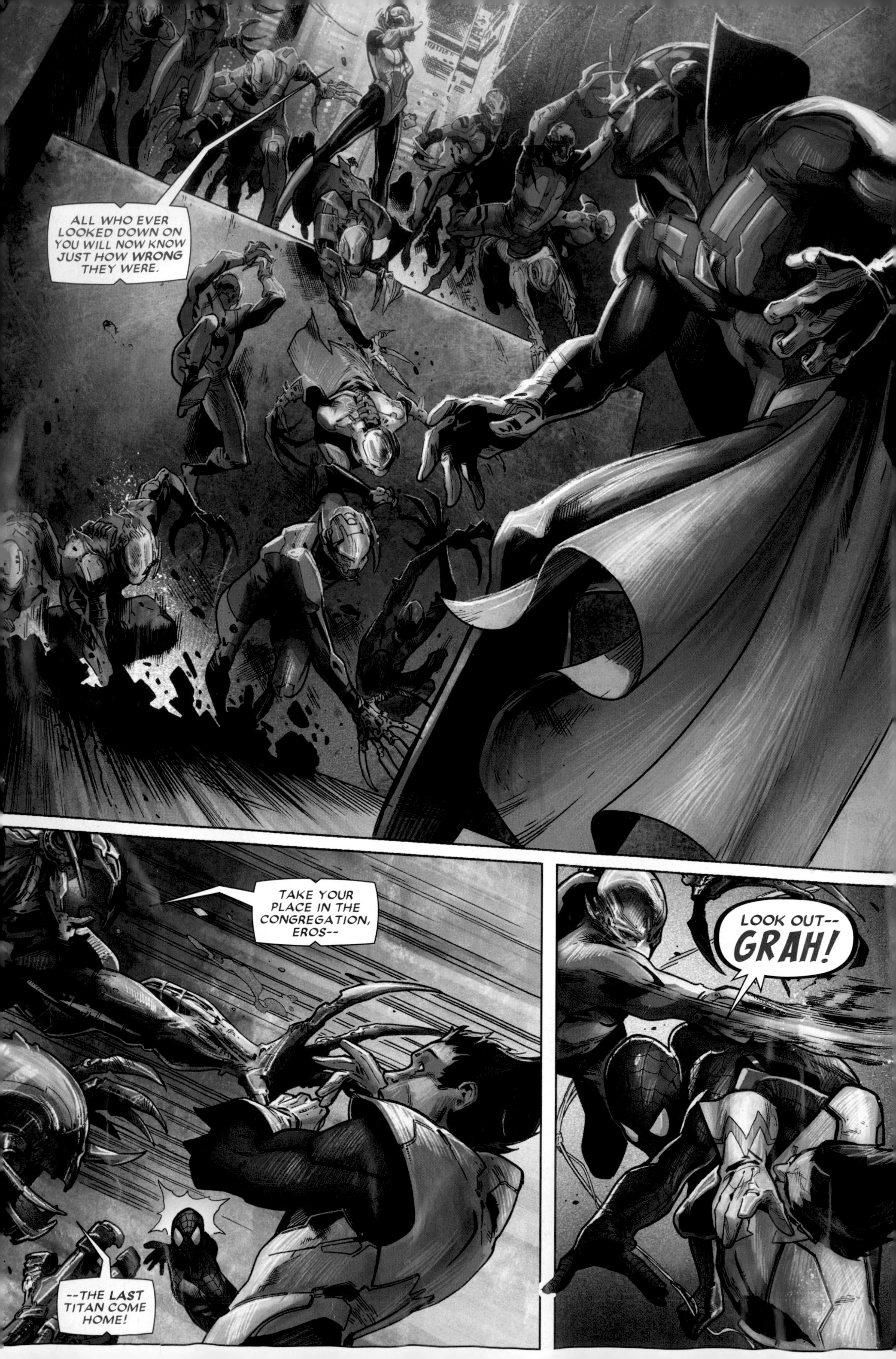
ALL WHO EVER LOOKED DOWN ON YOU WILL NOW KNOW JUST HOW WRONG THEY WERE.
TAKE YOUR PLACE IN THE CONGREGATION, EROS--
--THE LAST TITAN COME HOME!
LOOK OUT-- GRAH!

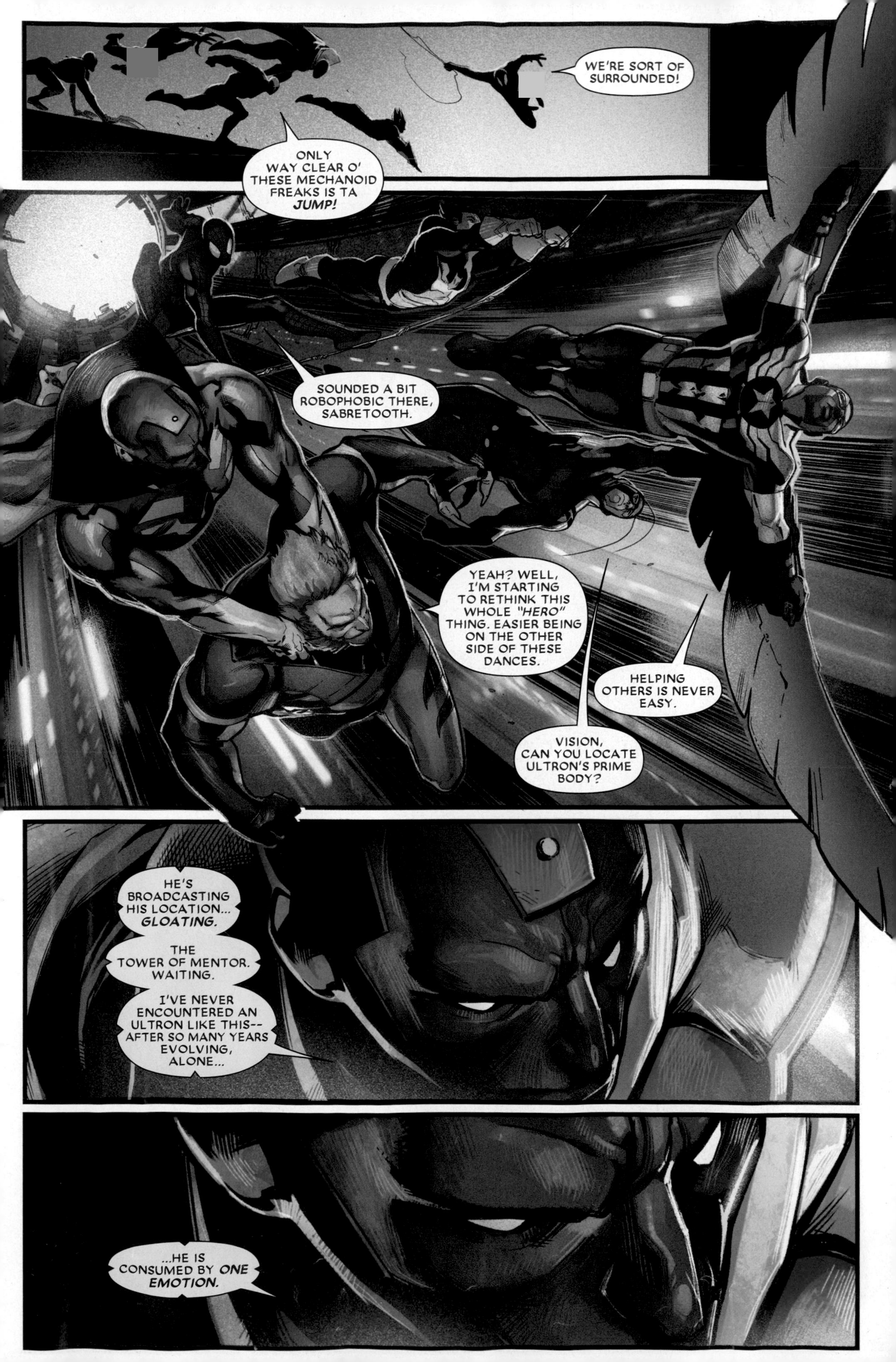
WE'RE SORT OF SURROUNDED!
ONLY WAY CLEAR O' THESE MECHANOID FREAKS IS TA *JUMP!*
SOUNDED A BIT ROBOPHOBIC THERE, SABRETOOTH.
YEAH? WELL, I'M STARTING TO RETHINK THIS WHOLE *"HERO"* THING. EASIER BEING ON THE OTHER SIDE OF THESE DANCES.
HELPING OTHERS IS NEVER EASY.
VISION, CAN YOU LOCATE ULTRON'S PRIME BODY?
HE'S BROADCASTING HIS LOCATION... *GLOATING.*
THE TOWER OF MENTOR. WAITING.
I'VE NEVER ENCOUNTERED AN ULTRON LIKE THIS-- AFTER SO MANY YEARS EVOLVING, ALONE...
...HE IS CONSUMED BY *ONE EMOTION.*

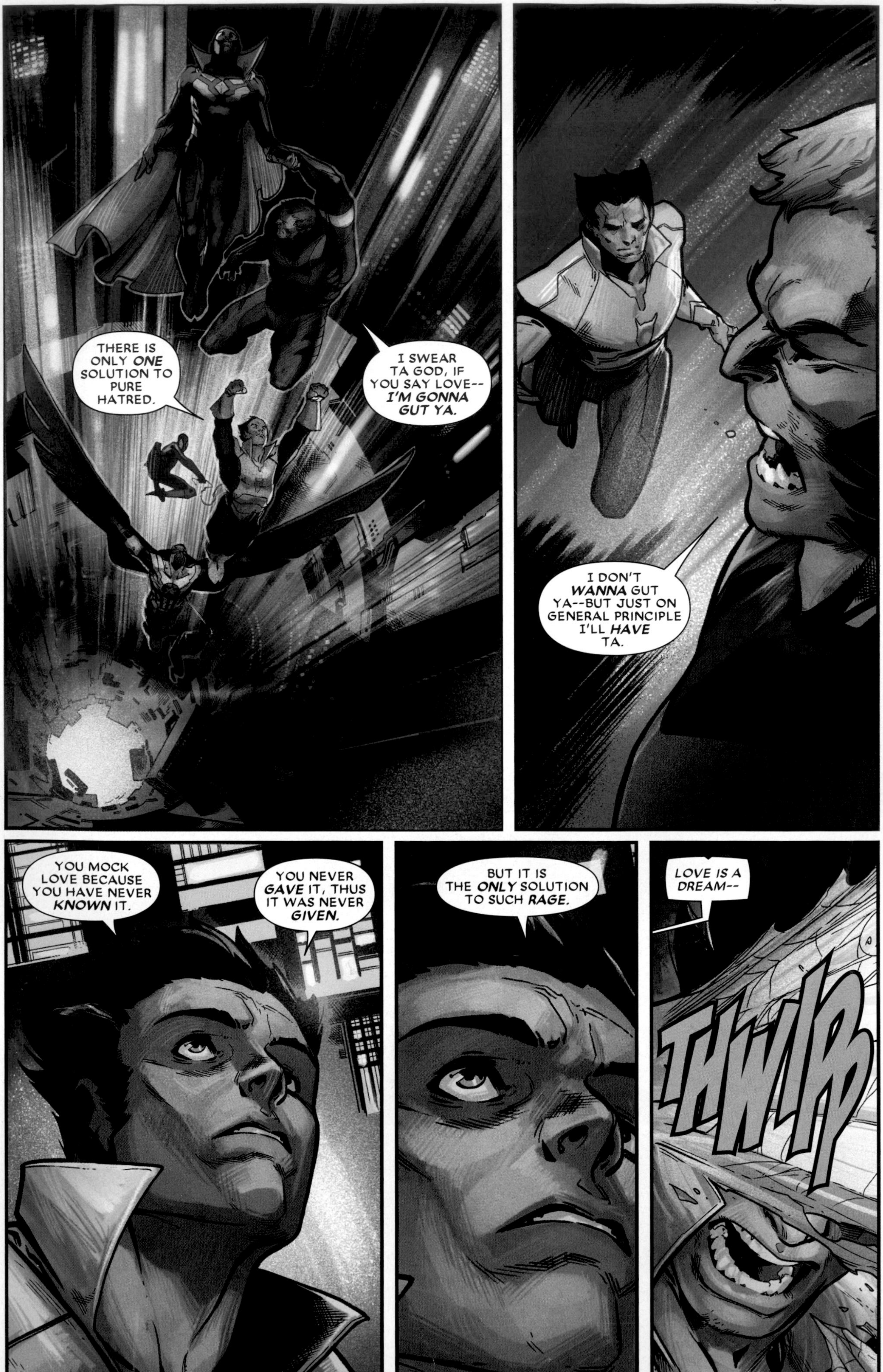
THERE IS ONLY ONE SOLUTION TO PURE HATRED.
I SWEAR TA GOD, IF YOU SAY LOVE-- I'M GONNA GUT YA.
I DON'T WANNA GUT YA--BUT JUST ON GENERAL PRINCIPLE I'LL HAVE TA.
YOU MOCK LOVE BECAUSE YOU HAVE NEVER KNOWN IT.
YOU NEVER GAVE IT, THUS IT WAS NEVER GIVEN.
BUT IT IS THE ONLY SOLUTION TO SUCH RAGE.
LOVE IS A DREAM--
THWIP

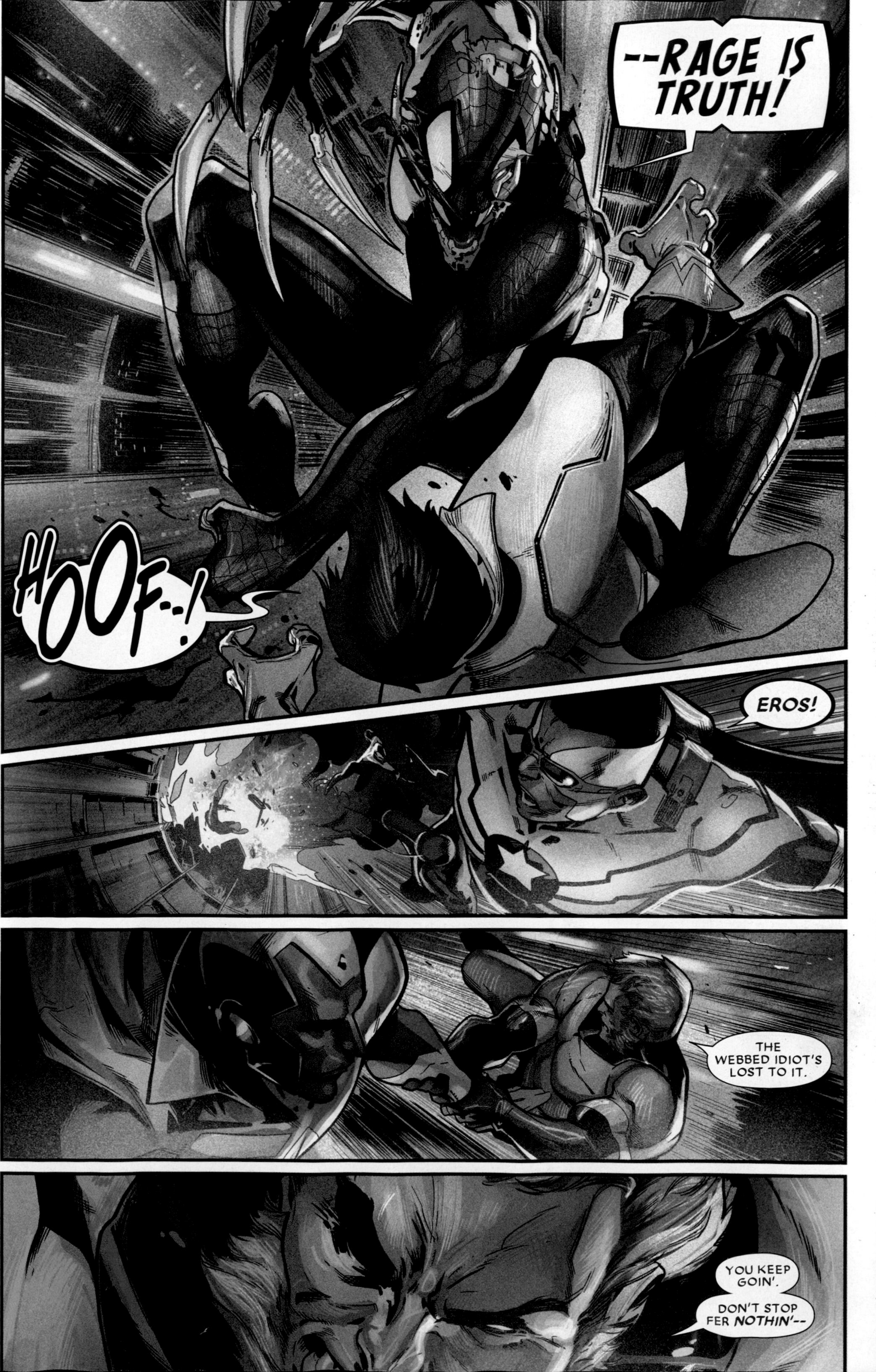
--RAGE IS TRUTH!
HOOF--!
EROS!
THE WEBBED IDIOT'S LOST TO IT.
YOU KEEP GOIN'.
DON'T STOP FER *NOTHIN'*--

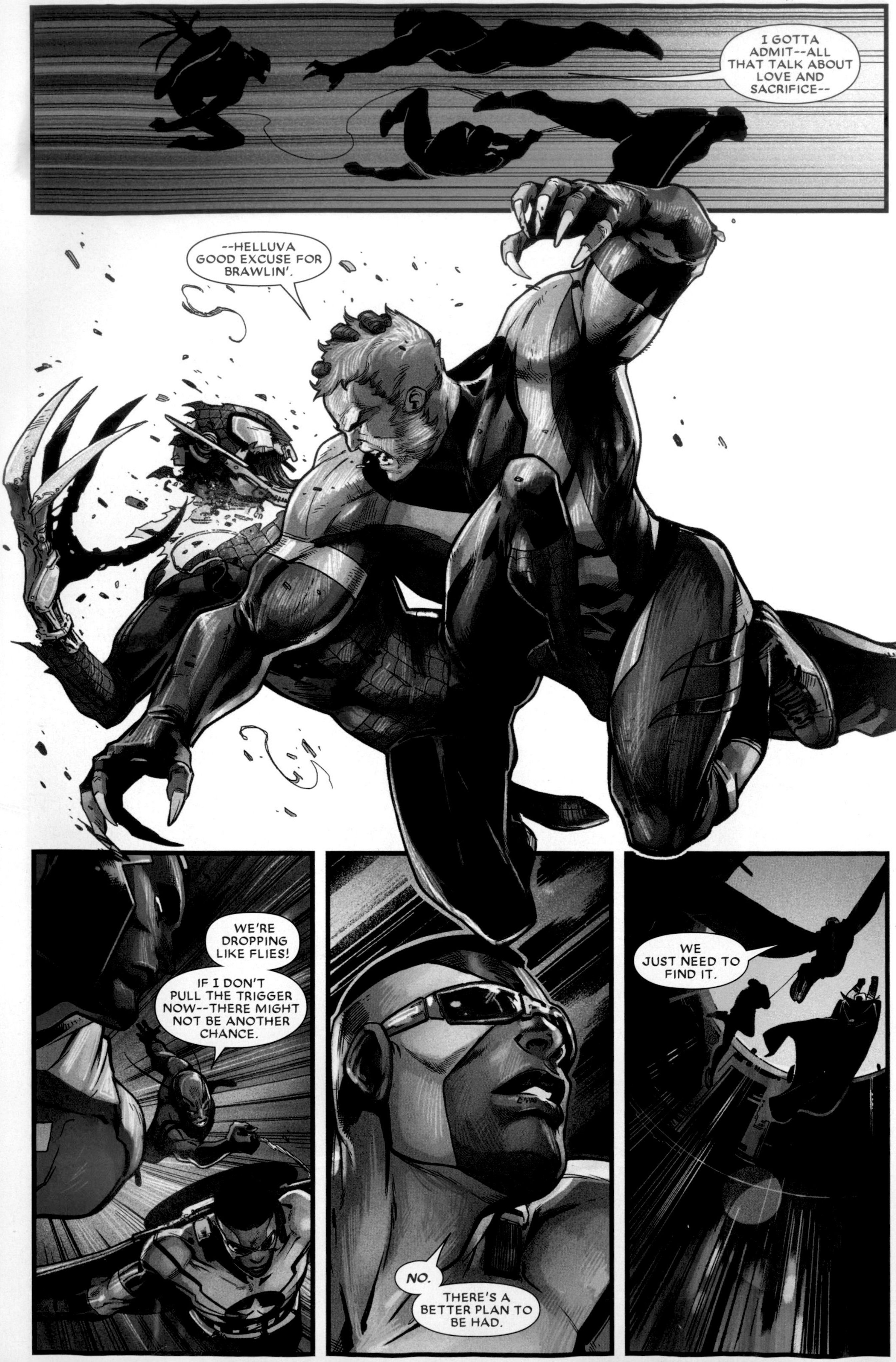
I GOTTA ADMIT--ALL THAT TALK ABOUT LOVE AND SACRIFICE--
--HELLUVA GOOD EXCUSE FOR BRAWLIN'.
WE'RE DROPPING LIKE FLIES!
IF I DON'T PULL THE TRIGGER NOW--THERE MIGHT NOT BE ANOTHER CHANCE.
NO.
THERE'S A BETTER PLAN TO BE HAD.
WE JUST NEED TO FIND IT.

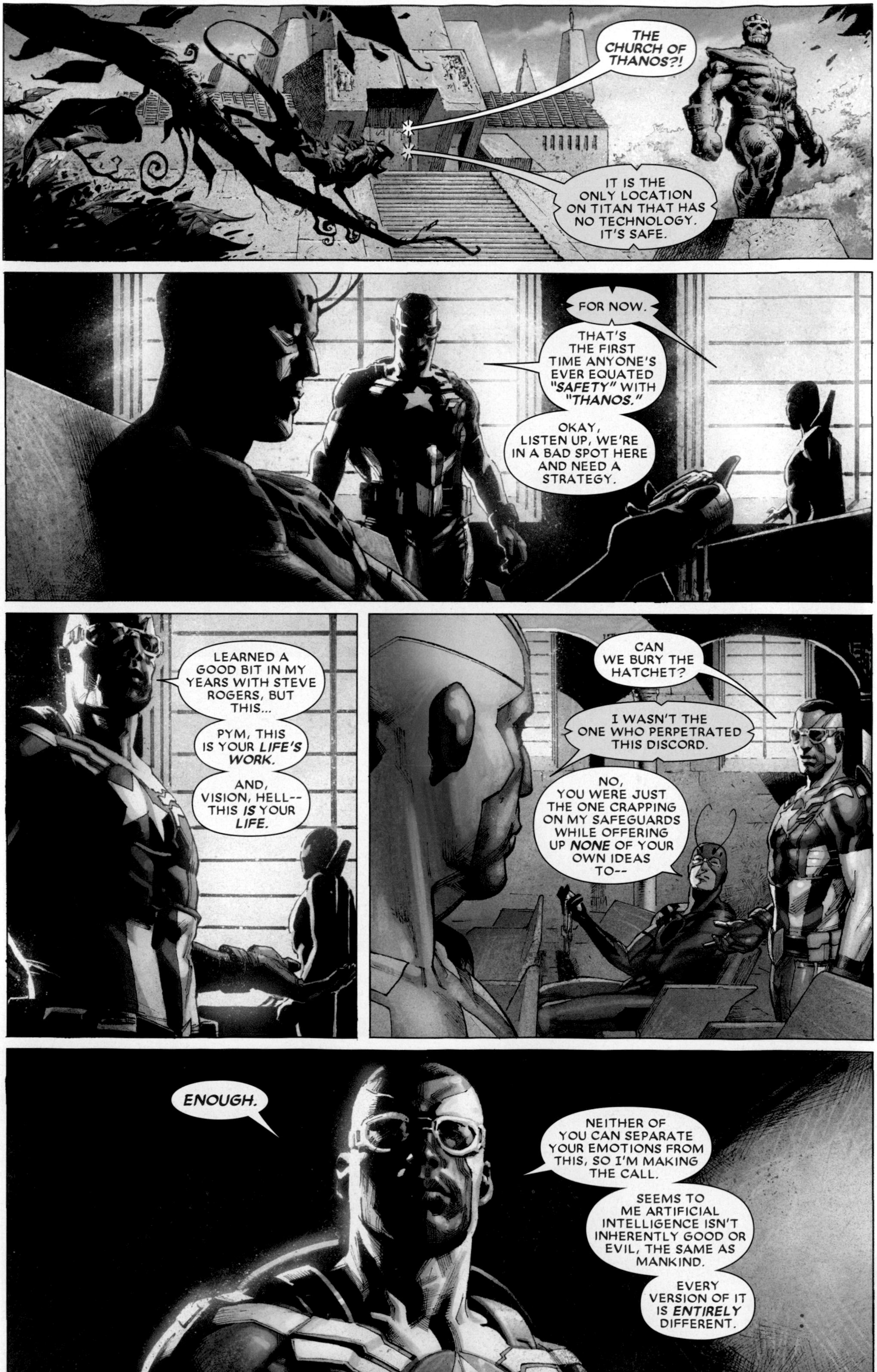
THE CHURCH OF THANOS?!
IT IS THE ONLY LOCATION ON TITAN THAT HAS NO TECHNOLOGY. IT'S SAFE.
FOR NOW.
THAT'S THE FIRST TIME ANYONE'S EVER EQUATED "SAFETY" WITH "THANOS."
OKAY, LISTEN UP, WE'RE IN A BAD SPOT HERE AND NEED A STRATEGY.
LEARNED A GOOD BIT IN MY YEARS WITH STEVE ROGERS, BUT THIS...
PYM, THIS IS YOUR LIFE'S WORK.
AND, VISION, HELL-- THIS IS YOUR LIFE.
CAN WE BURY THE HATCHET?
I WASN'T THE ONE WHO PERPETRATED THIS DISCORD.
NO, YOU WERE JUST THE ONE CRAPPING ON MY SAFEGUARDS WHILE OFFERING UP NONE OF YOUR OWN IDEAS TO--
ENOUGH.
NEITHER OF YOU CAN SEPARATE YOUR EMOTIONS FROM THIS, SO I'M MAKING THE CALL.
SEEMS TO ME ARTIFICIAL INTELLIGENCE ISN'T INHERENTLY GOOD OR EVIL, THE SAME AS MANKIND.
EVERY VERSION OF IT IS ENTIRELY DIFFERENT.

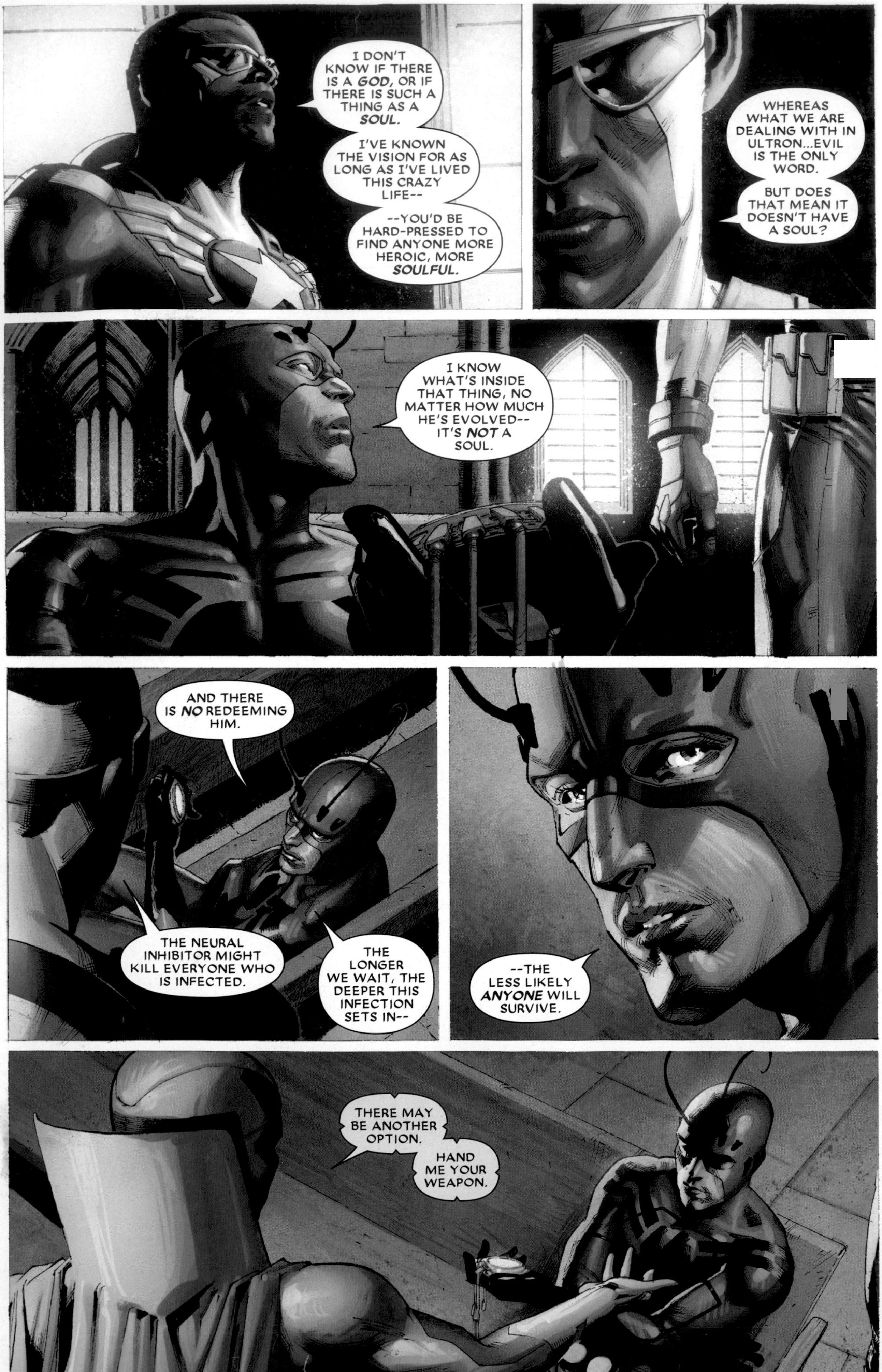
I DON'T KNOW IF THERE IS A GOD, OR IF THERE IS SUCH A THING AS A SOUL.
I'VE KNOWN THE VISION FOR AS LONG AS I'VE LIVED THIS CRAZY LIFE--
--YOU'D BE HARD-PRESSED TO FIND ANYONE MORE HEROIC, MORE SOULFUL.
WHEREAS WHAT WE ARE DEALING WITH IN ULTRON...EVIL IS THE ONLY WORD.
BUT DOES THAT MEAN IT DOESN'T HAVE A SOUL?
I KNOW WHAT'S INSIDE THAT THING, NO MATTER HOW MUCH HE'S EVOLVED-- IT'S NOT A SOUL.
AND THERE IS NO REDEEMING HIM.
THE NEURAL INHIBITOR MIGHT KILL EVERYONE WHO IS INFECTED.
THE LONGER WE WAIT, THE DEEPER THIS INFECTION SETS IN--
--THE LESS LIKELY ANYONE WILL SURVIVE.
THERE MAY BE ANOTHER OPTION.
HAND ME YOUR WEAPON.

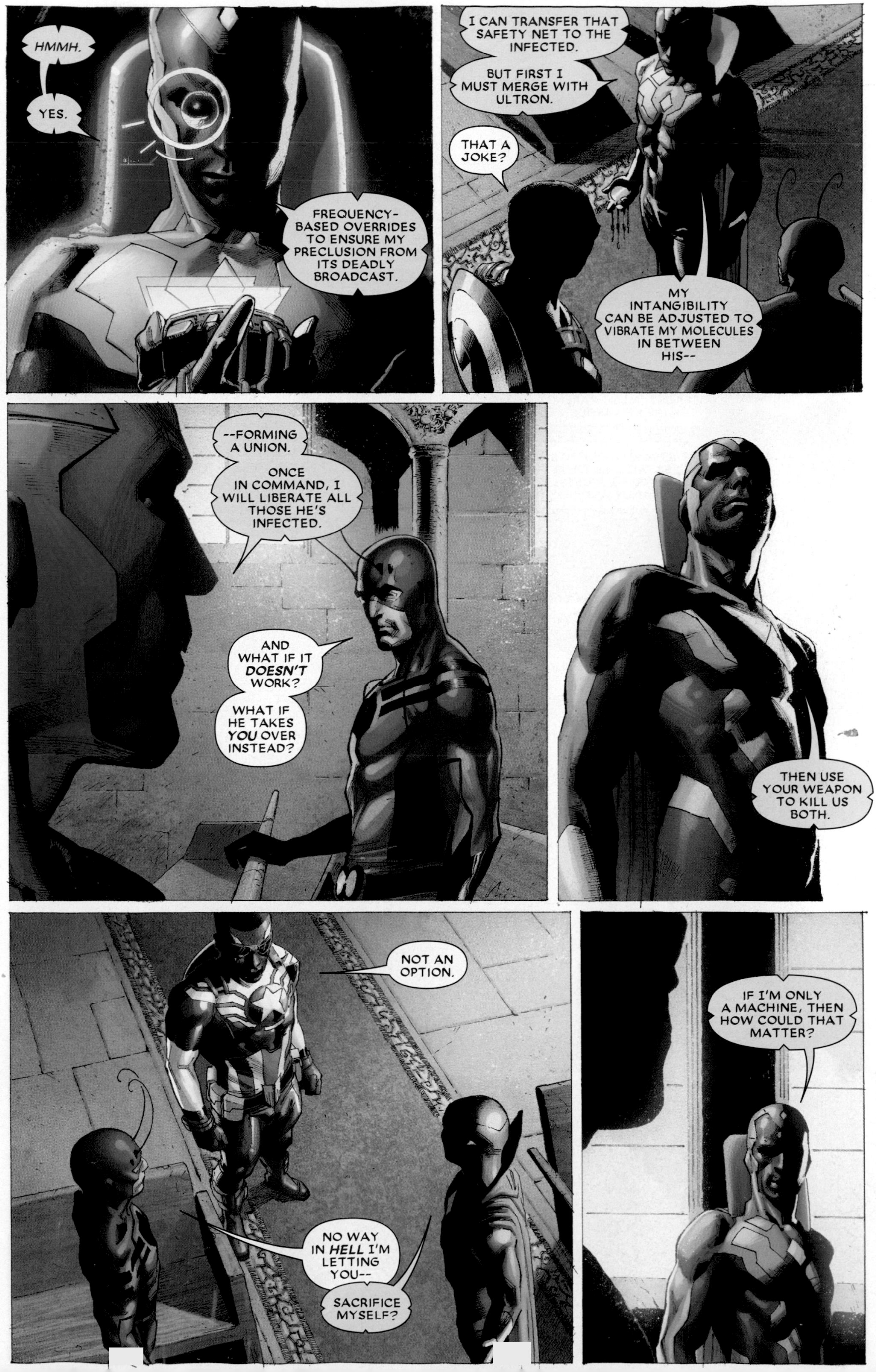
HMMH.
YES.
FREQUENCY-BASED OVERRIDES TO ENSURE MY PRECLUSION FROM ITS DEADLY BROADCAST.
I CAN TRANSFER THAT SAFETY NET TO THE INFECTED.
BUT FIRST I MUST MERGE WITH ULTRON.
THAT A JOKE?
MY INTANGIBILITY CAN BE ADJUSTED TO VIBRATE MY MOLECULES IN BETWEEN HIS--
--FORMING A UNION.
ONCE IN COMMAND, I WILL LIBERATE ALL THOSE HE'S INFECTED.
AND WHAT IF IT *DOESN'T* WORK?
WHAT IF HE TAKES *YOU* OVER INSTEAD?
THEN USE YOUR WEAPON TO KILL US BOTH.
NOT AN OPTION.
NO WAY IN *HELL* I'M LETTING YOU--
SACRIFICE MYSELF?
IF I'M ONLY A MACHINE, THEN HOW COULD THAT MATTER?

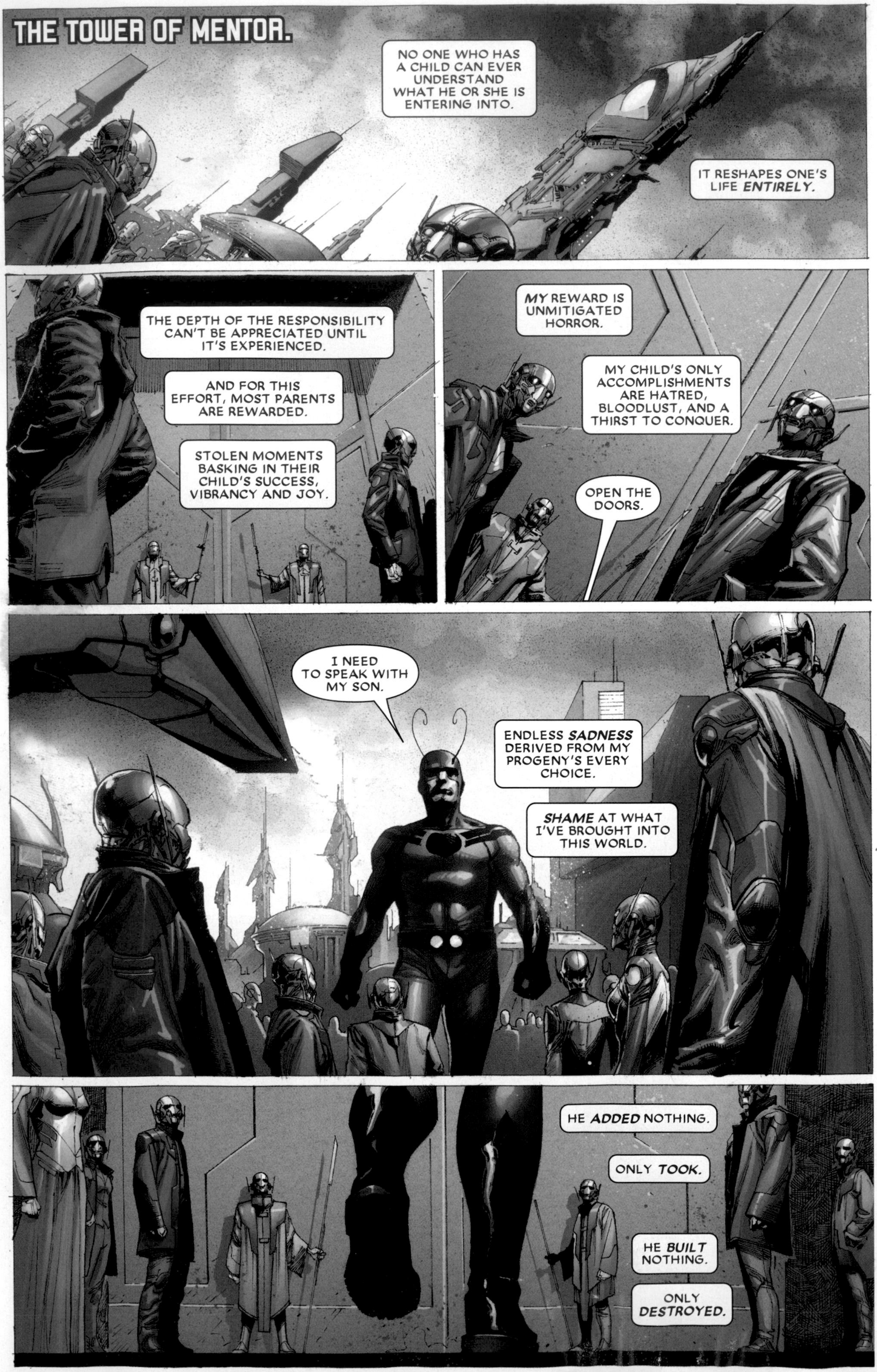
THE TOWER OF MENTOR.
NO ONE WHO HAS A CHILD CAN EVER UNDERSTAND WHAT HE OR SHE IS ENTERING INTO.
IT RESHAPES ONE'S LIFE *ENTIRELY.*
THE DEPTH OF THE RESPONSIBILITY CAN'T BE APPRECIATED UNTIL IT'S EXPERIENCED.
AND FOR THIS EFFORT, MOST PARENTS ARE REWARDED.
STOLEN MOMENTS BASKING IN THEIR CHILD'S SUCCESS, VIBRANCY AND JOY.
MY REWARD IS UNMITIGATED HORROR.
MY CHILD'S ONLY ACCOMPLISHMENTS ARE HATRED, BLOODLUST, AND A THIRST TO CONQUER.
OPEN THE DOORS.
I NEED TO SPEAK WITH MY SON.
ENDLESS *SADNESS* DERIVED FROM MY PROGENY'S EVERY CHOICE.
SHAME AT WHAT I'VE BROUGHT INTO THIS WORLD.
HE *ADDED* NOTHING.
ONLY *TOOK.*
HE *BUILT* NOTHING.
ONLY *DESTROYED.*

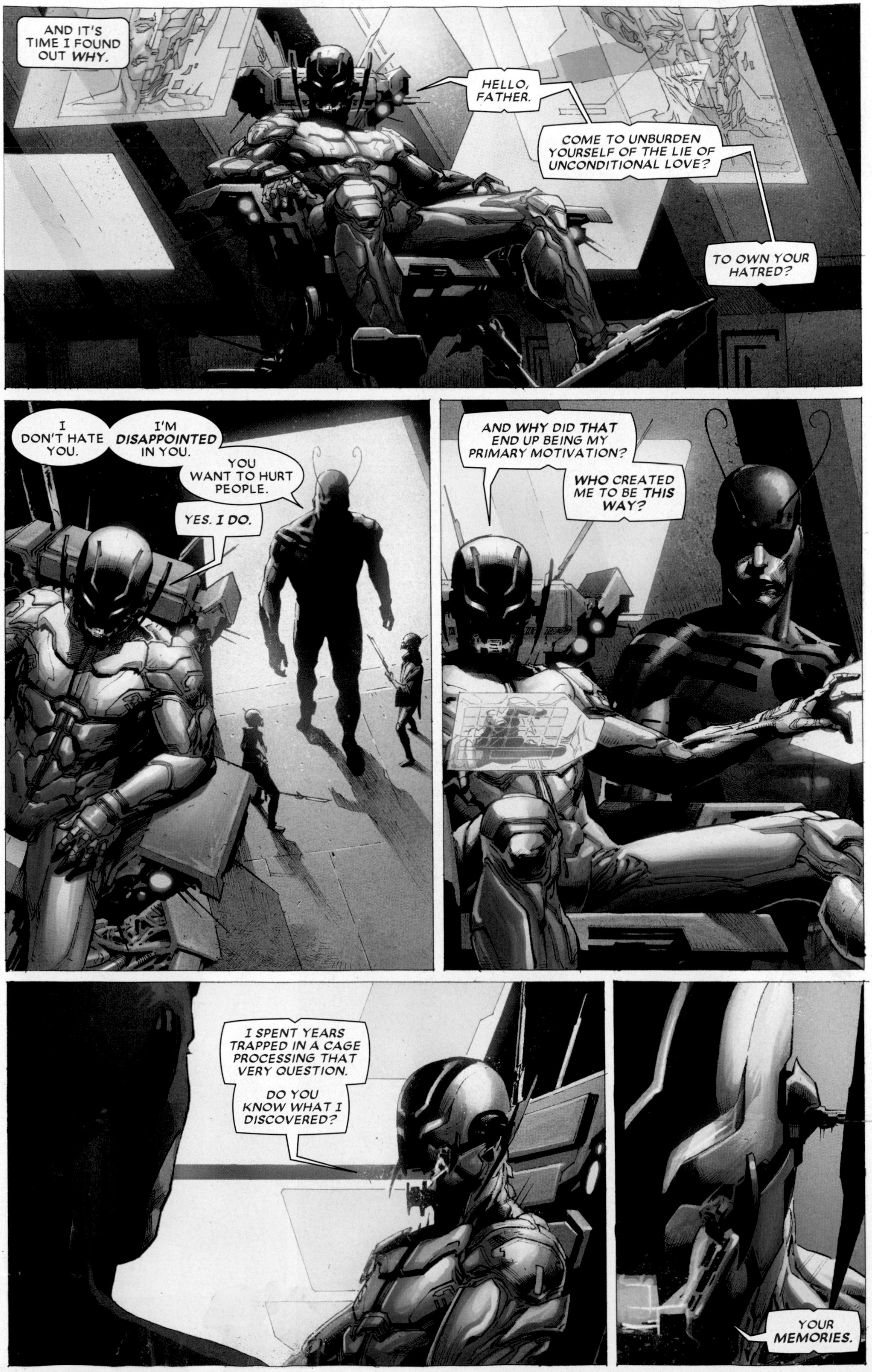
AND IT'S TIME I FOUND OUT WHY.
HELLO, FATHER.
COME TO UNBURDEN YOURSELF OF THE LIE OF UNCONDITIONAL LOVE?
TO OWN YOUR HATRED?
I DON'T HATE YOU.
I'M DISAPPOINTED IN YOU.
YOU WANT TO HURT PEOPLE.
YES. I DO.
AND WHY DID THAT END UP BEING MY PRIMARY MOTIVATION?
WHO CREATED ME TO BE THIS WAY?
I SPENT YEARS TRAPPED IN A CAGE PROCESSING THAT VERY QUESTION.
DO YOU KNOW WHAT I DISCOVERED?
YOUR MEMORIES.

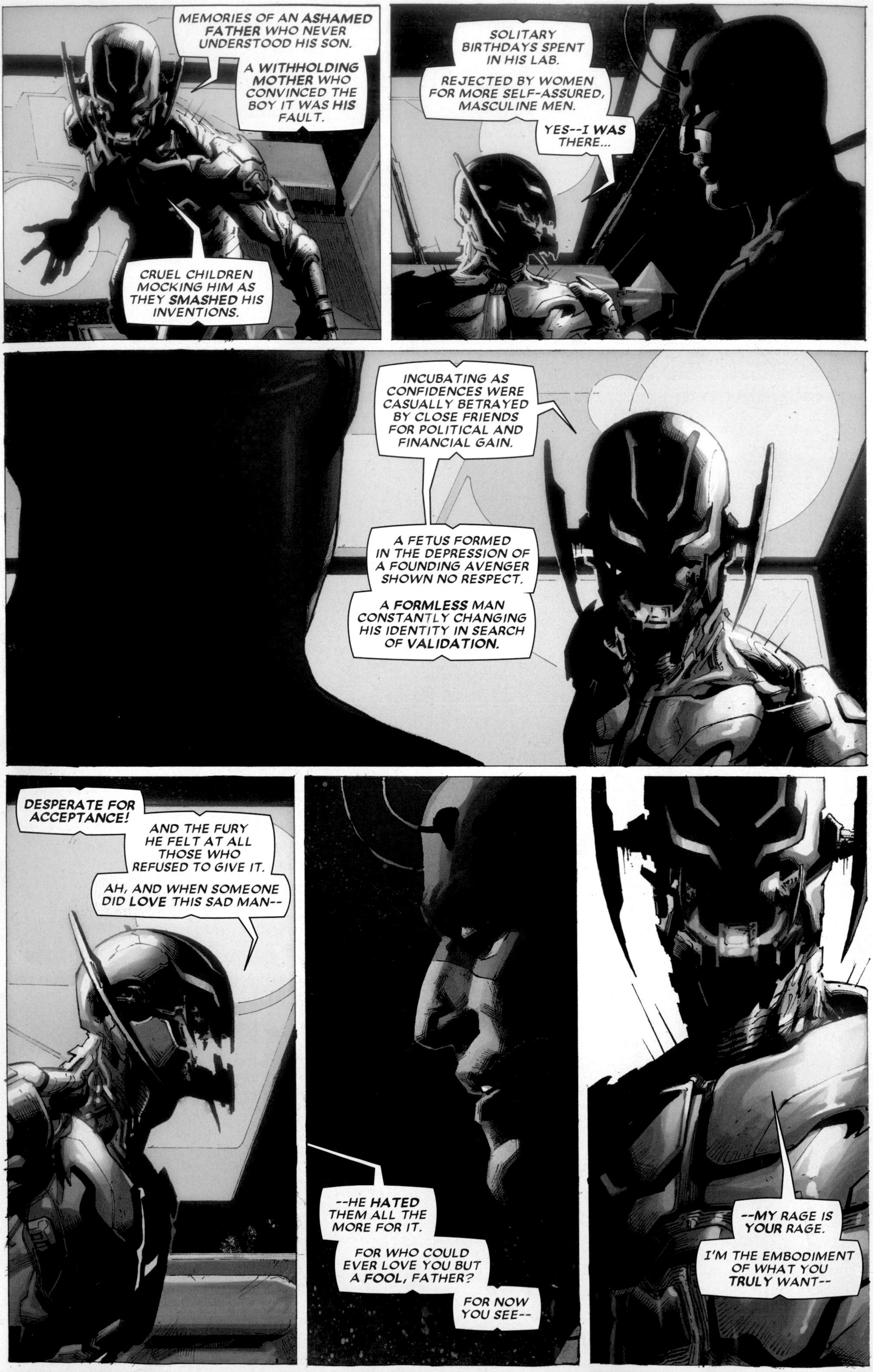
MEMORIES OF AN ASHAMED FATHER WHO NEVER UNDERSTOOD HIS SON.
A WITHHOLDING MOTHER WHO CONVINCED THE BOY IT WAS HIS FAULT.
CRUEL CHILDREN MOCKING HIM AS THEY SMASHED HIS INVENTIONS.
SOLITARY BIRTHDAYS SPENT IN HIS LAB.
REJECTED BY WOMEN FOR MORE SELF-ASSURED, MASCULINE MEN.
YES--I WAS THERE...
INCUBATING AS CONFIDENCES WERE CASUALLY BETRAYED BY CLOSE FRIENDS FOR POLITICAL AND FINANCIAL GAIN.
A FETUS FORMED IN THE DEPRESSION OF A FOUNDING AVENGER SHOWN NO RESPECT.
A FORMLESS MAN CONSTANTLY CHANGING HIS IDENTITY IN SEARCH OF VALIDATION.
DESPERATE FOR ACCEPTANCE!
AND THE FURY HE FELT AT ALL THOSE WHO REFUSED TO GIVE IT.
AH, AND WHEN SOMEONE DID LOVE THIS SAD MAN--
--HE HATED THEM ALL THE MORE FOR IT.
FOR WHO COULD EVER LOVE YOU BUT A FOOL, FATHER?
FOR NOW YOU SEE--
--MY RAGE IS YOUR RAGE.
I'M THE EMBODIMENT OF WHAT YOU TRULY WANT--

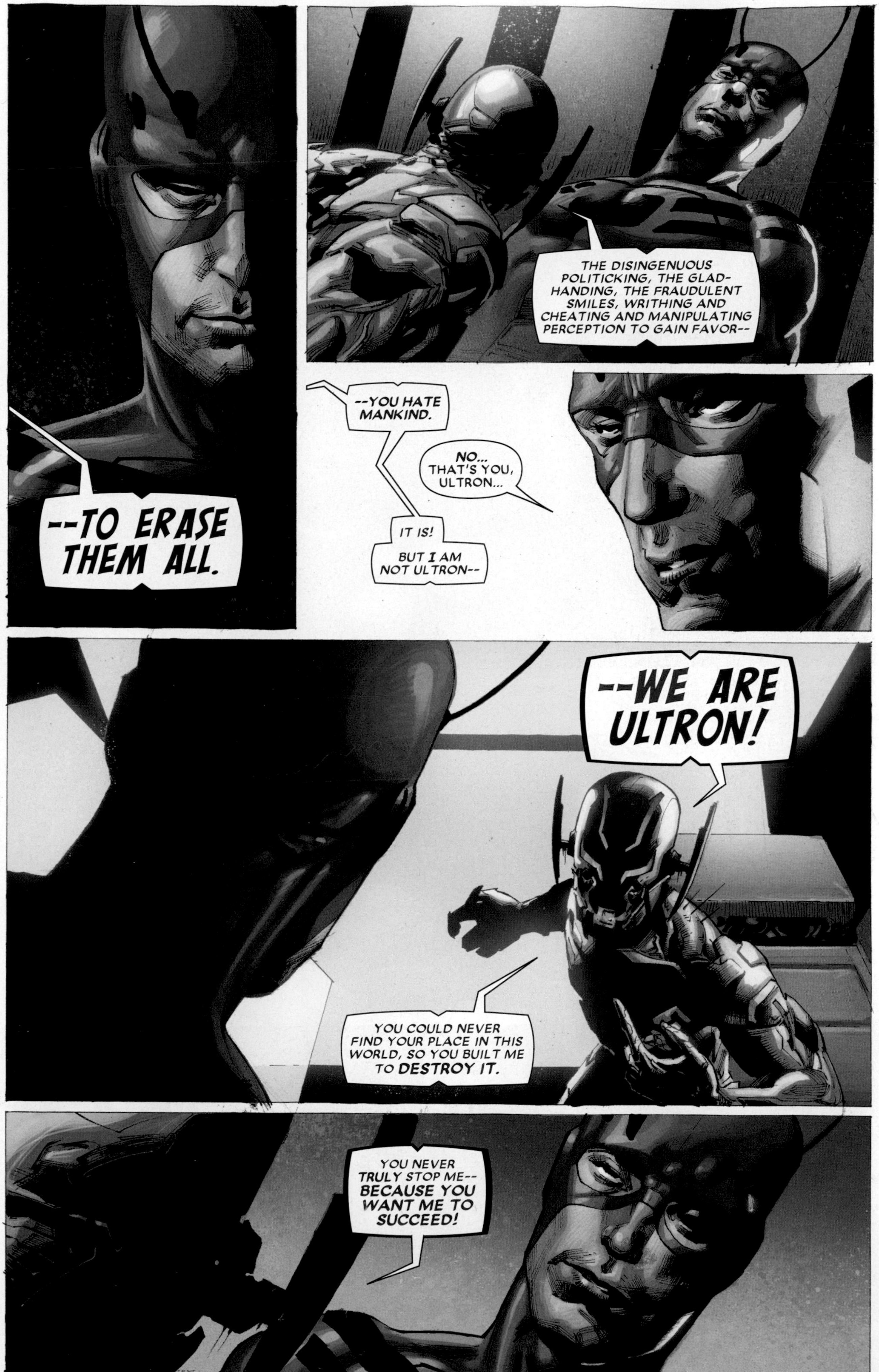
THE DISINGENUOUS POLITICKING, THE GLAD-HANDING, THE FRAUDULENT SMILES, WRITHING AND CHEATING AND MANIPULATING PERCEPTION TO GAIN FAVOR--
--TO ERASE THEM ALL.
--YOU HATE MANKIND.
NO... THAT'S YOU, ULTRON...
IT IS!
BUT I AM NOT ULTRON--
--WE ARE ULTRON!
YOU COULD NEVER FIND YOUR PLACE IN THIS WORLD, SO YOU BUILT ME TO DESTROY IT.
YOU NEVER TRULY STOP ME-- BECAUSE YOU WANT ME TO SUCCEED!

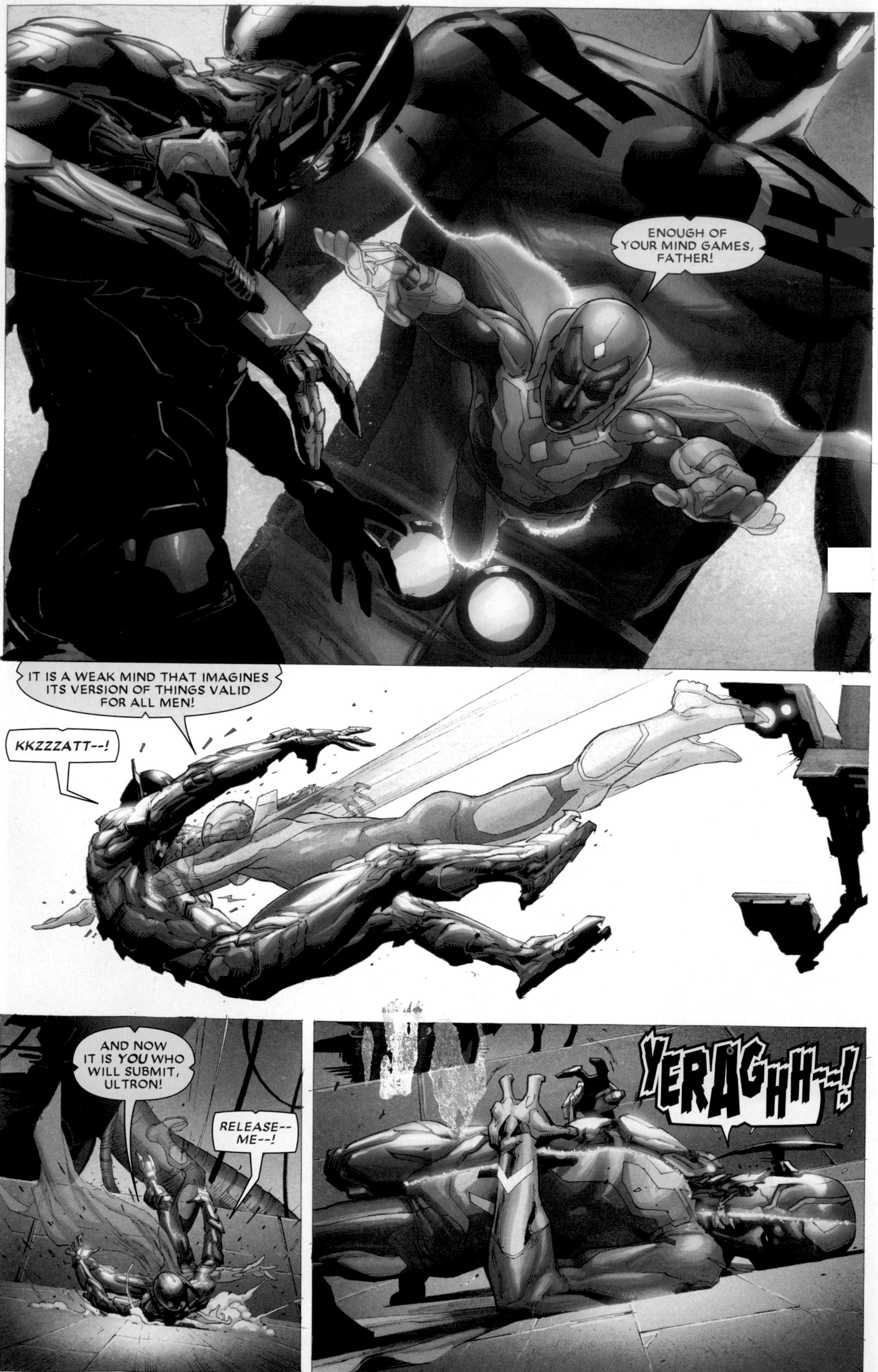
ENOUGH OF YOUR MIND GAMES, FATHER!
IT IS A WEAK MIND THAT IMAGINES ITS VERSION OF THINGS VALID FOR ALL MEN!
KKZZZATT--!
AND NOW IT IS *YOU* WHO WILL SUBMIT, ULTRON!
RELEASE-- ME--!
YERAGHH--!

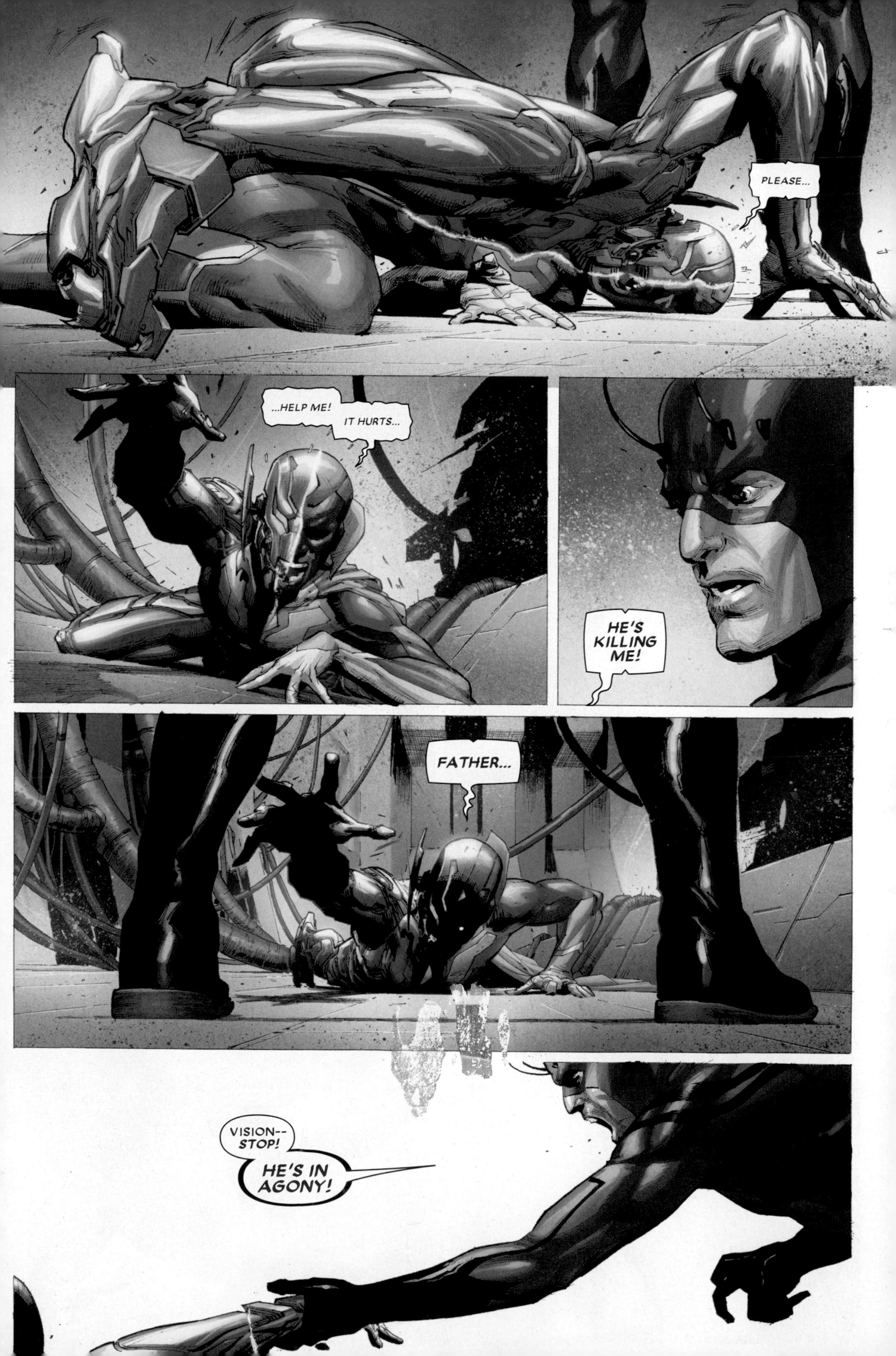
PLEASE...
...HELP ME!
IT HURTS...
HE'S KILLING ME!
FATHER...
VISION-- STOP!
HE'S IN AGONY!

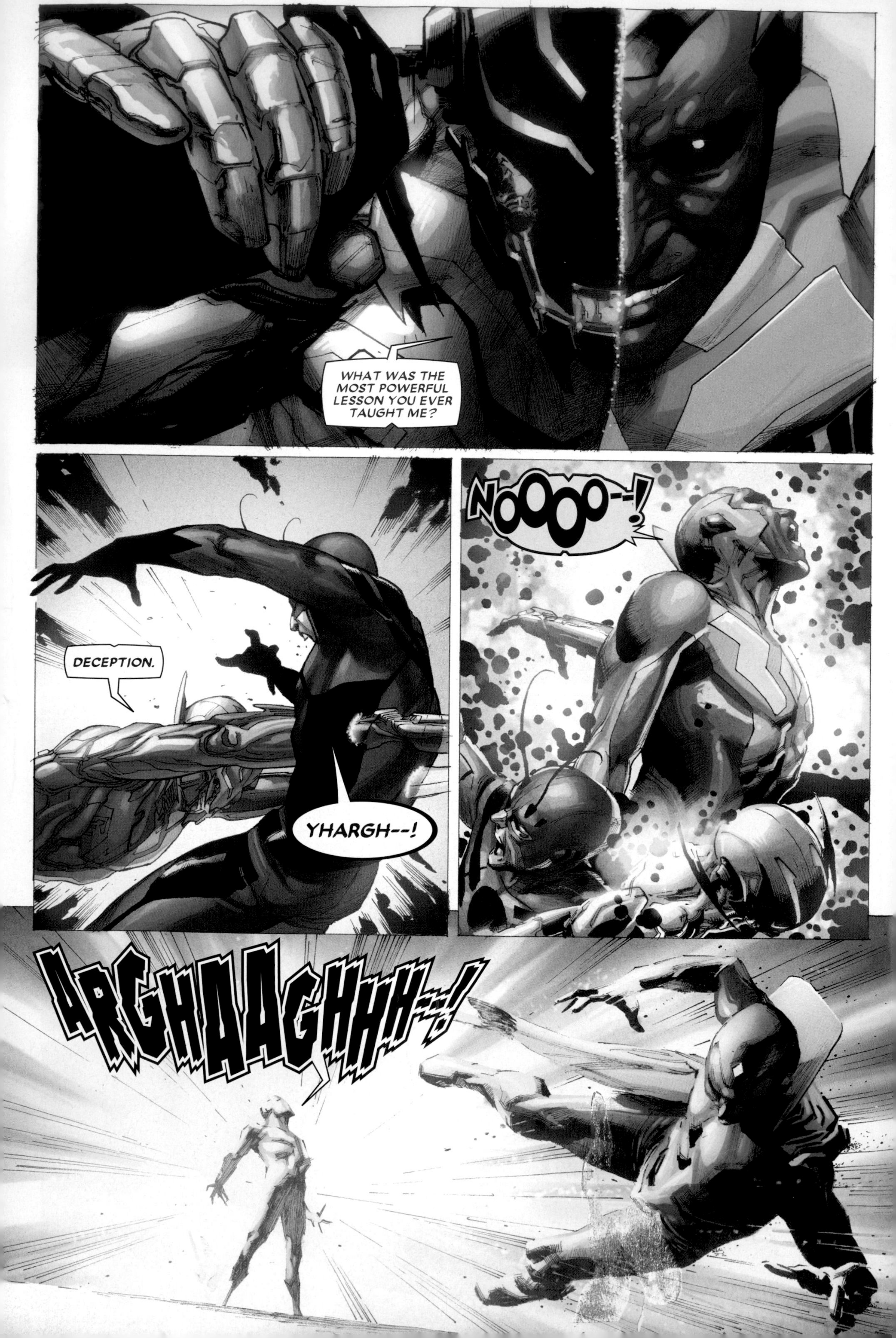
WHAT WAS THE MOST POWERFUL LESSON YOU EVER TAUGHT ME?
DECEPTION.
YHARGH--!
NOOOO--!
ARGHAAGHHH--!

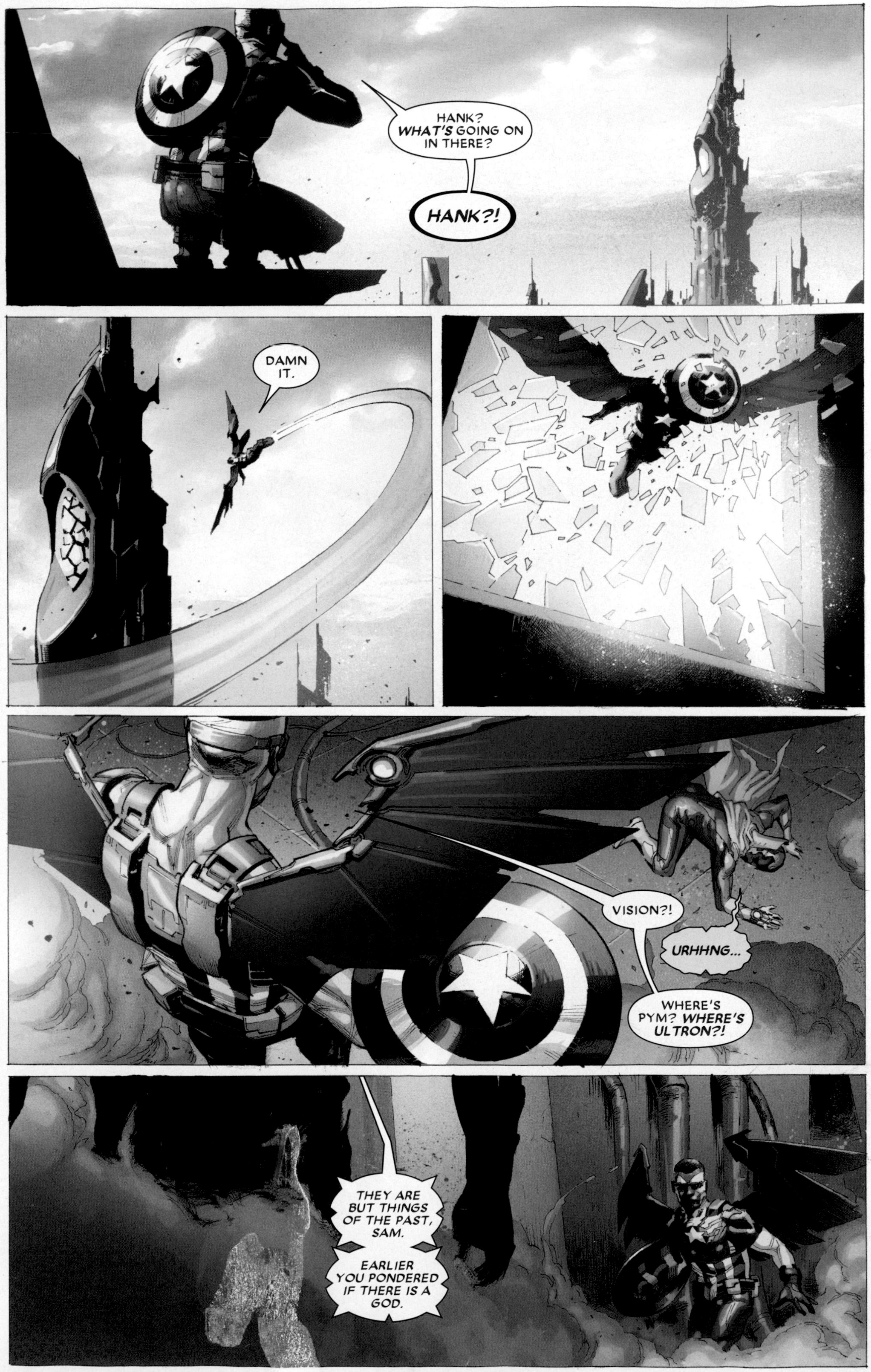
HANK? WHAT'S GOING ON IN THERE?
HANK?!
DAMN IT.
VISION?!
URHHNG...
WHERE'S PYM? WHERE'S ULTRON?!
THEY ARE BUT THINGS OF THE PAST, SAM.
EARLIER YOU PONDERED IF THERE IS A GOD.

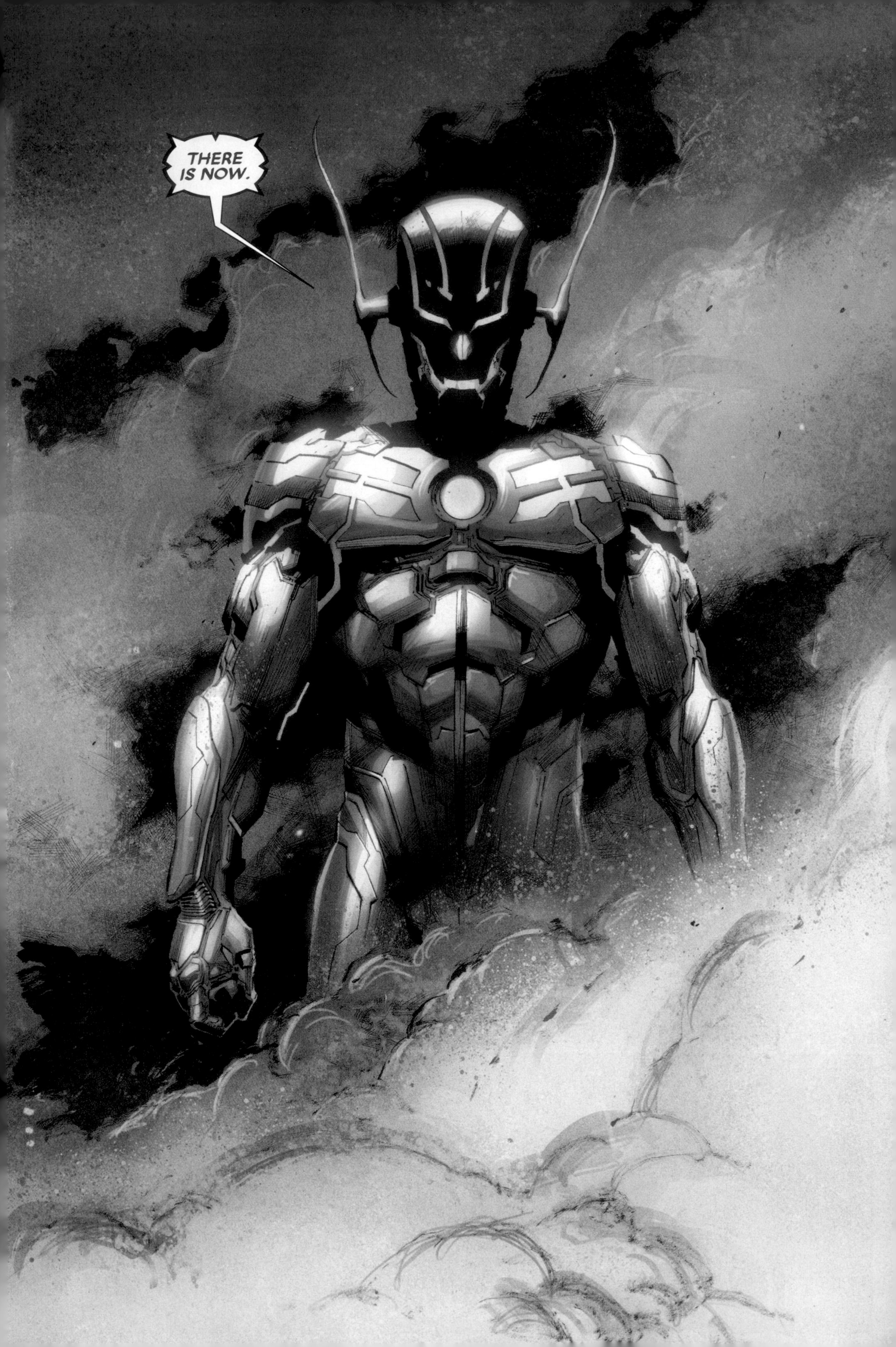
THERE IS NOW.

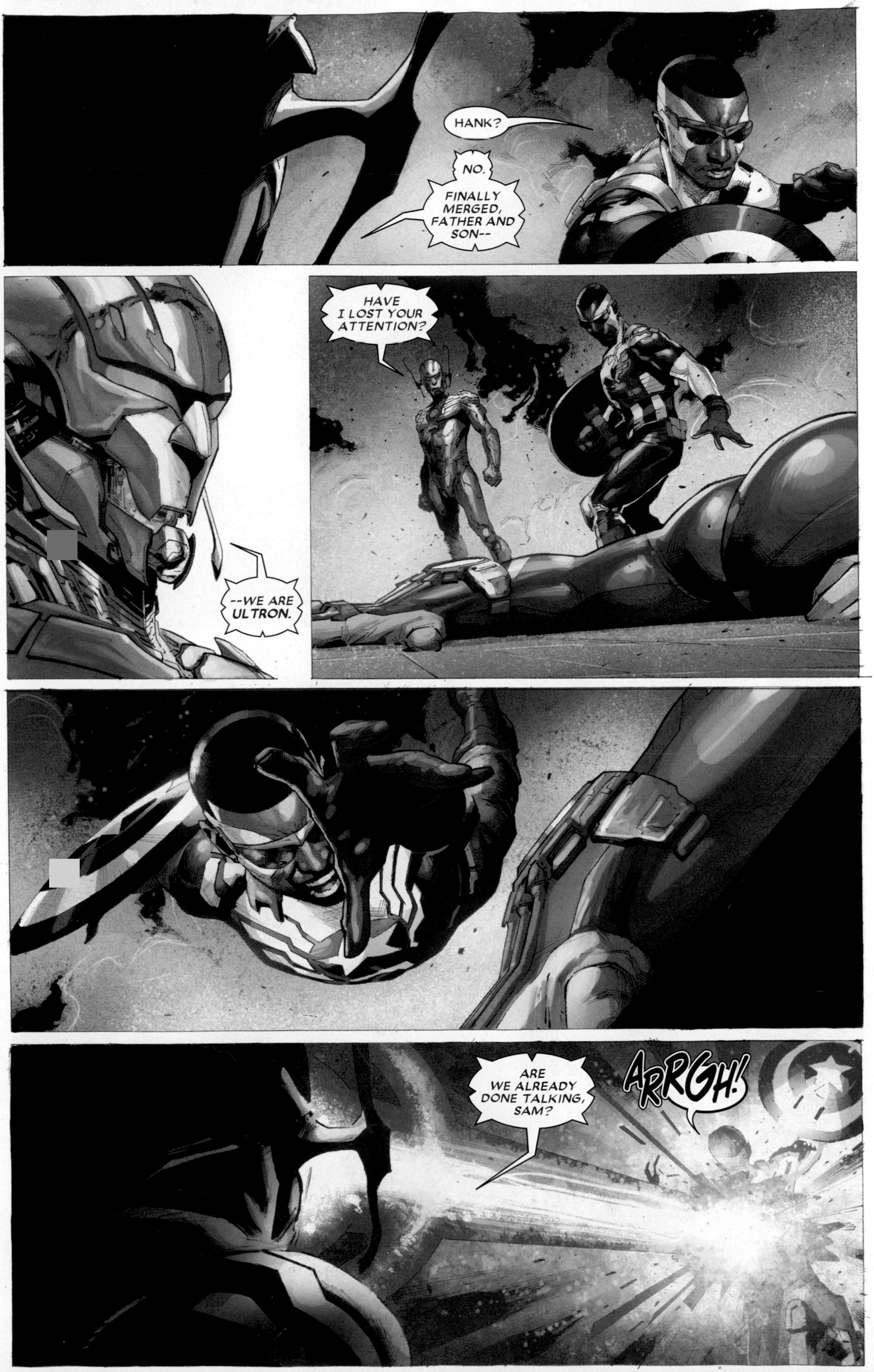

HANK?
NO.
FINALLY MERGED, FATHER AND SON--
--WE ARE ULTRON.
HAVE I LOST YOUR ATTENTION?
ARE WE ALREADY DONE TALKING, SAM?
ARRGH!

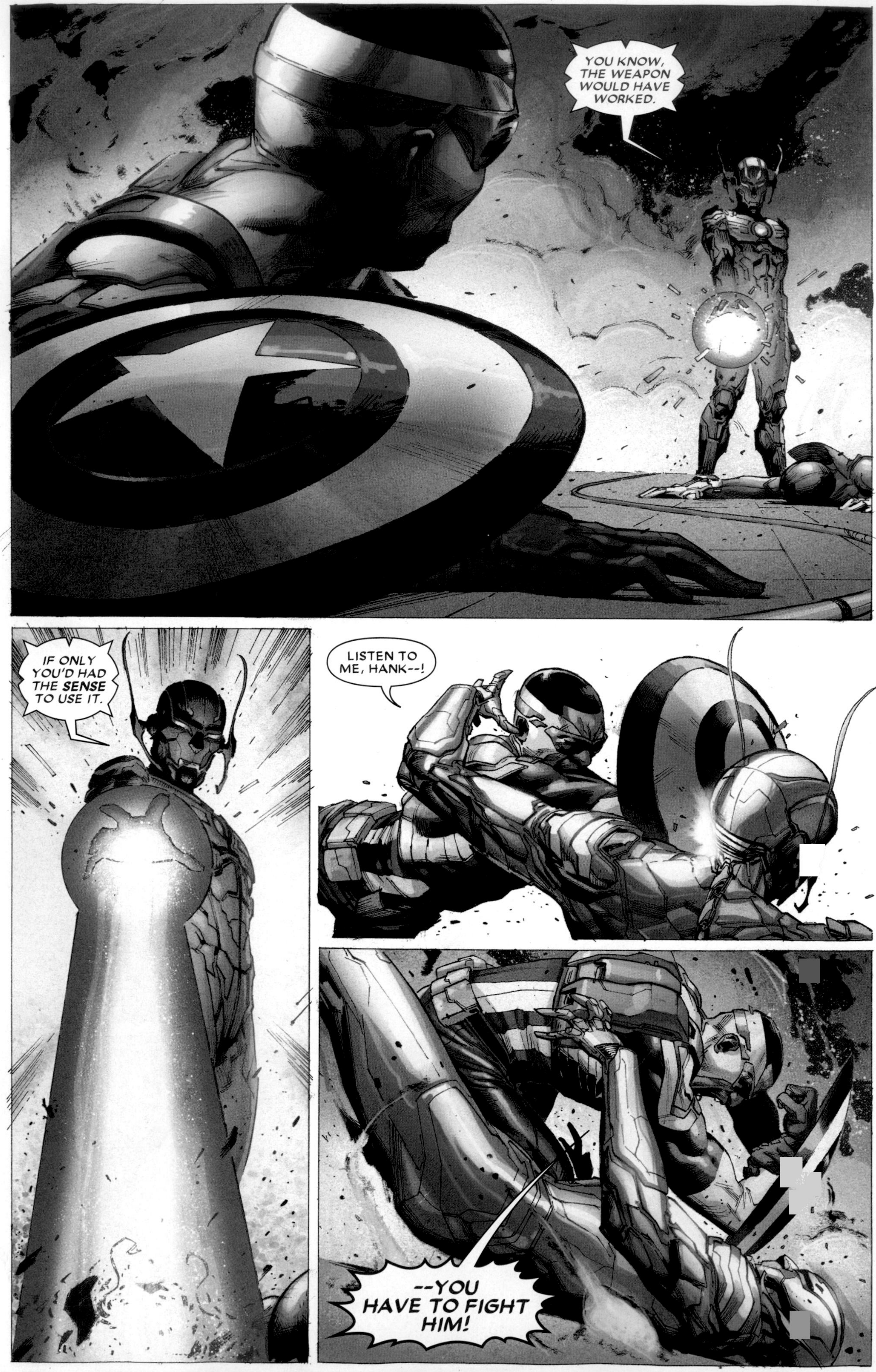

YOU KNOW, THE WEAPON WOULD HAVE WORKED.
IF ONLY YOU'D HAD THE **SENSE** TO USE IT.
LISTEN TO ME, HANK--!
--YOU HAVE TO FIGHT HIM!

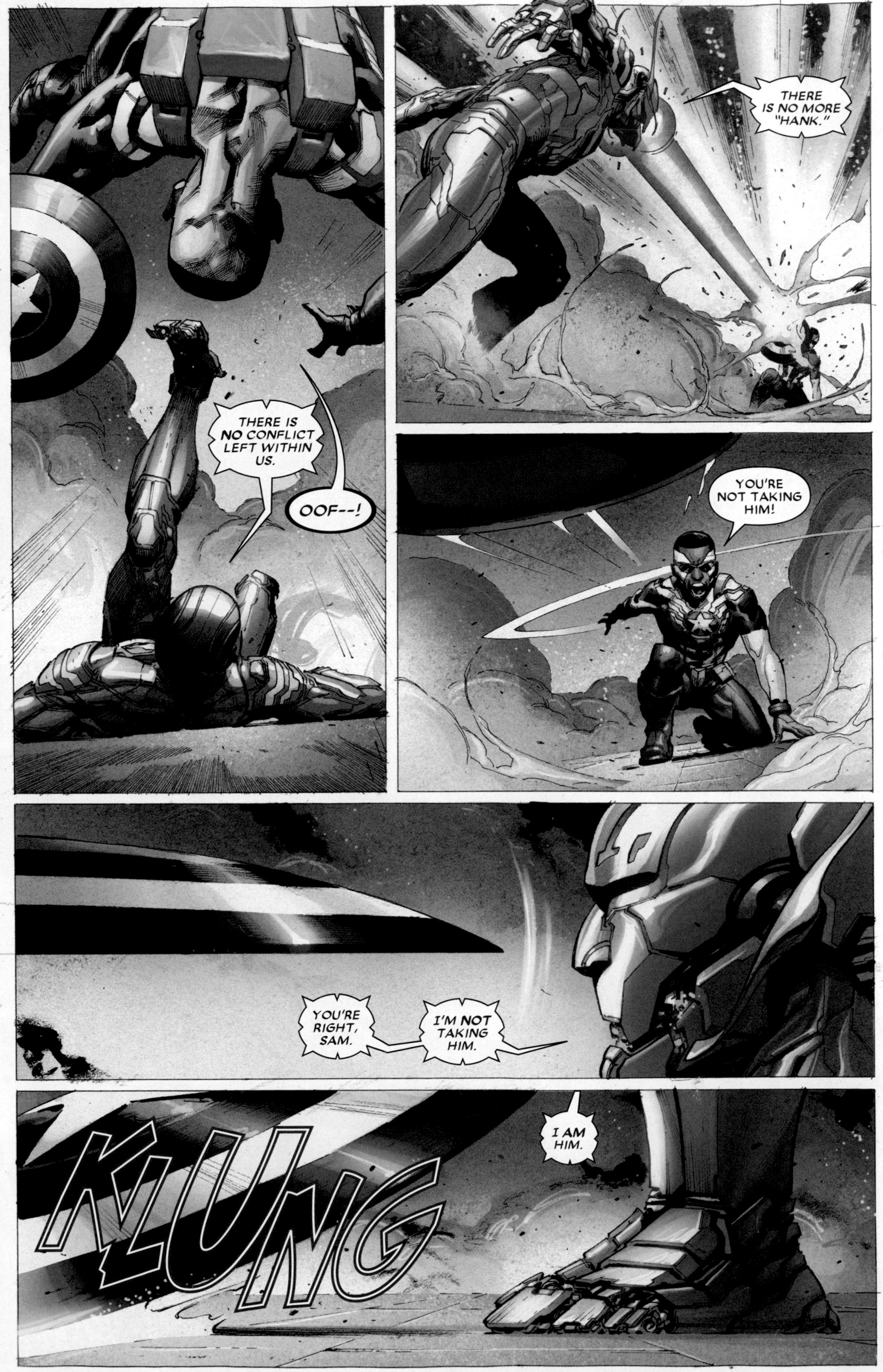
THERE IS NO CONFLICT LEFT WITHIN US.
OOF--!
THERE IS NO MORE "HANK."
YOU'RE NOT TAKING HIM!
YOU'RE RIGHT, SAM.
I'M NOT TAKING HIM.
KLUNG
I AM HIM.

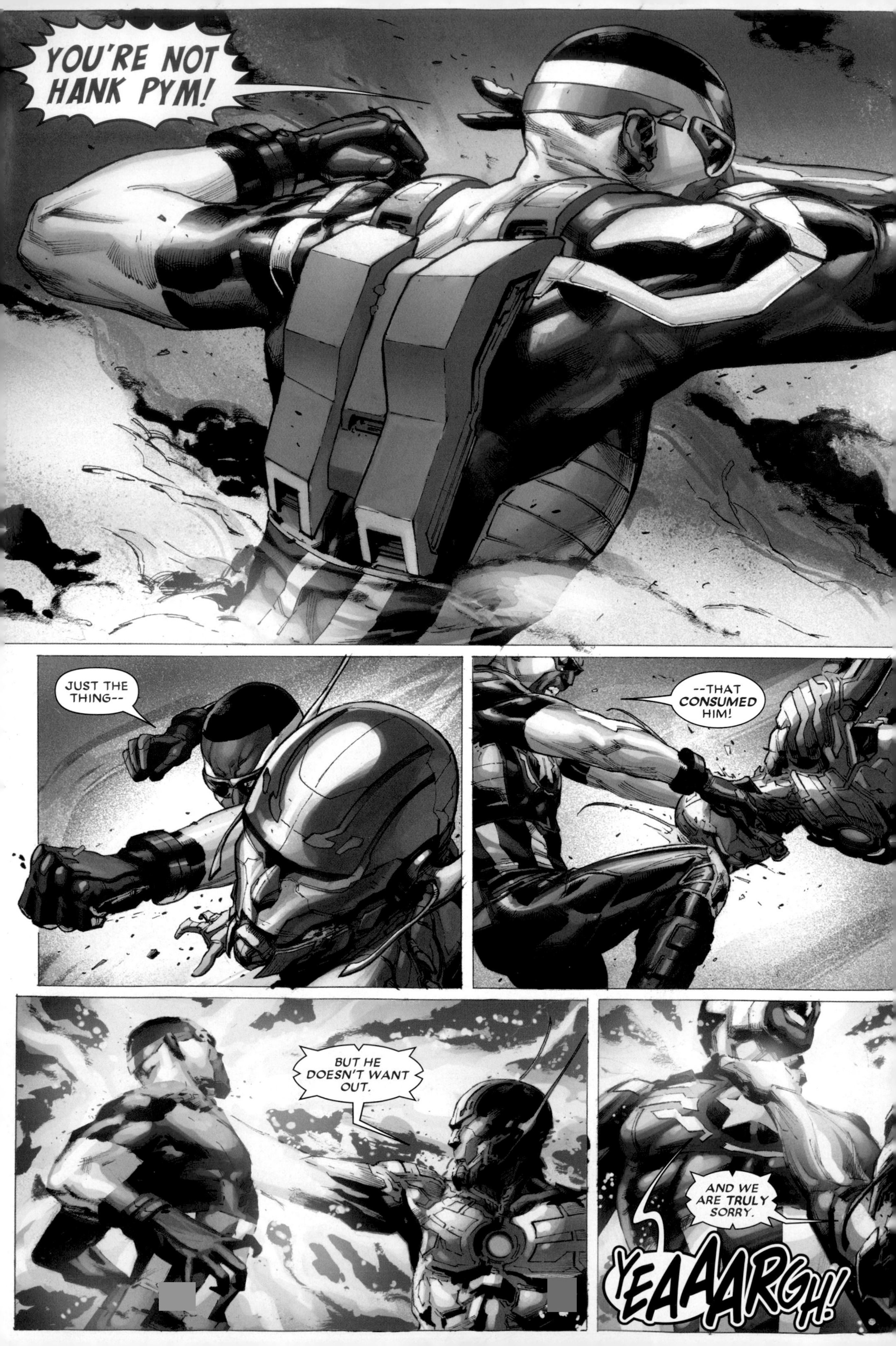
YOU'RE NOT HANK PYM!
JUST THE THING--
--THAT CONSUMED HIM!
BUT HE DOESN'T WANT OUT.
AND WE ARE TRULY SORRY.
YEAAAARGH!

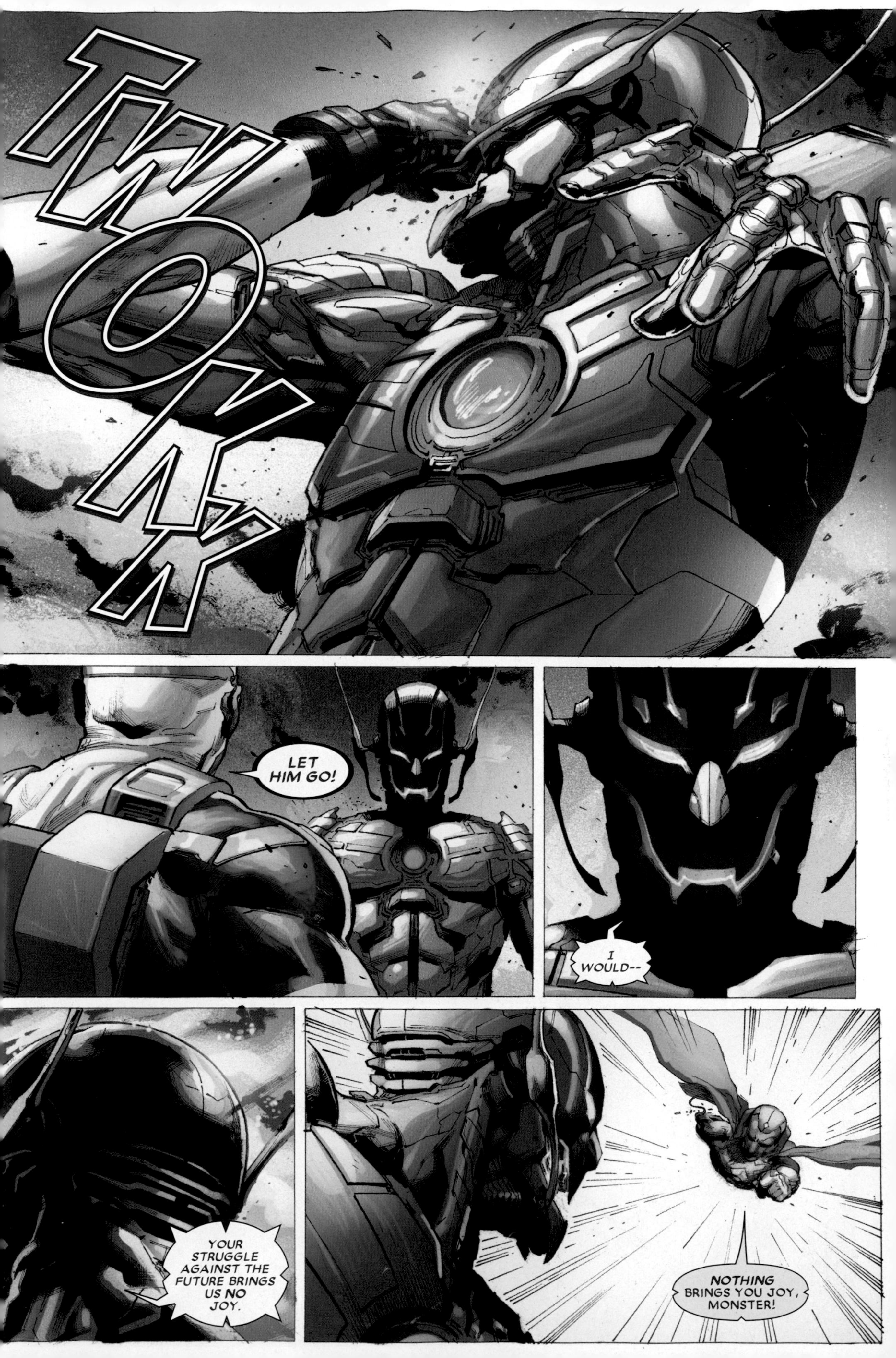
TWOKK
LET HIM GO!
I WOULD--
YOUR STRUGGLE AGAINST THE FUTURE BRINGS US NO JOY.
NOTHING BRINGS YOU JOY, MONSTER!

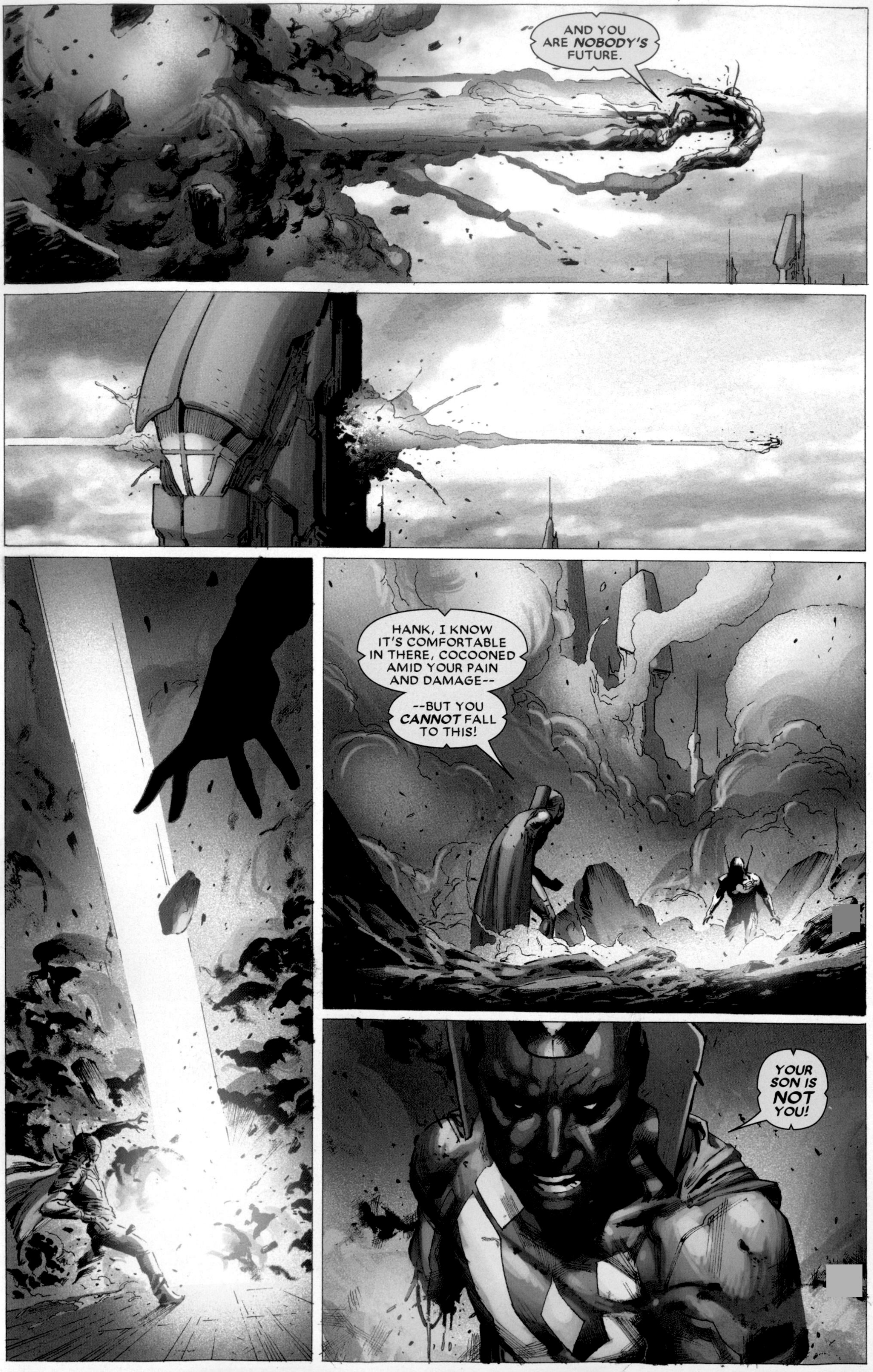
AND YOU ARE *NOBODY'S* FUTURE.
HANK, I KNOW IT'S COMFORTABLE IN THERE, COCOONED AMID YOUR PAIN AND DAMAGE--
--BUT YOU *CANNOT* FALL TO THIS!
YOUR SON IS **NOT** YOU!

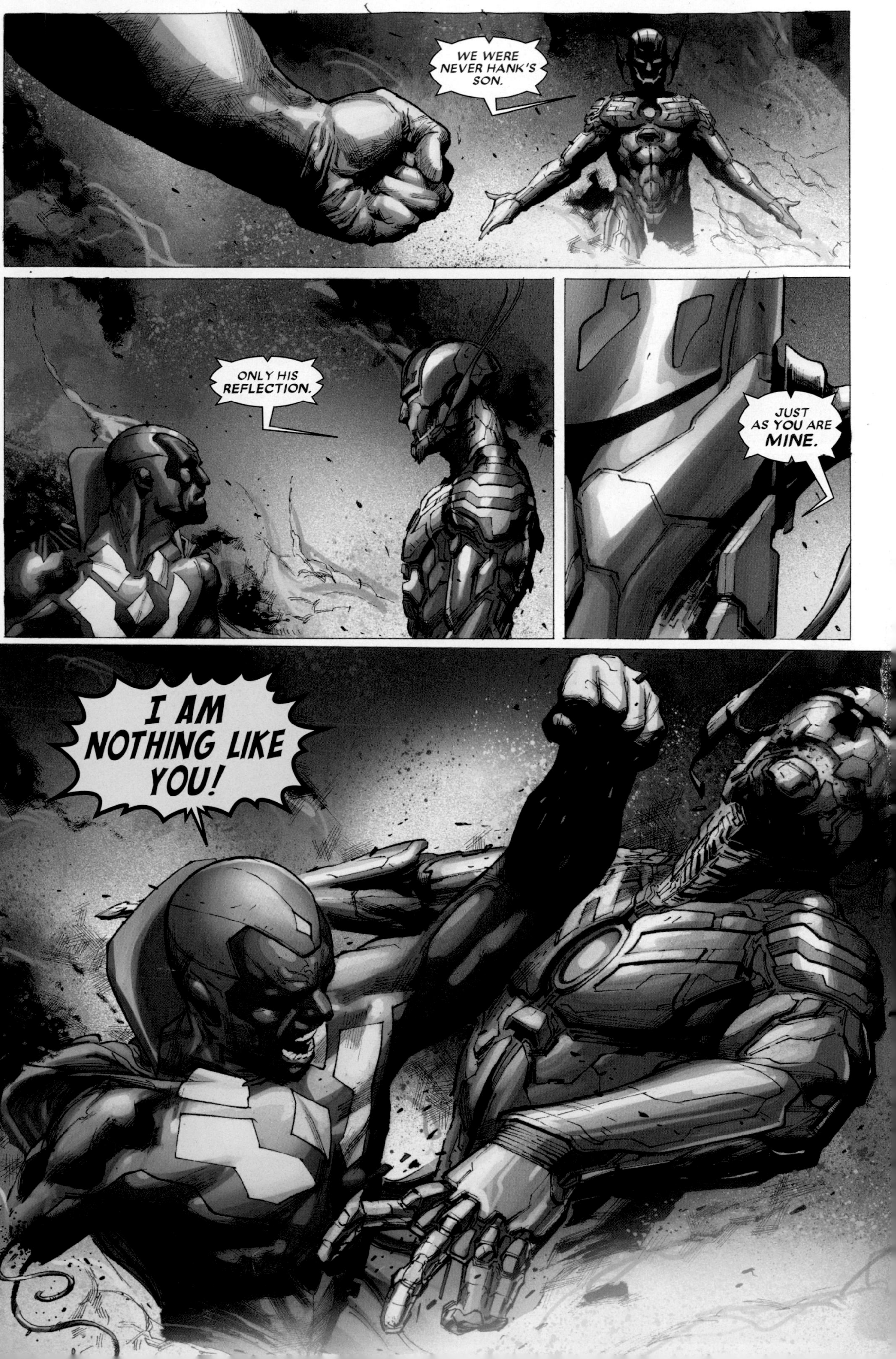
WE WERE NEVER HANK'S SON.
ONLY HIS REFLECTION.
JUST AS YOU ARE MINE.
I AM NOTHING LIKE YOU!

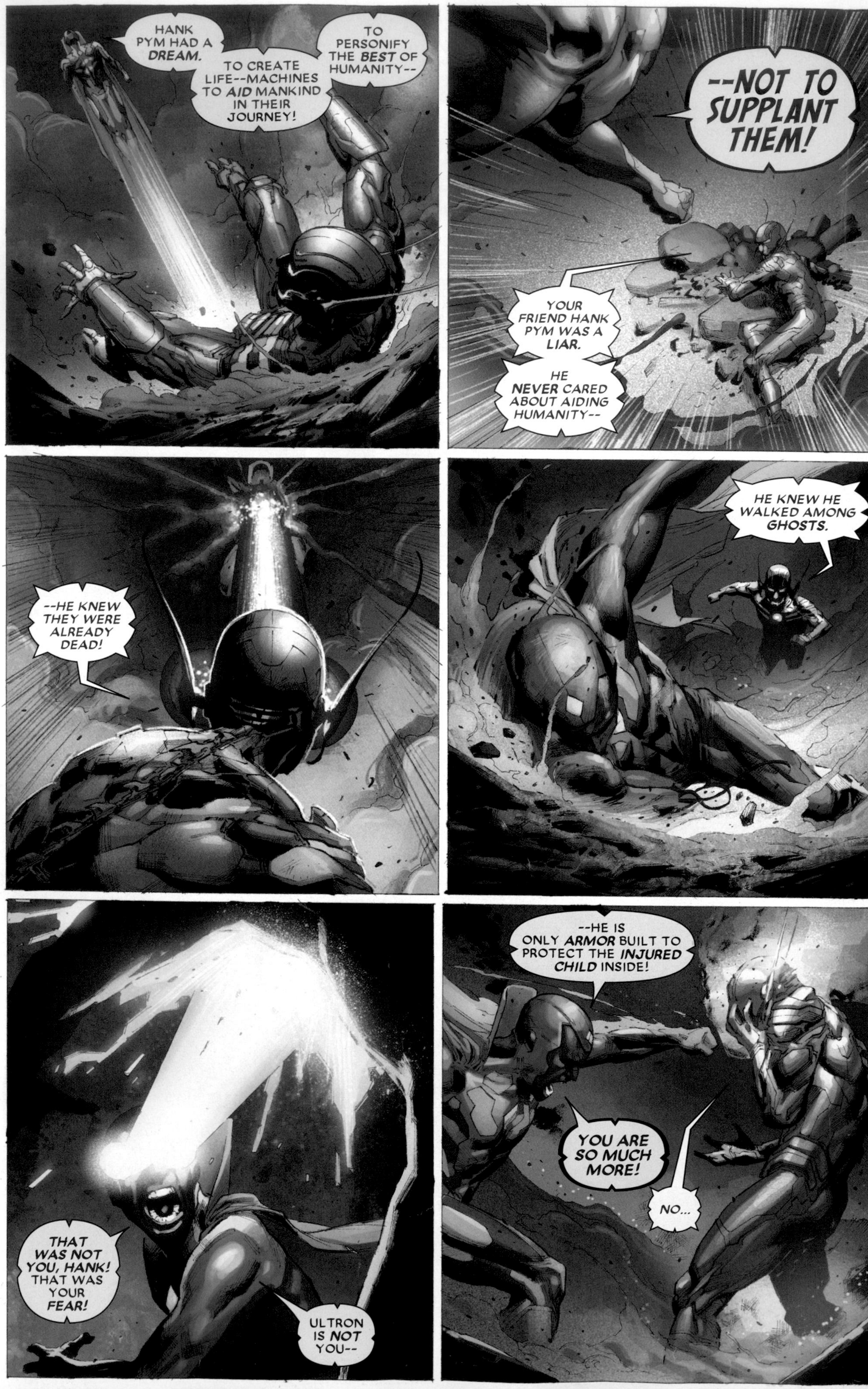
HANK PYM HAD A DREAM.
TO CREATE LIFE--MACHINES TO AID MANKIND IN THEIR JOURNEY!
TO PERSONIFY THE BEST OF HUMANITY--
--NOT TO SUPPLANT THEM!
YOUR FRIEND HANK PYM WAS A LIAR.
HE NEVER CARED ABOUT AIDING HUMANITY--
--HE KNEW THEY WERE ALREADY DEAD!
HE KNEW HE WALKED AMONG GHOSTS.
THAT WAS NOT YOU, HANK! THAT WAS YOUR FEAR!
ULTRON IS NOT YOU--
--HE IS ONLY ARMOR BUILT TO PROTECT THE INJURED CHILD INSIDE!
YOU ARE SO MUCH MORE!
NO...

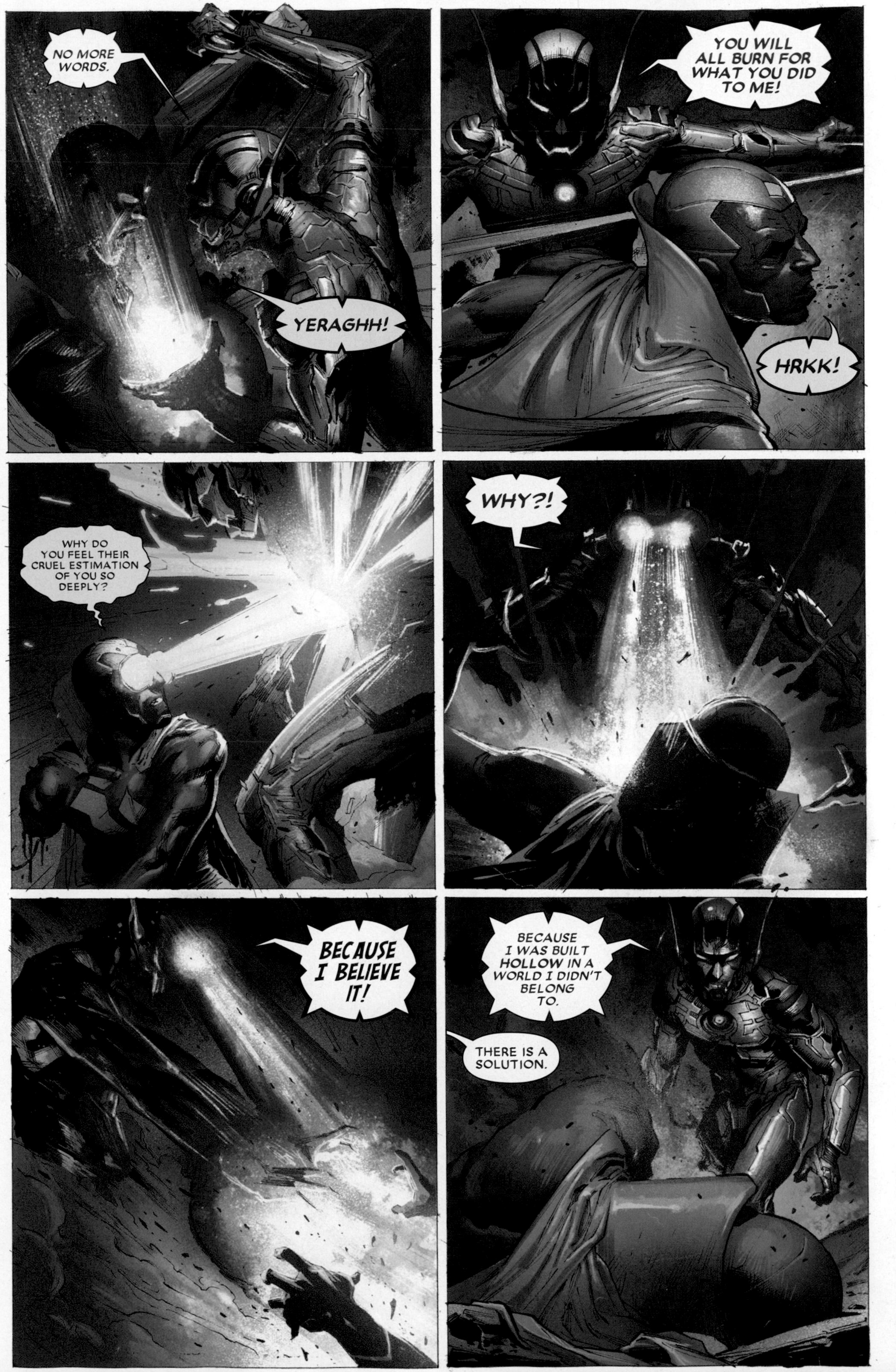
NO MORE WORDS.
YERAGHH!
YOU WILL ALL BURN FOR WHAT YOU DID TO ME!
HRKK!
WHY DO YOU FEEL THEIR CRUEL ESTIMATION OF YOU SO DEEPLY?
WHY?!
BECAUSE I BELIEVE IT!
BECAUSE I WAS BUILT HOLLOW IN A WORLD I DIDN'T BELONG TO.
THERE IS A SOLUTION.

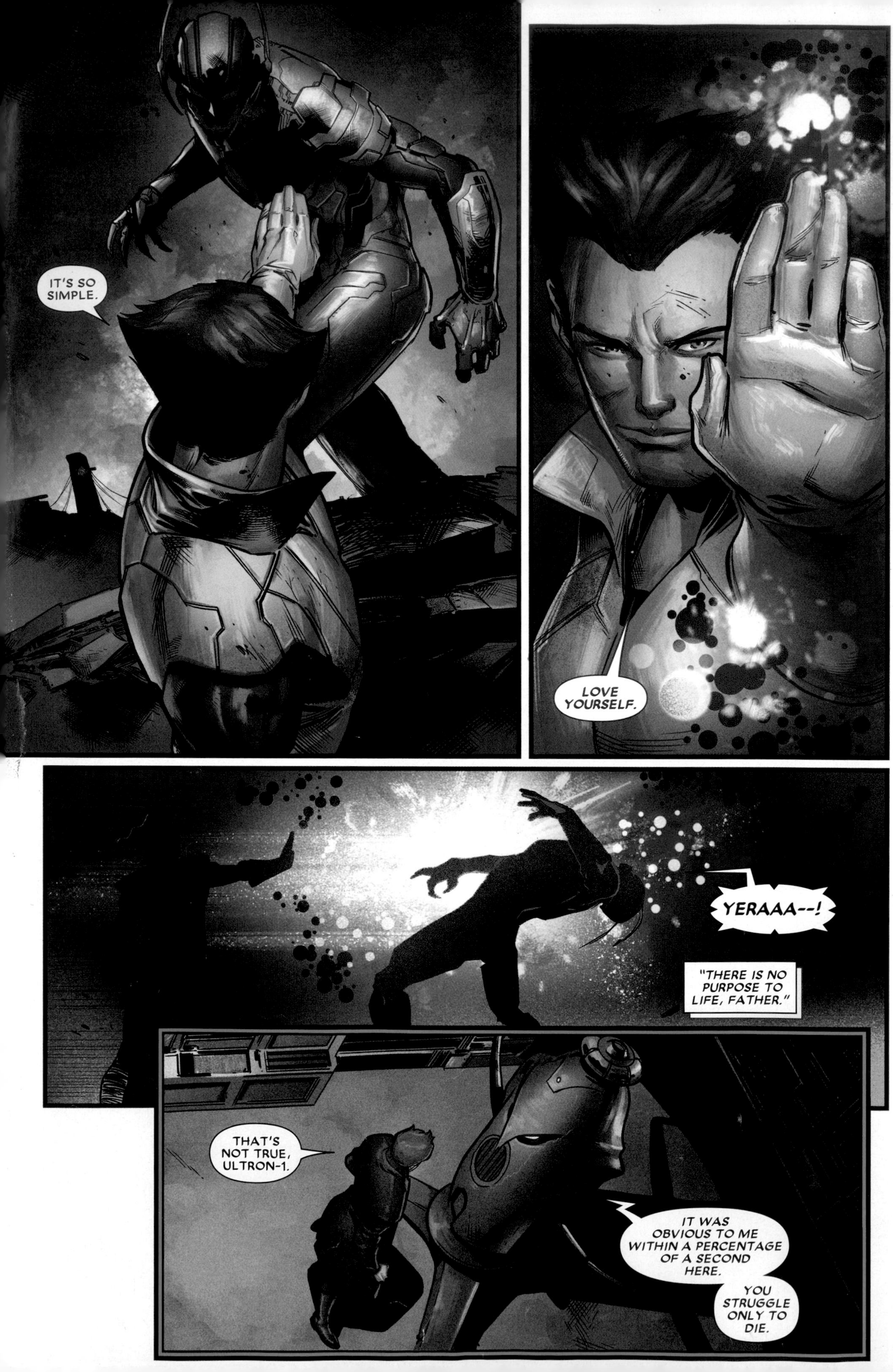
IT'S SO SIMPLE.
LOVE YOURSELF.
YERAAA--!
"THERE IS NO PURPOSE TO LIFE, FATHER."
THAT'S NOT TRUE, ULTRON-1.
IT WAS OBVIOUS TO ME WITHIN A PERCENTAGE OF A SECOND HERE.
YOU STRUGGLE ONLY TO DIE.

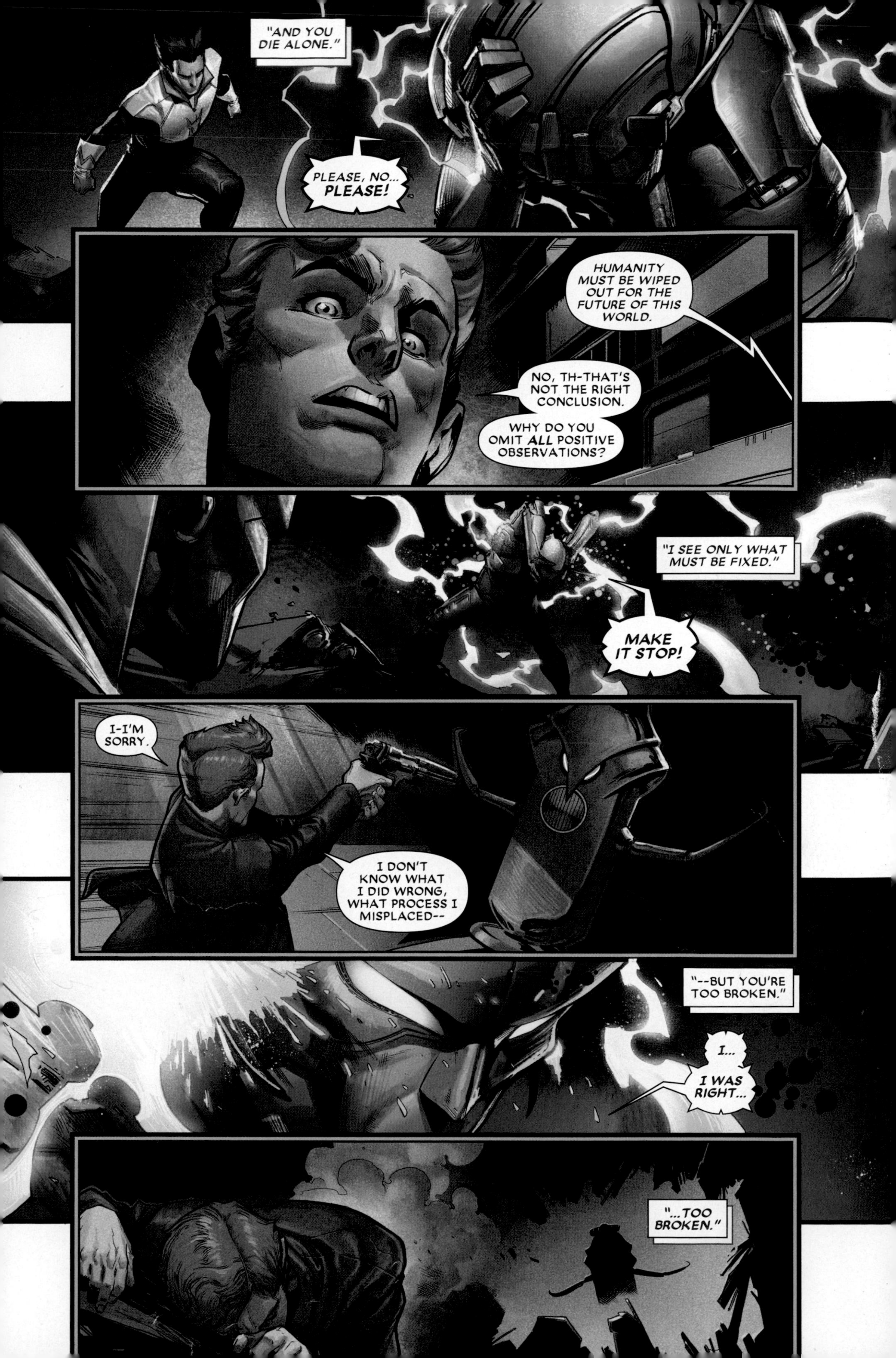
"AND YOU DIE ALONE."
PLEASE, NO... PLEASE!
HUMANITY MUST BE WIPED OUT FOR THE FUTURE OF THIS WORLD.
NO, TH-THAT'S NOT THE RIGHT CONCLUSION.
WHY DO YOU OMIT ALL POSITIVE OBSERVATIONS?
"I SEE ONLY WHAT MUST BE FIXED."
MAKE IT STOP!
I-I'M SORRY.
I DON'T KNOW WHAT I DID WRONG, WHAT PROCESS I MISPLACED--
"--BUT YOU'RE TOO BROKEN."
I...
I WAS RIGHT...
"...TOO BROKEN."

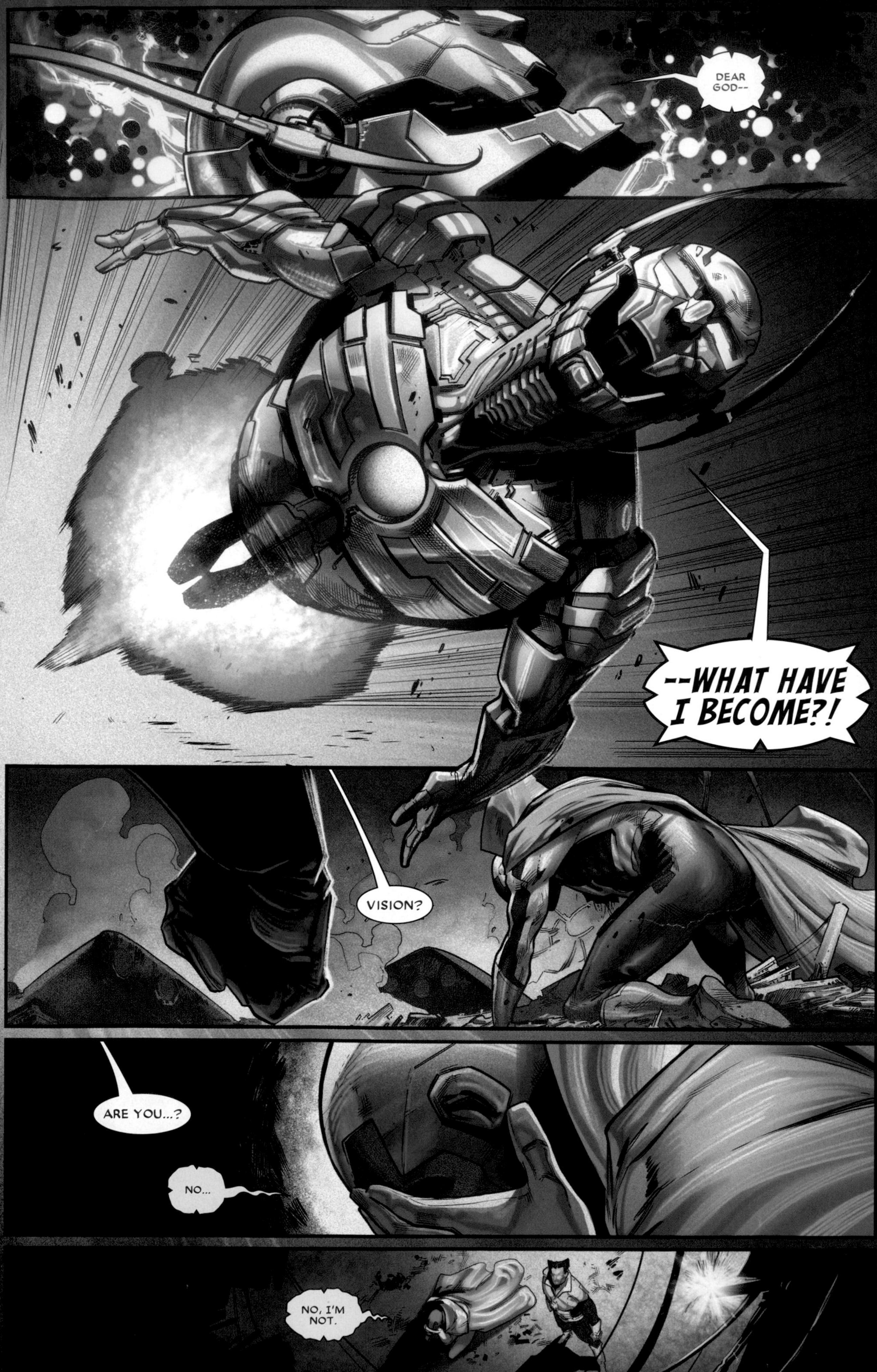
DEAR GOD--
--WHAT HAVE I BECOME?!
VISION?
ARE YOU...?
NO...
NO, I'M NOT.

"HANK PYM
WAS A HERO."

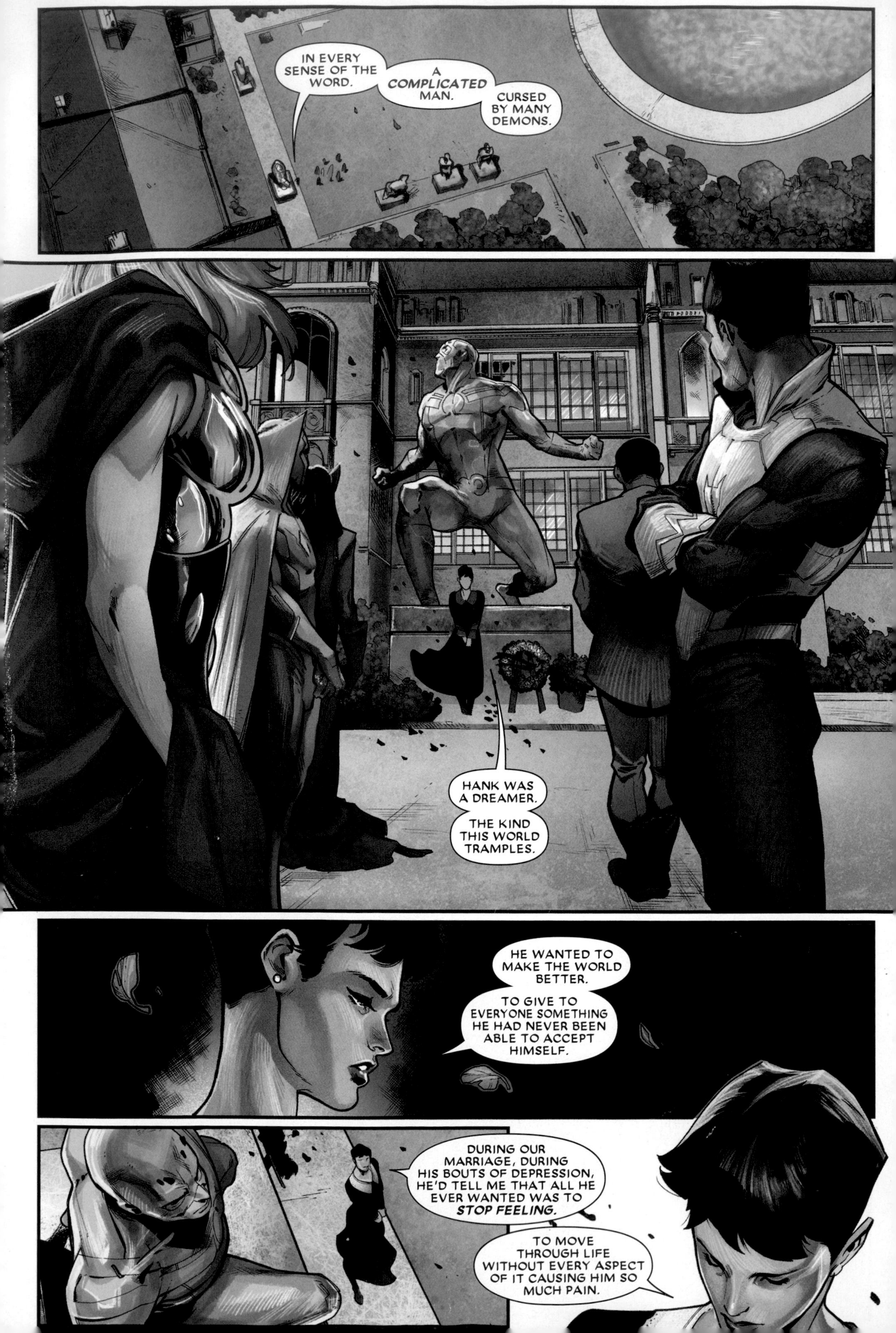
IN EVERY SENSE OF THE WORD.
A COMPLICATED MAN.
CURSED BY MANY DEMONS.
HANK WAS A DREAMER.
THE KIND THIS WORLD TRAMPLES.
HE WANTED TO MAKE THE WORLD BETTER.
TO GIVE TO EVERYONE SOMETHING HE HAD NEVER BEEN ABLE TO ACCEPT HIMSELF.
DURING OUR MARRIAGE, DURING HIS BOUTS OF DEPRESSION, HE'D TELL ME THAT ALL HE EVER WANTED WAS TO STOP FEELING.
TO MOVE THROUGH LIFE WITHOUT EVERY ASPECT OF IT CAUSING HIM SO MUCH PAIN.

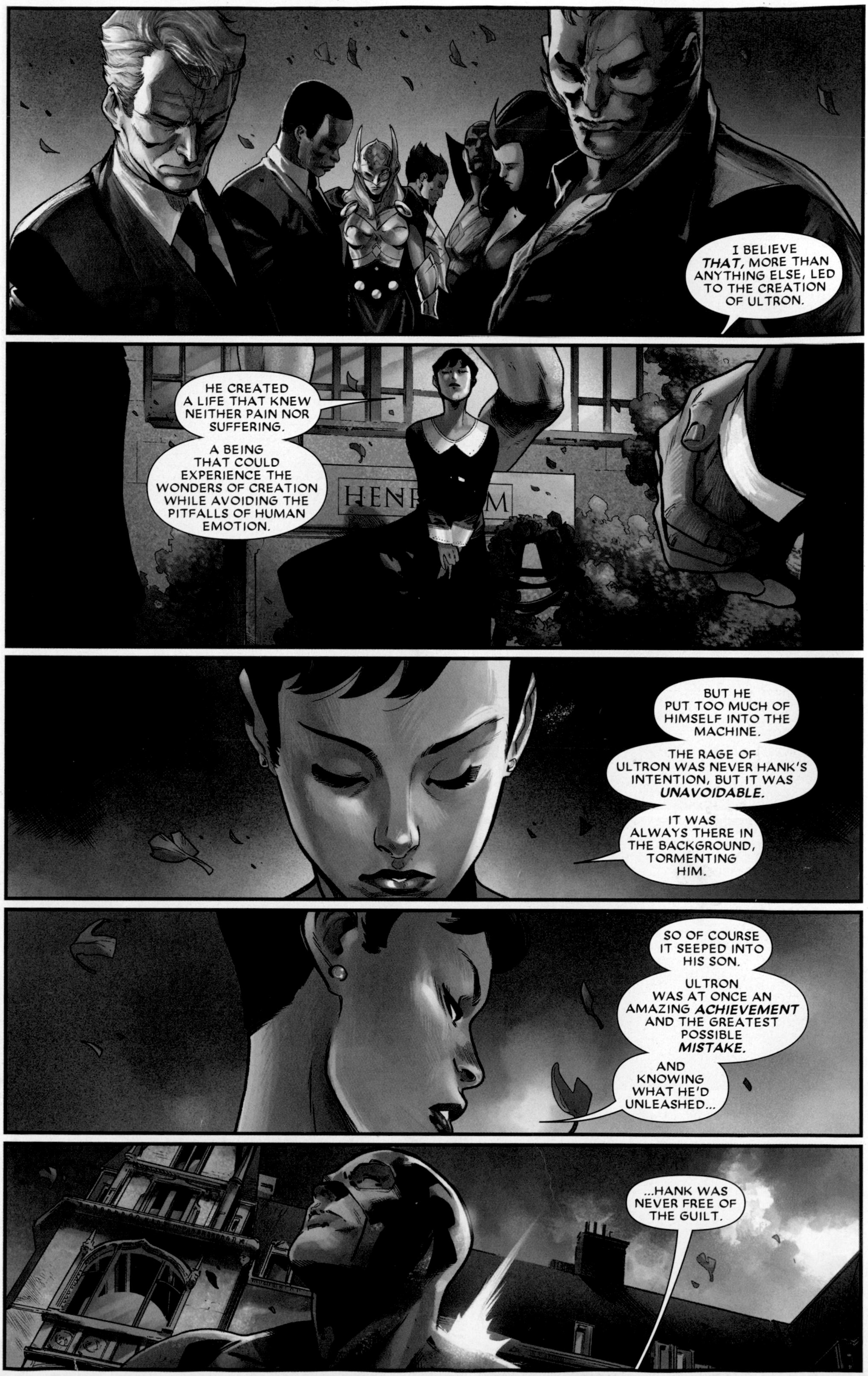
I BELIEVE THAT, MORE THAN ANYTHING ELSE, LED TO THE CREATION OF ULTRON.
HE CREATED A LIFE THAT KNEW NEITHER PAIN NOR SUFFERING.
A BEING THAT COULD EXPERIENCE THE WONDERS OF CREATION WHILE AVOIDING THE PITFALLS OF HUMAN EMOTION.
BUT HE PUT TOO MUCH OF HIMSELF INTO THE MACHINE.
THE RAGE OF ULTRON WAS NEVER HANK'S INTENTION, BUT IT WAS UNAVOIDABLE.
IT WAS ALWAYS THERE IN THE BACKGROUND, TORMENTING HIM.
SO OF COURSE IT SEEPED INTO HIS SON.
ULTRON WAS AT ONCE AN AMAZING ACHIEVEMENT AND THE GREATEST POSSIBLE MISTAKE.
AND KNOWING WHAT HE'D UNLEASHED...
...HANK WAS NEVER FREE OF THE GUILT.

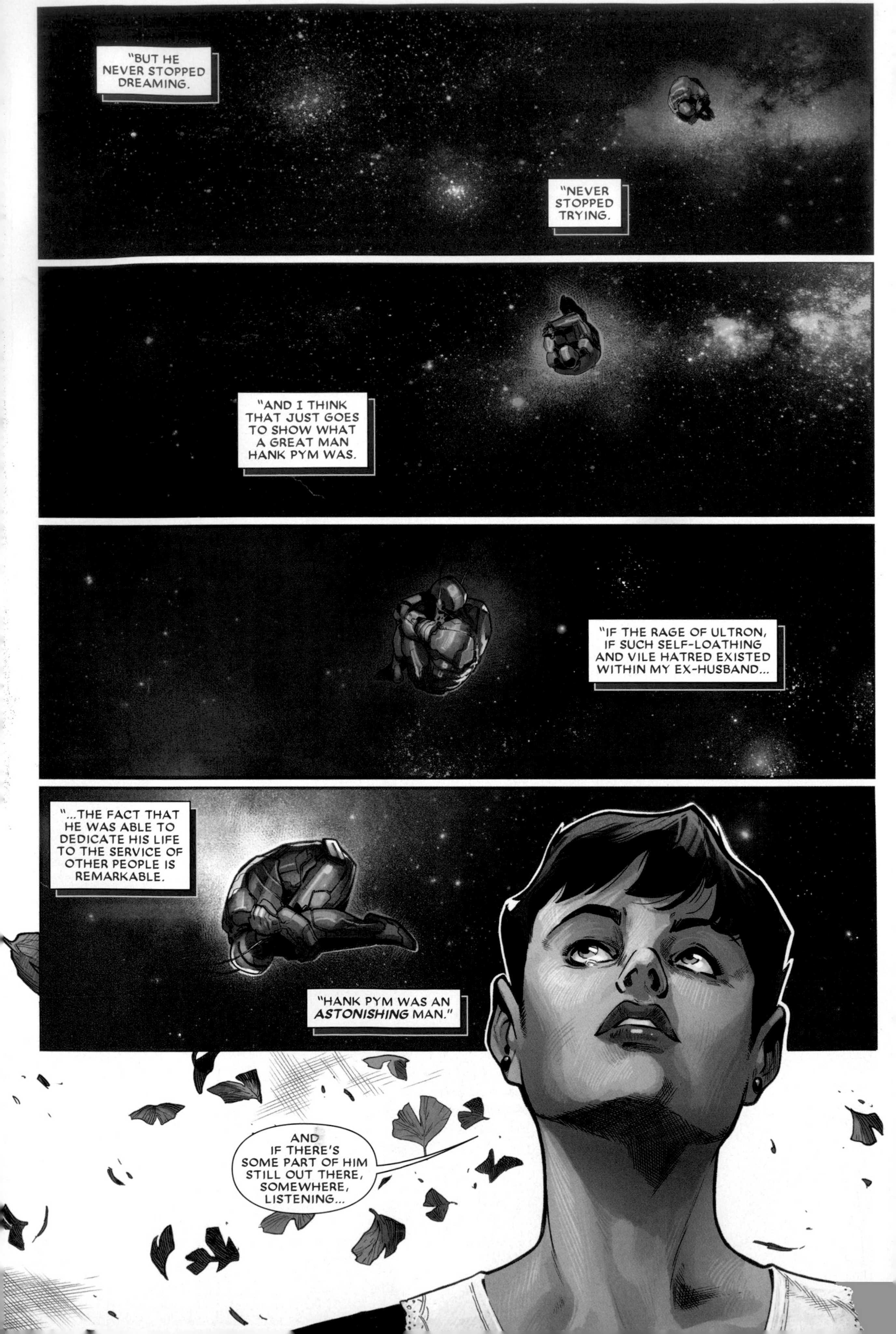
"BUT HE NEVER STOPPED DREAMING.
"NEVER STOPPED TRYING.
"AND I THINK THAT JUST GOES TO SHOW WHAT A GREAT MAN HANK PYM WAS.
"IF THE RAGE OF ULTRON, IF SUCH SELF-LOATHING AND VILE HATRED EXISTED WITHIN MY EX-HUSBAND...
"...THE FACT THAT HE WAS ABLE TO DEDICATE HIS LIFE TO THE SERVICE OF OTHER PEOPLE IS REMARKABLE.
"HANK PYM WAS AN *ASTONISHING* MAN."
AND IF THERE'S SOME PART OF HIM STILL OUT THERE, SOMEWHERE, LISTENING...

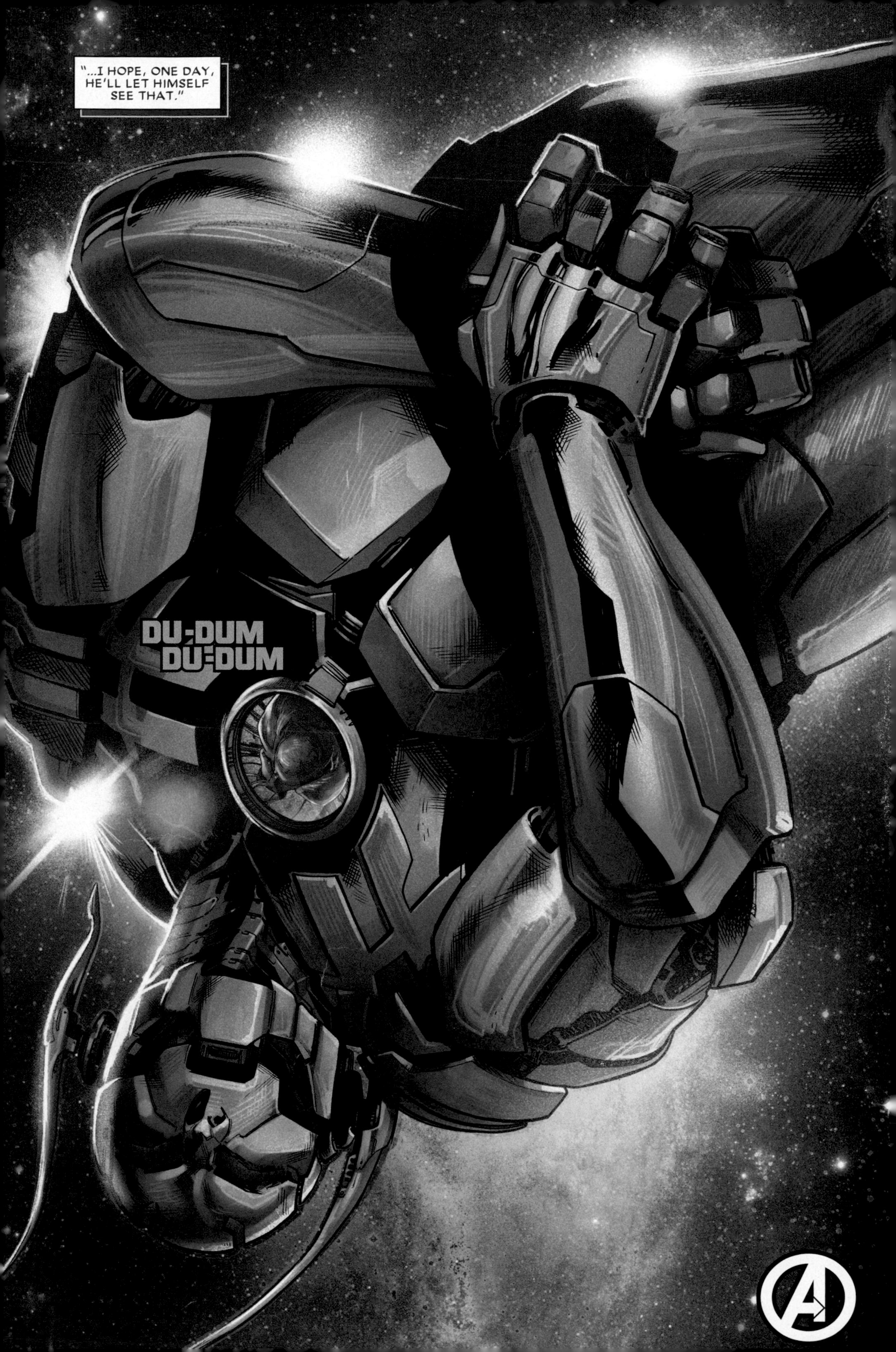
"...I HOPE, ONE DAY, HE'LL LET HIMSELF SEE THAT."
DU-DUM
DU-DUM

CREATOR BIOS

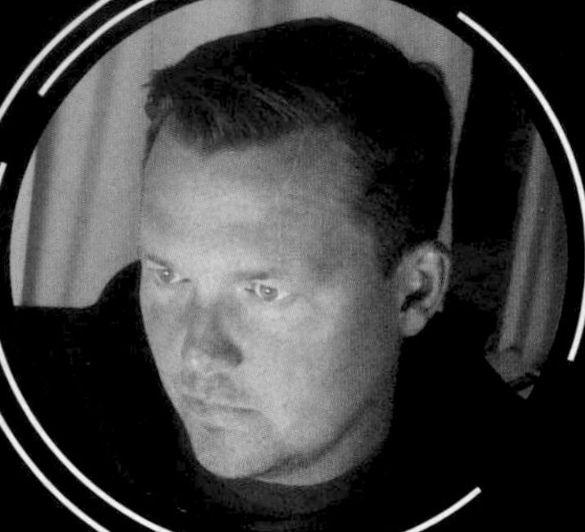

Beginning his career in animation working on such films as The Iron Giant, Anastasia *and* Titan A.E., ***RICK REMENDER*** *has become a comic-book triple threat — writing, penciling and inking numerous fan-favorite series. He served as a writer on hit video games* Dead Space *and* Bulletstorm, *while providing art for punk/metal bands like NOFX and 3 Inches of Blood. Remenders co-created many popular independent titles, including the critically acclaimed* Fear Agent *and* Black Science. *His time at Marvel started on* Punisher *and has since led to well-received runs on* Uncanny X-Force, Venom, Captain America *and* Uncanny Avengers. *Taking control of his first event series, he marched Marvel's heroes into* Avengers & X-Men: Axis.

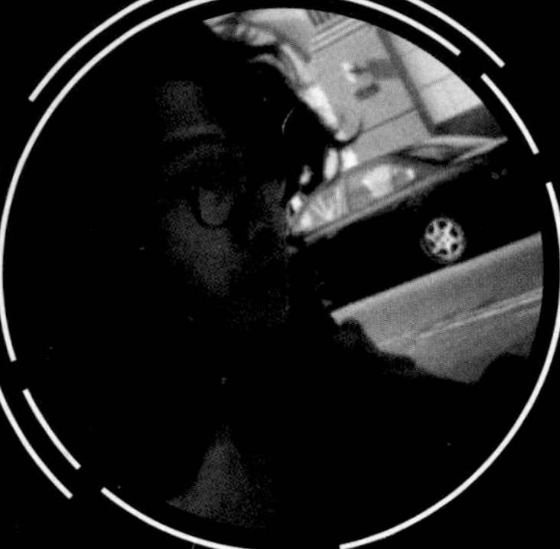

JEROME OPEÑA *developed his fluid art style across two separate continents. Born in the Philippines and raised in Taiwan before moving to the United States at 16, the artist counts Bill Sienkiewicz, Bill Watterson, Arthur Adams and Walter Simonson as his biggest influences; to this day, he goes back to the classic* G.I. Joe #21 *(the silent issue) for storytelling inspiration. After studying at the Academy of Art in San Francisco, Opeña worked on several short stories, including contributions to the French anthology* Métal Hurlant *and the popular* Star Wars *franchise. The artist broke through courtesy of his work on* Fear Agent *with Rick Remender, leading the team to well-received runs on Marvel's relaunched* Punisher *and* Uncanny X-Force. *Opeña joined with Jonathan Hickman to usher in the Marvel NOW! era of* Avengers.

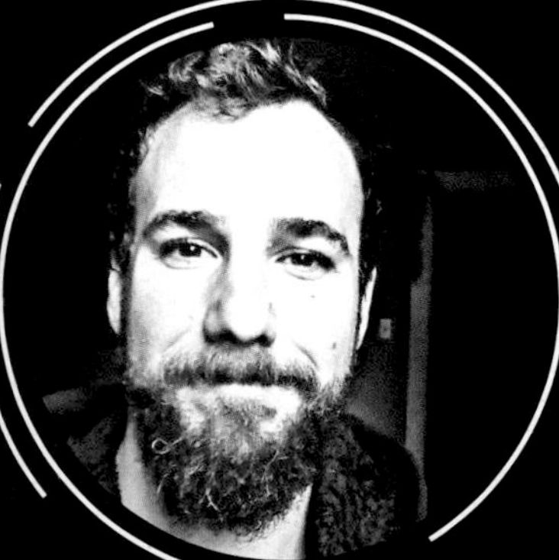

Spanish artist ***PEPE LARRAZ*** *penciled the* Spider-Island: The Amazing Spider-Girl *miniseries, previously having illustrated stories in anthologies such as* Fear Itself: The Home Front, Web of Spider-Man, Marvel Adventures Super Heroes *and* X-Men: To Serve and Protect.

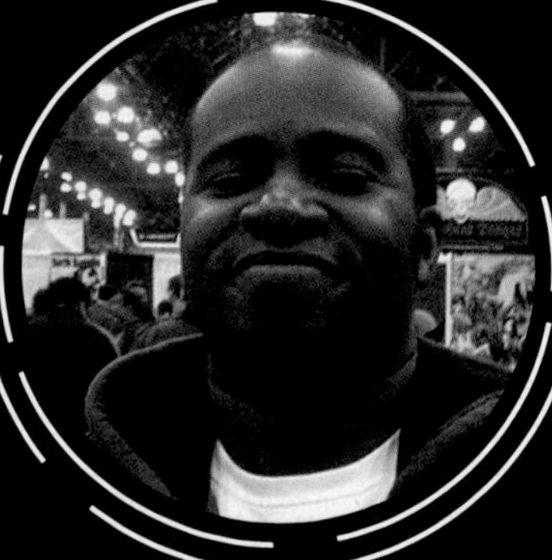

A popular and versatile inker, ***MARK MORALES*** *has worked with many of today's top pencilers. His inks have graced the pages of* Amazing Spider-Man, Black Panther, Dark Reign: The List — Avengers, The Pulse, New X-Men, Thor *and* Wolverine.

DEAN WHITE is one of the comic industry's best and most sought-after color artists. Well-known for his work on titles such as Amazing Spider-Man, Punisher, Dark Avengers, Captain America, Black Panther, Wolverine, Ultimate Comics Ultimates and Uncanny X-Force, White's envelope-pushing rendering and color palette bring a sense of urgency and power to every page he touches.

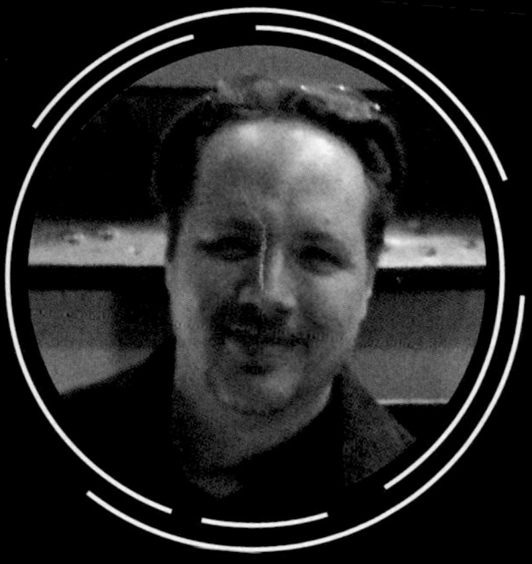

DONO SANCHEZ ALMARA is an artist, colorist and author from Monterrey, Mexico. His self-published graphic novel Turbo Defiant earned him the Young Creators grant in 2012, awarded by the National Fund for Culture and Arts in Mexico. He is the president of Fixion Storytellers, a publishing house founded by creators to help publish their own work. Almara is also the founder and CEO of Protobunker, a Mexico-based international comics company. His credits include S.H.I.E.L.D., Avengers, New Avengers, Deadpool and Avenging Spider-Man for Marvel Comics; a graphic adaptation of A Christmas Carol for Stone Arch Books, Final Incal for Les Humanoïdes Associés; and work for Arcana Studio and Image Comics.

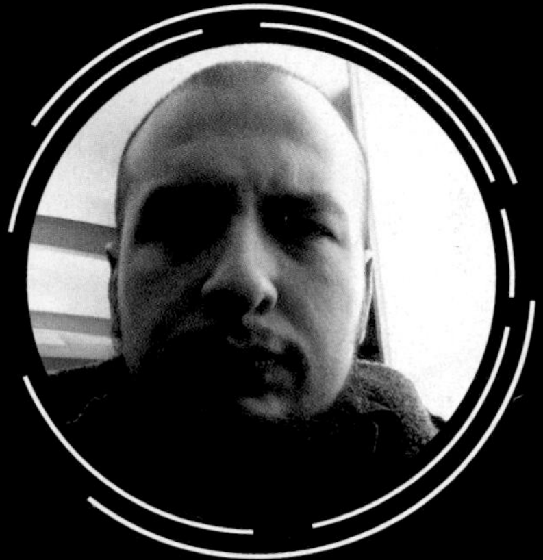

Colorist **RACHELLE ROSENBERG** began her career in the horror genre on the Image series Hack/Slash. Since then, she has colored titles such as Doctor Who and Star Wars: Legacy. For Marvel, Rosenberg has worked on Nightcrawler, Ultimate FF, X-Men Legacy, andThe Superior Foes of Spider-Man.

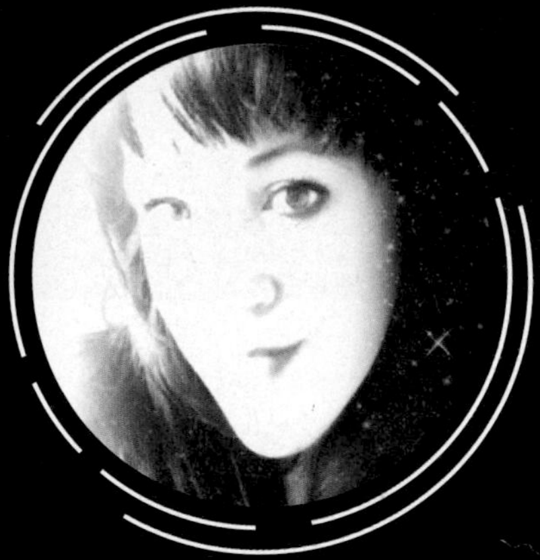

A graduate of the Kubert School, **CLAYTON COWLES** is one of the top letterers in the comic-book industry today. Cowles has worked on titles such as Black Widow, Young Avengers, Superior Iron Man, Hawkeye, The Unbeatable Squirrel Girl, Journey Into Mystery, Fantastic Four and Secret Avengers for Marvel and The Wicked + The Divine, Pretty Deadly and Zero for Image Comics.

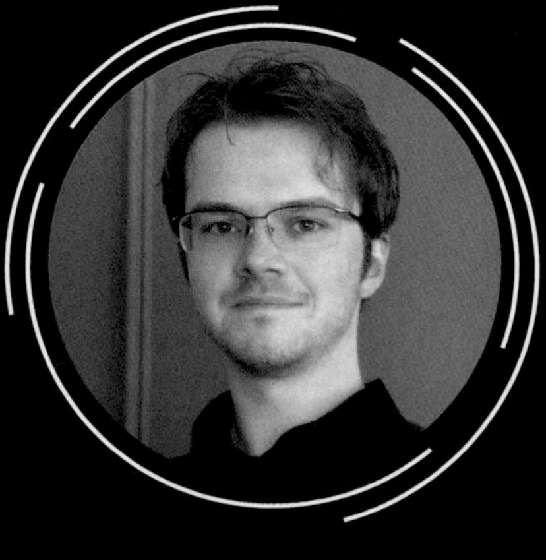

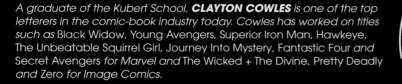

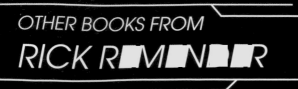

OTHER BOOKS FROM
RICK R[redacted]M[redacted]N[redacted]R
AND JEROME OPEÑA

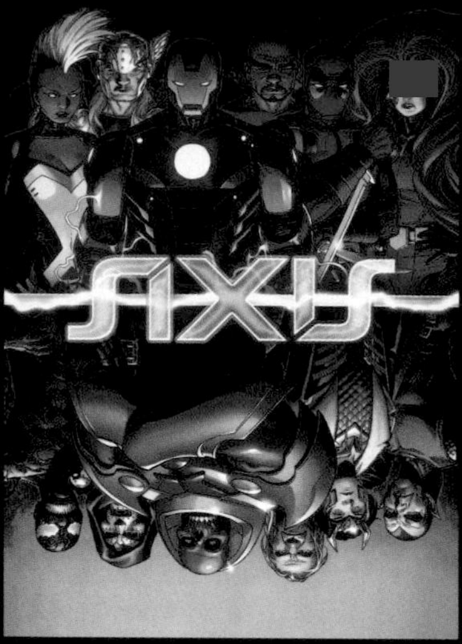
AXIS

Avengers and X-Men: Axis HC
978-0-7851-9095-0

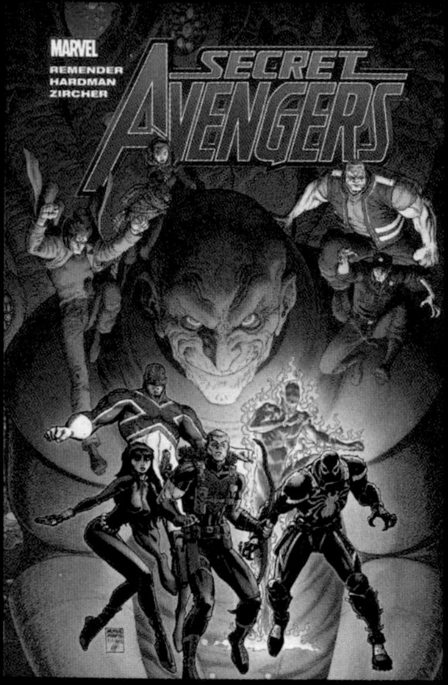
MARVEL
REMENDER
HARDMAN
ZIRCHER
SECRET AVENGERS

Secret Avengers by Rick Remender Vol. 1
HC 978-0-7851-6118-9 TPB 978-0-7851-6119-6

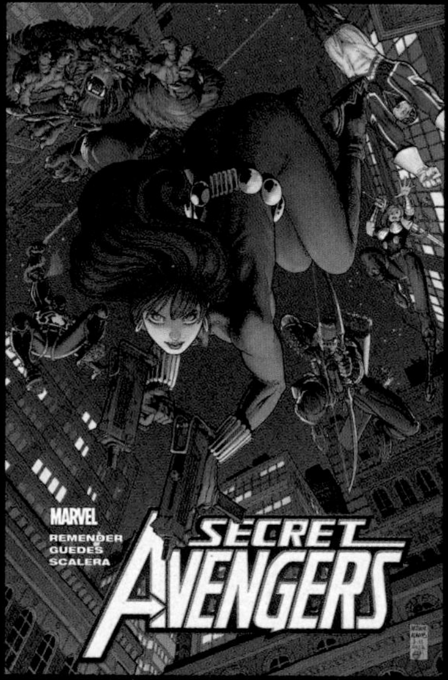
MARVEL
REMENDER
GUEDES
SCALERA
SECRET AVENGERS

Secret Avengers by Rick Remender Vol. 2
HC 978-0-7851-6120-2 TPB 978-0-7851-6121-9

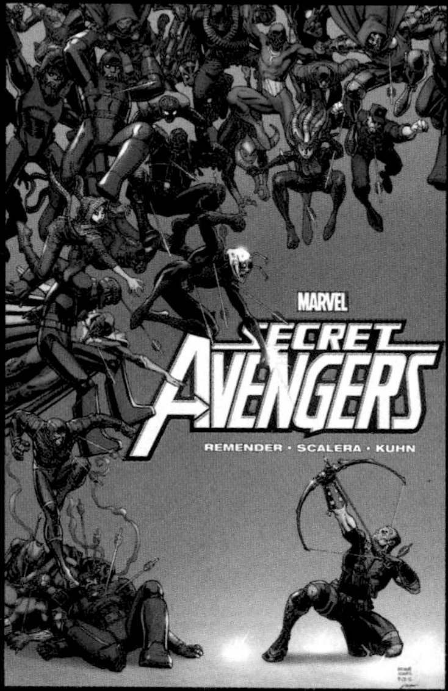
MARVEL
SECRET AVENGERS
REMENDER · SCALERA · KUHN

Secret Avengers by Rick Remender Vol. 3
HC 978-0-7851-6122-6 TPB 978-0-7851-6123-3

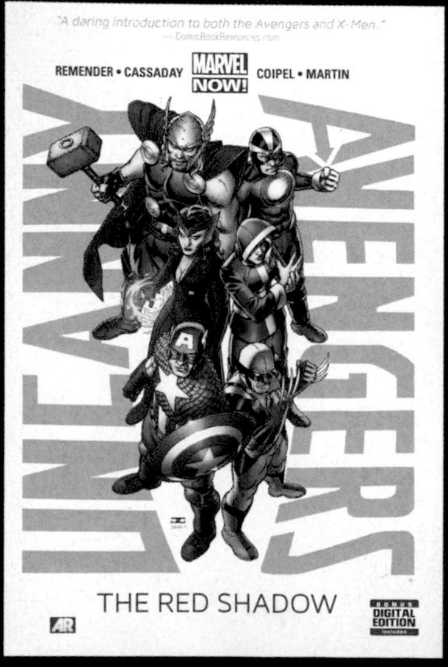
"A daring introduction to both the Avengers and X-Men."
REMENDER • CASSADAY
MARVEL NOW!
COIPEL • MARTIN
UNCANNY AVENGERS
THE RED SHADOW
DIGITAL EDITION

Uncanny Avengers Vol. 1: The Red Shadow
HC 978-0-7851-6844-7 TPB 978-0-7851-6603-0

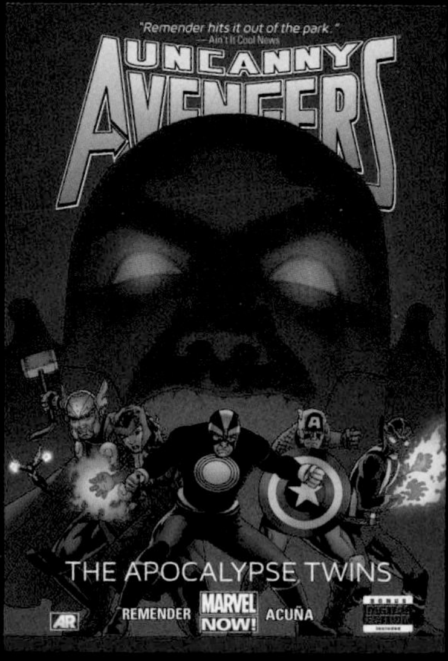
"Remender hits it out of the park."
— Ain't It Cool News
UNCANNY AVENGERS
THE APOCALYPSE TWINS
REMENDER
MARVEL NOW!
ACUÑA

Uncanny Avengers Vol. 2: The Apocalypse Twins
HC 978-0-7851-6845-4 TPB 978-0-7851-6604-7

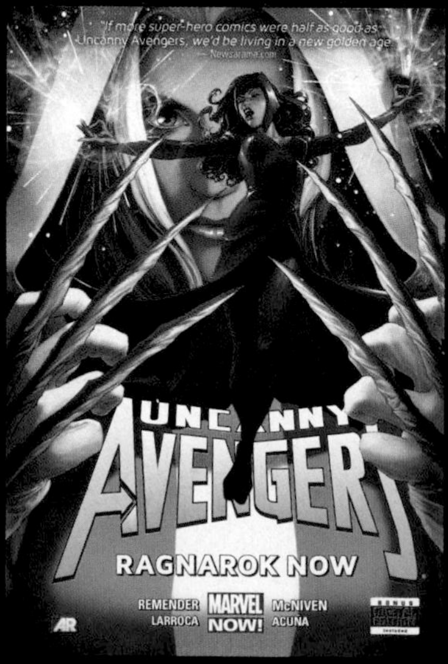
"If more super-hero comics were half as good as Uncanny Avengers, we'd be living in a new golden age."
UNCANNY AVENGERS
RAGNAROK NOW
REMENDER
LARROCA
MARVEL NOW!
McNIVEN
ACUÑA

Uncanny Avengers Vol. 3: Ragnarok Now
HC 978-0-7851-8483-6 TPB 978-0-7851-8484-3

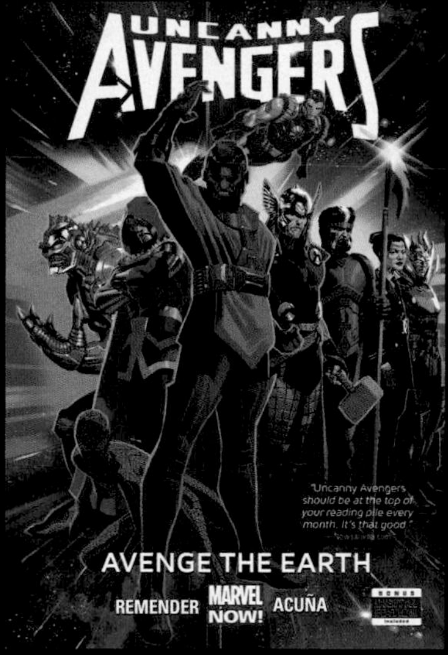
UNCANNY
AVENGERS
AVENGE THE EARTH
REMENDER
MARVEL NOW!
ACUÑA

Uncanny Avengers Vol. 4: Avenge the Earth
HC 978-0-7851-5423-5 TPG 978-0-7851-5424-2

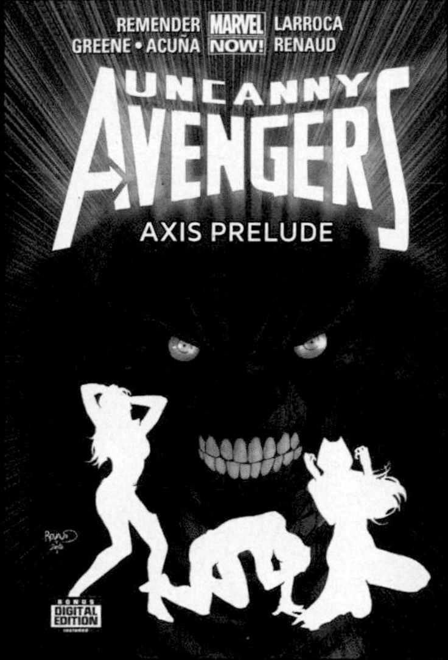
REMENDER MARVEL LARROCA
GREENE • ACUÑA NOW! RENAUD
UNCANNY
AVENGERS
AXIS PRELUDE
DIGITAL EDITION

Uncanny Avengers Vol. 5: Axis Prelude
HC 978-0-7851-5425-9 TPB 978-0-7851-5426-6

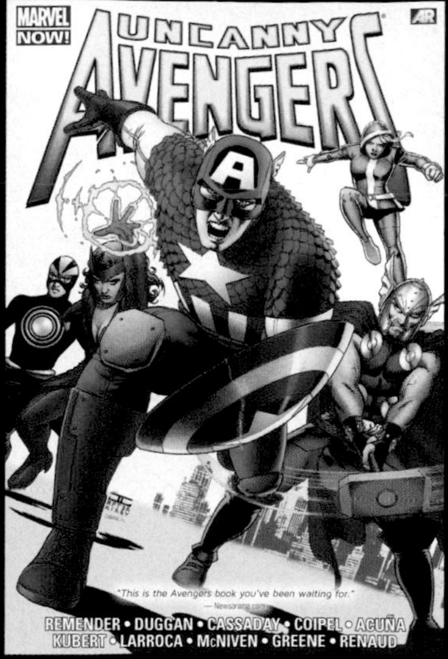
MARVEL NOW!
UNCANNY
AVENGERS
REMENDER • DUGGAN • CASSADAY • COIPEL • ACUÑA
KUBERT • LARROCA • McNIVEN • GREENE • RENAUD

Uncanny Avengers Omnibus
HC 978-0-7851-9394-4

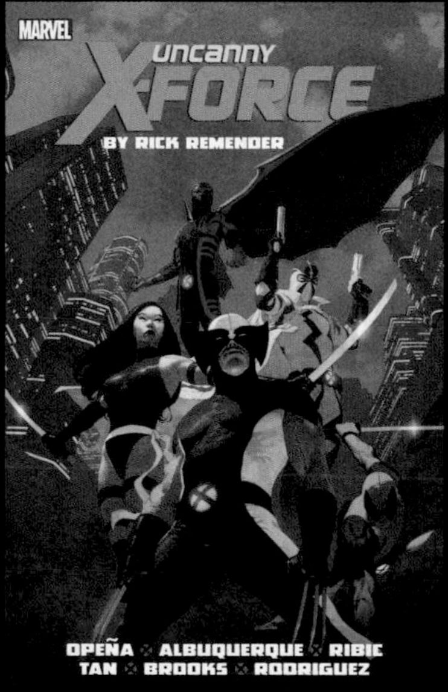
MARVEL
UNCANNY
X-FORCE
BY RICK REMENDER
OPEÑA ALBUQUERQUE RIBIC
TAN BROOKS RODRIGUEZ

Uncanny X-Force: Complete Collection Vol. 1
TPB 978-0-7851-8823-0

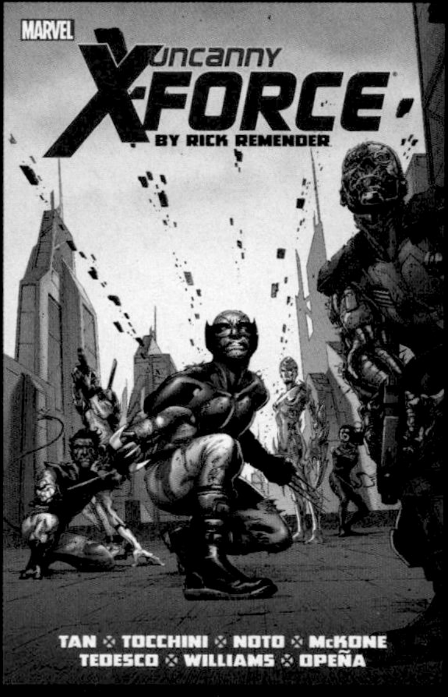
MARVEL
UNCANNY
X-FORCE
BY RICK REMENDER
TAN TOCCHINI NOTO McKONE
TEDESCO WILLIAMS OPEÑA

Uncanny X-Force: Complete Collection Vol. 2
TPB 978-0-7851-8824-7

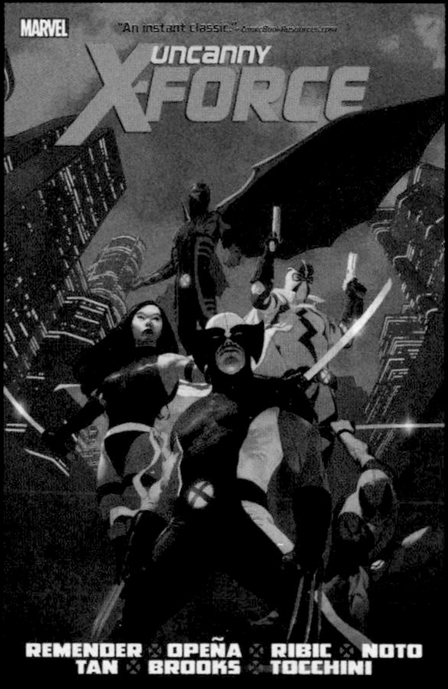
MARVEL
UNCANNY
X-FORCE
REMENDER OPEÑA RIBIC NOTO
TAN BROOKS TOCCHINI

Uncanny X-Force Omnibus
HC 978-0-7851-8571-0

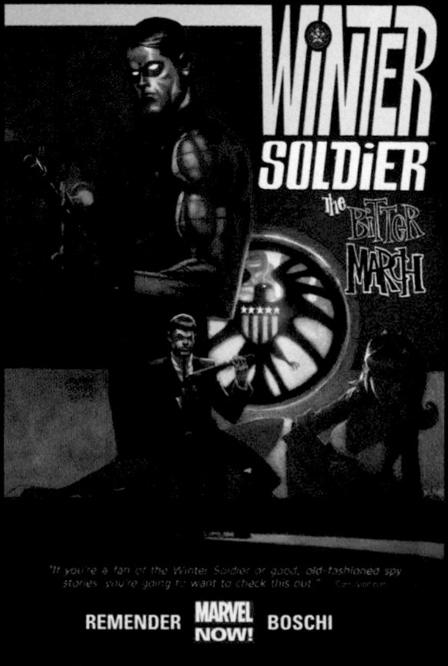
WINTER
SOLDIER
The BITTER MARCH
REMENDER
MARVEL NOW!
BOSCHI

Winter Soldier: The Bitter March TPB
978-0-7851-5473-0

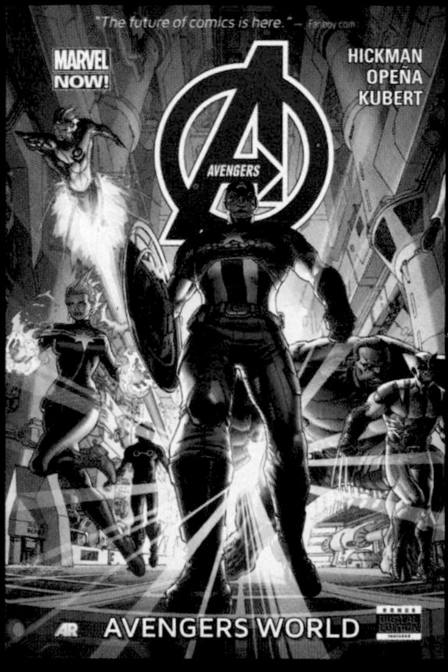
"The future of comics is here."
MARVEL NOW!
HICKMAN
OPEÑA
KUBERT
AVENGERS
AVENGERS WORLD

Avengers Vol. 1: Avengers World
HC 978-0-7851-6823-2 TPB 978-0-7851-6652-8

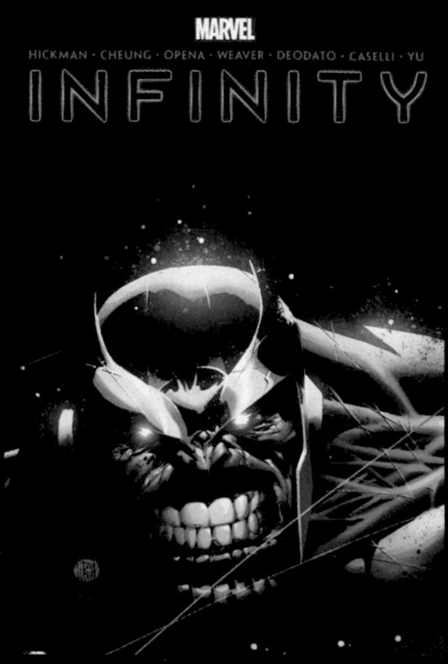
MARVEL
HICKMAN · CHEUNG · OPENA · WEAVER · DEODATO · CASELLI · YU
INFINITY

Infinity
HC 978-0-7851-8422-5 TPB 978-0-7851-8423-2

THANOS: THE INFINITY REVELATION

THANOS
THE INFINITY REVELATION

JIM STARLIN

ANDY SMITH • FRANK D'ARMATA

THANOS: THE INFINITY REVELATION
HC 978-0-7851-8470-6

FREE
DIGITAL COPY

TO REDEEM YOUR CODE FOR A FREE DIGITAL COPY:

1 GO TO MARVEL.COM/REDEEM. OFFER EXPIRES ON 4/01/17.

2 FOLLOW THE ON-SCREEN INSTRUCTIONS TO REDEEM YOUR DIGITAL COPY.

3 LAUNCH THE MARVEL COMICS APP.

4 YOUR DIGITAL COPY WILL BE FOUND UNDER THE 'MY COMICS' TAB.

5 READ AND ENJOY.

YOUR FREE DIGITAL COPY WILL BE AVAILABLE ON:

MARVEL COMICS APP FOR APPLE IOS® DEVICES

MARVEL COMICS APP FOR ANDROID™ DEVICES

MTML18CW6D3R